WENSLEY CLARKSON

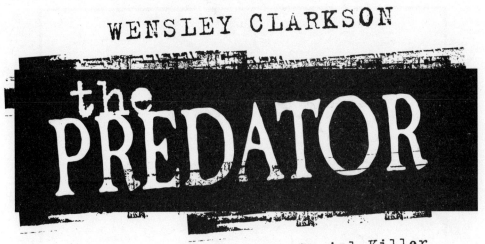
the PREDATOR

Portrait of a Global Serial Killer

JOHN BLAKE

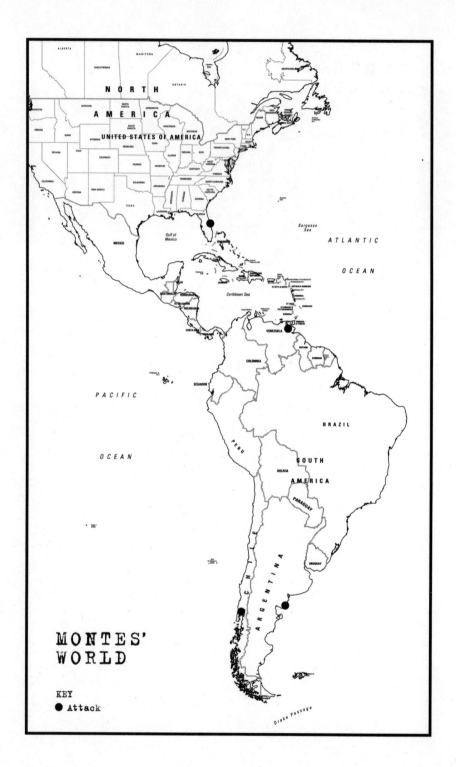

MONTES'
WORLD

KEY
● Attack

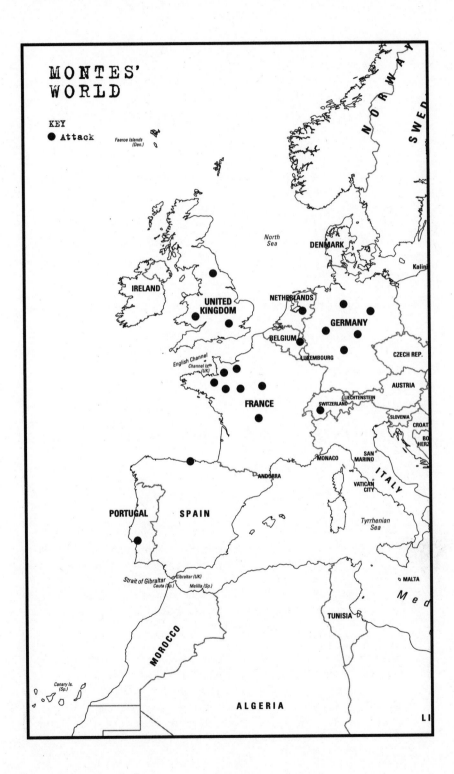

MONTES' WORLD

KEY
● Attack

Published by John Blake Publishing Ltd,
3 Bramber Court, 2 Bramber Road,
London W14 9PB, England

www.blake.co.uk

First published in hardback in 2007

ISBN: 978-1-84454-290-1

British Library Cataloguing-in-Publication Data:

A catalogue record for this book is available from the British Library.

Design by www.envydesign.co.uk

Printed in Great Britain by Creative Print and Design, Wales

1 3 5 7 9 10 8 6 4 2

Papers used by John Blake Publishing are natural, recyclable products made
from wood grown in sustainable forests. The manufacturing processes conform
to the environmental regulations of the country of origin.

Dedicated to all those who suffered at the hands of
Francisco Javier Arce Montes.

Author's Note
and
Acknowledgements

Although no-one has been convicted of many of the murders associated with Montes' reign of terror, the information contained in this book that points to him being the perpetrator of these crimes is based on confidential interviews with police forces directly involved with the cases.

The name of the central figure in this story, Francisco Javier Arce Montes, was shortened by most media sources to Francisco Montes. To avoid confusion, I have called him this, except when describing his childhood and when quoting acquaintances who used a fuller form.

In direct quotations, where it seems that a word was inadvertently omitted, it has been added for clarity. A few mistakes of punctuation, grammar or spelling have been corrected in preference to using the intrusive editorial 'sic'. Some names have been changed because many of those linked to Montes still fear his retribution. Many scenes have been constructed from available documents and allegations provided to this author.

Author's Note and Acknowledgements

I wish to express my gratitude to the following individuals, without whose kind support this book would not have been possible. In Gijon, Spain, the Montes family and friends, local expert Luis Alvarez Mayo, Francisco Benito, Octavio Villa, Gustavo Martinez, Jesus San Roman, Dr Felix Margolyes, Dr Rubero Prieto Rodriguez Ponga, Tino Diaz, Jose Ricardo Gonzales Fernandez, Marcelino Gutierrez, Father Fernando Fueyo Garcia, Claudio Alvar-Gonzalo Torrerro, Marcia Porto, Carmen Figar, Maria Fuentes, Juan Casares, Emmanuel Legin, Mark Griffiths, James Shelby, Jerome Morienere, Justin Webster, Dave Chandler, Paco Veglona, Jim McNally, Geoff Garvey.

My thanks also to my publisher, John Blake.

And to Jean-Pierre Michel, the head of the French police task force, who spent many fruitless years hunting down Francisco Montes. 'Clouseau' Michel and three other French lawyers and law-enforcement officials repeatedly failed to reply to my requests for an interview for this book.

The man that wandereth out of the
Way of understanding
Shall remain in the congregation of
The dead.
Proverbs 21:16

BOOK 1

THE PREDATOR STRIKES

'ONCE THEY ARE FOCUSED ON YOU, HAVE YOU WHERE
YOU ARE VULNERABLE, YOU'RE ALL THEIRS. WHAT PEOPLE CAN
DO IS NOT TRUST SOMEONE YOU DON'T KNOW AND TO ALWAYS
BE AWARE OF WHAT'S GOING ON AROUND YOU. WHEN YOU
DROP YOUR GUARD — THAT'S WHEN A SERIAL KILLER MOVES.'

Los Angeles serial killer Richard 'Night Stalker' Ramirez.

1

The most striking feature of petite, brunette student Christine Le Menes was her crystal-clear blue eyes. Yet it was the shy manner of the young-looking 19-year-old that caught the attention of the tall, dark man who had just stopped his car to ask directions. Spotting her across the reception area of the youth hostel in the Dutch city of Utrecht, he was taken aback when she smiled in his direction. He wasn't used to people even noticing him. He watched her walk along the corridor to her room and noted precisely where it was located. Outside, he carefully counted the windows so that he could pinpoint which one was hers. As he got into his car and drove off, he was determined to return.

But first the stranger found the nearest pharmacy and bought a bottle of Afranil tablets, the anti-depressants he'd been using ever since he was a troubled teenager. Long ago he'd discovered that if he knocked them back with enough whisky they quelled the nervousness he felt whenever he was in the presence of other people. The potent mix of drugs and booze not only helped him lose all his inhibitions but also sparked a sexual urge that always demanded to be satisfied.

Tonight he was in his rusting UK-registered white VW Beetle, though no one paid much attention to what he was driving. That just about summed him up. Few people ever noticed anything about him, except for his bushy eyebrows and long hooked nose, which later many said made him look like a 'wolf-man'. Besides, Utrecht is a busy university city, filled with an ever-changing sea of faces. It was an easy place to get lost in.

As on so many other nights in the stranger's often miserable life, all his money had gone on pills and alcohol. He got back into his car, drove a few blocks and parked in a darkened side street. There he took the plastic container of tablets from his pocket, spread four into the palm of his hand and threw them all into his mouth at once. Then he grabbed the bottle of whisky, unscrewed the top and gulped back a mouthful. Glugging hungrily at the bottle, he almost choked as the whisky and the pills collided in his throat.

It was a warm, muggy, late-spring night in 1981. For a few moments he contemplated his strange, transient existence and how it always took a mouthful of booze and pills to drown out the depression and fear. Then he waited patiently for the surge of raw excitement to kick in. He needed it to escape the cold, harsh reality of his life. For as long as he could remember it had been this way. Ever since he was a child he had suffered an overwhelming feeling of rejection every time his mother called him cruel names and told him she was ashamed of him.

But all those bad memories were gradually wiped out as the chemicals kicked in. Sweating profusely, he restarted the

Beetle and cruised back towards the centre of town, driving up and down the dingy streets, casting an eye at every woman walking along the pavement. He was thinking about sex. Were any of the women prostitutes? But, even if they were, he thought, he had no money to offer them. In any case, he didn't like that sort of woman. The ones who had already been soiled by other men.

By day the tall, dark stranger sometimes found work as a waiter, keeping himself to himself. But by night he'd long since grown used to turning into a reckless figure the moment his 'fuel' took effect. All he ever needed was the mere sight of a suitable young female prey and he'd take his chances. That night he drove in ever-widening circles around the city centre, all the while thinking more and more vividly about his raging desire and how, surely, he could find a girl who would sate his lust. He later recalled, 'When I get these urges nothing can stop me until I've satisfied them.'

As he drove he continued to watch people walking along the streets or sitting in their cars waiting at red lights. That was when he thought about his ideal woman. She had to be clean and pure, untouched by anyone before him. But the time and place had to be just right if he was going to find that dream girl.

Under the influence of the chemical cocktail, time flashed past, until eventually he started to come down. The euphoric rushes he had so relished were fading, to be gradually replaced by an anxiety and edginess that could only be relieved with another hit of booze and pills.

After stopping the car in a side street, he washed more pills down with whisky. Then he pulled away erratically and headed back to the outskirts of Utrecht. It was only then that his befuddled brain remembered the pretty young girl in the youth hostel from earlier that day. It was definitely a situation he could exploit, though it would be riskier going into a hostel than finding a woman on the streets. Buzzing again, he drove on without a map, his dark narrow eyes squinting through the narcotic haze for signs that he was heading in the right direction. His eyes snapped around, searching the night, adjusting to the darkness, looking for the place where he knew he could satisfy his lust.

Eventually he parked on a narrow street running parallel to the main road. He sat in the car for a few moments to compose himself. He checked in all directions to make sure no one was watching him. Satisfied that he was unobserved, he got out of the Beetle and walked through a small alleyway towards the main road, staying in the shadows and taking long, silent steps.

Above, grey clouds raced across the sky as the moonlight bathed everything in an eerie bluish glow. He kept imagining her face as he pounced. How he'd wipe that smile off it. He pictured her young, ripe body and savoured her look of fear. Then he reached the youth hostel. It was a scruffy, two-storey, barracks-style building with an alley to the right of it that ran through to an area at the rear. The wall running alongside the alley was low and would be easy to climb over.

He walked down the alley, counting the windows carefully, fuelled by the image of her face. He couldn't believe his luck when he saw her window was open. Swiftly climbing the wall, he made for the room occupied by 19-year-old Christine Le Menes.

Originally from Paris, Christine was travelling around Europe before starting university in the autumn. She had long, dark hair, was five feet four inches tall and weighed no more than eight stone. She had been travelling alone because that was the type of person she was. In some ways her background was like that of the man who was heading for her room at that moment. Both were detached loners who felt at odds with society.

That night she'd left her window open because she found it hard to sleep unless fresh air was circulating in the room. Outside the hostel, the stranger crept quietly towards the window. He wasn't worried if there were other girls in the room. His mission was to get to her and no one would stand in his way. He would make sure she was his, whatever the circumstances. He'd do what the hell he wanted.

Not for one second did he doubt he had the right to invade her privacy in this way, for he had no idea of morals and what was 'acceptable'. And he certainly didn't care what other people thought of him. Long ago he had learned not to listen to the opinions of others. Nor did he have any mercy. It had been knocked out of him during childhood.

Silently he opened the window further. Then, with ease but carefully, he hoisted himself over the sill and inside. Now he stood perfectly still in the darkened room, as quiet as a cat stalking its prey.

Staying low and moving on the balls of his feet, he took in the scene as his eyes adjusted to the darkness of the room. He made out the form of Christine Le Menes, sleeping deeply in a big dark-blue sleeping bag on the bottom level of a bunk bed. Her breathing was fast and nervous-sounding. It made him stop for a moment and think. Her pretty, elfin-like features seemed to tell him that she was a troubled person, like him.

He cast his eyes around the room carefully to see if anyone else was there. When he realised Christine was alone, he stepped towards her rucksack on the floor next to the bed and opened it quietly. He wanted to know more about her. Soundlessly, he went through its contents, all the time staring at the sleeping form, sexual tension racking up all through him. His breathing quickened. His face contorted with anticipation, he bent down and carefully began to unzip the sleeping bag. He could feel blood pulsating at his temples and behind his eyes.

Now highly excited by the prospect of what was about to happen, he continued to pull down the zip until he could see her body covered only by a flimsy T-shirt and panties. He slipped his hand between her legs. Suddenly Christine woke up. For a split second she stared in shock at her assailant. Then she tried to push his hand away but he kept it there. She could smell his rancid, alcohol-soaked breath on her face. He slammed his other hand over her mouth, then raised her chin and looked deeply into her eyes. Her body was shaking violently with fear. She struggled to breathe. He took his hand away and said in broken French, 'Don't scream or I'll have to kill you.'

She nodded just as he clamped his hand over her mouth once more. Her eyes were now wide open, filled with watery fear. Her pupils dilated wildly. For a moment she wondered if it was all a nightmare. But then she felt the pain of his fingers probing her and knew this was an appalling reality.

He pulled the zip of the sleeping bag down further and tried to climb on top of her. She was too scared to fight back and just lay there, afraid to utter a word. Convinced that she was in some way actually enjoying the situation, he spoke to her. 'You like it, don't you?' he asked. When she didn't reply he took it as encouragement and continued his assault.

Fascinated by her reaction, he stood up and excited himself for some five minutes, watching her face constantly. When he was finished, he sat on the edge of the bed and began talking to her about himself. He had been expecting her to scream and try to escape, but she seemed calm and composed and he liked that about her. As she lay on her sleeping bag, she switched on the bedside light to get a better look at him. Then, as he carried on talking, she even got up and walked around in a casual manner.

It felt to him as if she was treating him more like a boyfriend than a man who had just sexually assaulted her. He told her he was a terrorist from ETA, the Spanish Basque separatist movement, who was on the run and needed her help. She was intrigued.

Christine recalled that he spoke to her in a soothing Spanish accent as he insisted he meant her no harm and pleaded for her help. 'Stupidly, I believed him,' she explained. 'At the time I was very naïve. His story appealed to my romantic temperament. I gradually fell for his charms. I looked upon him as a romantic sort of bohemian type.'

In a few short minutes in that hostel bedroom, Christine's fear fell away, to be replaced by an overwhelming feeling of love and generosity towards this strange intruder. Later she said she felt nothing but sorrow for this predator who had invaded her room and subjected her to a gross form of sexual humiliation. When he told her how he'd first spotted her in the hostel reception earlier that same day and felt an instant attraction, she even felt a little flattered. For Christine had little self-esteem and, just like her assailant, she felt ignored by the world at large.

The stranger continued to talk as he sat on the bed, but

Christine made no attempt to raise the alarm. Something very strange was happening to her: she was drawn to this man because he seemed so vulnerable – just like her. Later she would tell a friend that she had looked on this predatory man as a sort of wild animal who could be tamed.

Moments later they showered together and caressed each other lovingly. Then Christine and her sexual assailant made love on the bed where, just minutes earlier, he had forced himself upon her.

The stranger couldn't quite believe what was happening. As his chemically induced euphoria subsided, he found himself in a complete daze, unable to comprehend why this girl seemed genuinely to like him despite his having assaulted her. He later claimed it was the first time in his life he'd properly made love to a woman.

Afterwards, they lay on the bed together and talked further about their lives. Both had suffered from extreme loneliness during childhood and this shared experience seemed to be forging a bond between them. It was, he later said, as if the previous pain they had both gone through meant that she could forgive his appalling assault on her. Christine was looking for happiness in a cold, hard world in just the same way that he was.

They agreed to keep in touch after she returned home to Paris. He couldn't quite believe what was happening to him. For the first time he felt true love for a member of the opposite sex. He had an overwhelming desire to be with her. The next morning he left the hostel feeling a sense of elation that he'd thought he would never experience in his entire life. It was as if he had turned a corner and suddenly discovered that it wasn't so bad after all to be alive.

Not long afterwards, they spent a romantic week together in Amsterdam but then Christine became aware of an aggressive streak in the strange man she had first met in such an unusual way. After a furious row, she returned to her parents' home in Paris, determined to forget him. But two weeks later he turned up on her doorstep. She weakened and he ended up moving into her parents' house.

In time, they set up home together in Nancy, in north-eastern France. Christine became pregnant and her loner of a lover was overjoyed to learn that he was to be a father. He got a job as a waiter and made a real effort to stay off both drink and pills.

Christine's parents had no idea how their daughter had met this weird man, but from the start they had hoped it was just a passing phase for her. Her pregnancy and his wish to marry her left them shattered. Naturally he saw things rather differently. He looked on Christine as a chance to free himself from the evil desires and habits which had tortured his mind since childhood.

So, when he saw the virulent opposition of Christine's parents to their marrying, he became violent and bitter towards her because of their rejection of him. Tensions soon mounted and the two lovers argued. Christine, heavily pregnant, fled back to her family. She saw little more of him for the rest of her pregnancy, but when their son was born in Paris he turned up in the maternity ward, made a scene and had to be ejected by staff. By this time, Christine had become deeply afraid of him but, she later told friends, her main concern was to protect her child. She left her family's home and told her parents not to let him know where she was living. In trying to avoid any contact with him, she began a life lived virtually on the run.

Initially Christine moved to Brittany to work as a teacher,

but he eventually tracked her down and turned up every six months or so, begging her to let him see their son. Each time she refused. Friends later described Christine as being in a constant state of terror about her mysterious former lover. She herself later said that she was deeply afraid of what he was capable of doing to her. Eventually she moved to the small town of Vitre, near Rennes, the principal city of Brittany. But every time he had a reason to drive through France he tried to seek her out.

One of her friends explained, 'She was terrified of him and she is still afraid of him to this day.' However, as Christine herself later admitted, she never once suspected that her rejection of him was about to unleash a monster capable of raping and killing dozens of other young girls.

2

Not long after splitting up with Christine Le Menes, the stranger with the unnerving, wolf-like features spotted a pretty 19-year-old British student called Deborah Feltham in another youth hostel, this time in the French city of Tours. Haunted by Christine's rejection and his childhood miseries, he now felt an even more overwhelming hatred of women.

Currently enjoying the challenge of a gap year in France, Deborah had been living in Bordeaux and working as an assistant teacher of English in a secondary school. She had taught pupils the lyrics to songs by groups such as the Beatles and the Stray Cats.

Deborah also travelled all over France, staying in youth hostels and camping. She visited Tours with two British boys she had met in Paris on a teacher-training course and they stayed in a youth hostel along with three or four other people. There Deborah noticed a gaunt-looking man with a beard and bushy eyebrows hanging around one afternoon, although she didn't pay much attention to him.

Later that night she was in bed in the women's dormitory when the door creaked open. She raised her head slightly from the pillow and immediately recognised, standing in the doorway, the man from earlier that day. She assumed he was either lost or a peeping Tom and decided to pretend to be asleep in the hope that he would go away. But he didn't; instead, he stared at her in the darkness. She leaned over to the next bed and tapped the shoulder of the only other woman in the dormitory, but she was fast asleep and didn't respond.

The tall, dark stranger continued to stare at Deborah. 'I began to get frightened,' she recalled. 'Really frightened.' He was blocking the door, so she felt trapped. She yelled at him in French to go away, but he didn't flinch. Again and again she shouted and called for help, but nobody heard her as the men's dormitory was on the other side of the building. Still he didn't move. He just stared hard at her.

She thought about grabbing the penknife in her rucksack but was afraid that if she got up he would do something to her. Then, after what seemed like hours but was probably only a few minutes, the man pushed the door open wider and took a step towards her. Deborah leaped from the bed and ran screaming towards the doorway, managing to dart around the man and race along the corridor to the male side of the hostel. There she pleaded with a man to go and check if the other woman in her dormitory was safe.

They caught the strange man in the hallway and he was ejected from the youth hostel without the police being called. Eventually Deborah and her friends went to bed but she spent the rest of the night awake with her penknife clutched in her hand under the pillow. The following day she thought she saw him hanging around again but because he hadn't actually attacked her she didn't bother to alert the police.

It was 20 years later that Deborah recognised him from the pictures in the newspapers and was chilled to the bone. The shock left her wondering how many other young women he had preyed on and how many, unlike her, hadn't escaped. How many reported it to the police? And how many could not?

The tall, dark stranger didn't care about the feelings of any of his victims. Fired up by booze and pills, his burning hatred of women had manifested itself in a warped desire to exact revenge on them all.

The man with the wolf-like features had been a regular visitor to Britain ever since his late teens. He liked the cosmopolitan atmosphere of Earl's Court, in west London, where he often took part-time jobs as a waiter and rented a room for a few months at a time. But he particularly liked the English countryside, which was always filled with young people travelling alone.

At weekends he would drive out of London either north or west on one of the motorways. He would always try to find a young girl to attack on a lonely road, and here his Youth Hostels Association membership came in handy, allowing him to stay in out-of-the-way places.

One weekend in the middle of 1984, he drove up to York, which he knew, from previous visits, was always full of school parties visiting the famous cathedral and other sightseeing spots dating back nearly 2,000 years to the Roman occupation of Britain. For hours, he strolled around in the parks and along the crowded pavements without finding a girl he could attack. He began to grow angry and frustrated but continued to hunt even as darkness fell and most of the school groups dispersed. In one quiet street on the edge of the city, he tried to abduct a 12-year-old schoolgirl, but she screamed, fought him off and ran away.

As usual, he wasn't unduly worried about the police being out looking for him after the earlier failed abduction. Even so, he decided it would be better to find a youth hostel, as he knew that they were often full of the sort of girls he found attractive. After all, that was how he'd met the love of his life, Christine Le Menes.

Before long, he found a hostel on the edge of York called the Holgate Centre. Minutes after arriving, he entered the room of an eight-year-old schoolgirl. The child awoke as he tried to touch her. When she screamed in terror he fled, and she watched his shadowy figure running out of the room. 'I'll never forget that face as long as I live,' the girl later said. Her mother – a teacher at her school – was sleeping in the next room and was alerted by her daughter's scream.

When the mother confronted the stranger in the hallway, he claimed to be lost. The police were called but he was released without charge after a few hours. Officers later said they were convinced by his story and had no reason to detain him. If they'd searched his car, they would have found a hammer and rope, as well as three false number plates he had been using on his car for months.

The man with the wolf-like features also frequently stayed in Germany. He liked being there because it was clean and efficiently run, unlike his native Spain, where everything seemed dirty and neglected. He picked up German easily because he had a good ear for languages. Sometimes he wondered why his parents hadn't allowed him to go to university, because many were impressed with his ability to speak English and French. He liked being able to use a number of languages because it put the people he met at ease and so made it easier for him to pounce.

In Germany he got a job as a waiter and rented a modest flat in the university town of Tubingen. He was delighted to be as far away as possible from Spain. He also liked being in a town filled with 20,000 students, many of them still in their teens. By now he'd got into the habit of drifting around Europe in a cheap second-hand car, living on a shoestring budget and getting work whenever he needed it to finance his drink and drugs habits.

Now he found himself out on the streets of Tubingen hunting once again. He was so sexually charged by mental images of what he'd done to women in the past that he felt as if he was ready to explode if he didn't get what he required. And that was to hurt, to control, to be the one in charge, and to have sex with a pure, young girl who had never in her life been near a man. All the while memories of his one and only real lover, Christine Le Menes, continued to lurk in the back of his mind. Was it really all his fault? If she had not rejected him, maybe he might have been able to rid himself of these evil urges. He often thought about that. But he didn't like taking responsibility for his actions. He needed someone to blame for his deviant existence, and Christine and his mother both fitted that bill perfectly.

Tubingen is a neat, fairly prosperous town with a population of 85,000. He enjoyed cruising its late-night streets in search of girls, but he knew he'd never get away with kidnapping them in busy neighbourhoods. So, when the pills and booze really kicked in, he usually headed for the countryside and the dark recesses of the nearby Black Forest, a hunting district if ever there was one. He had with him some rope, a knife and a few other instruments of terror that would come in useful when he found the latest girl of his dreams.

He liked the freedom of being out on the road in his car. It meant he could reinvent himself as anyone he wanted, and he enjoyed role playing. He would replay in his mind how he told Christine Le Menes that he was a Basque terrorist on the run after he broke into her room, which had led them to fall in love. He liked being thought of as somebody, even though in reality he was a nobody. By now most of his life was no more than a detached fantasy. And within his dream world the biggest driving force was his bitterness over the way Christine had treated him. He still sometimes returned to Brittany, where she lived with their son, and begged her to let him establish some kind of relationship with his child, but she always refused. At times, he wondered if she suspected the full horror of the darkness that had enveloped him.

Now he was driving out of Tubingen towards the Black Forest in his quest to find someone young and pure to satisfy his monstrous desires. Over the previous 18 months, he had carried out a string of rapes and sex attacks on young female hitchhikers on the edge of the forest, nearly all of them in broad daylight. He was driving his latest car, a Dutch-registered 1600-cc white Toyota Corolla, having concluded that picking up hitchhikers was a lot easier than breaking into youth hostels. Once he had a young girl in his car, he would drive her to an isolated spot on the edge of the forest, where he would produce a knife and threaten to kill her unless she did exactly what he wanted.

On this particular spring evening, 22 April 1988, he found

himself a 14-year-old girl out recklessly thumbing a ride after an argument with her parents. As she got into his car, the teenager gave no thought to the possible danger. His eyes flashed with excitement when she sat beside him. He even smiled to himself as he asked her in near-perfect German, 'Surely your parents have told you not to take lifts from strange men?'

She giggled shyly at him in a sweet, innocent fashion. Later she would recall that his voice was so soft and almost feminine that she felt sure he was trustworthy. As usual, he pretended he had to take a short diversion to pick up something from a friend, but instead drove her to a lonely wooded spot and raped her at knifepoint before leaving her by the edge of the road stranded, terrified and distressed. By pure luck, a police patrol car passed the spot shortly afterwards and found his battered victim. An alert was put out for the stranger in the car after the young girl told officers she remembered the distinctive registration number. But he seemed to have disappeared without trace.

A month later, on 14 May, the sex attacker was arrested on the German–Dutch border because he had stupidly not changed the number plates since his attack on the 14-year-old girl. Inside the Toyota, German border police found a set of Dutch plates which turned out to have belonged to another Toyota he had once owned but had since dumped in a scrapyard near Utrecht.

Bizarrely, even after this arrest for rape, the man's fingerprints were not taken.

Weeks later, the 14-year-old was so scared of the prospect of having to give evidence against her attacker that she committed suicide. For that rape and two previous ones, the stranger with the wolf-like looks was jailed for five and half years by a court in Tubingen.

However, halfway through his sentence he was deported to his native Spain to serve the remaining time. Incredibly, he was trusted to travel alone, and the Spanish authorities have no record of him ever having arrived at a jail there. The German police even asked Interpol to issue a search notice for him requesting that he finish his prison sentence. Police from both countries eventually decided that he had disappeared into thin air and it was unlikely they would ever track him down. But at least he would no longer be a drain on the public purse.

3

After his premature release from jail in Germany, the tall, dark stranger slipped back deeper still into his addiction to prescription drugs washed down with vast amounts of whisky.

For this truly evil man, a heartless rape or murder was like a fine Rioja wine. You needed to make it last and get the most out of it.

Buoyed by strong anti-depressants, he genuinely believed that the devil would always protect him and enable him to attack any woman he wanted. He looked on his arrest and imprisonment in Germany as a consequence of his own stupidity in not changing the number plates on his car.

He knew the drugs made him paranoid and prone to stupid mistakes. If he was to continue to succeed in his perverted missions, he needed to avoid such errors. He dreaded further imprisonment and promised himself he would be more careful in future.

He bought himself some new 'tools', including rope, tape

and a knife. He also purchased a big box of cotton wool and alcohol cleanser. From now on, his 'conquests' would be immaculately clean. The first thing I'll do, he decided, is cleanse their bodies so that I can't catch any germs from touching them. They will prefer it that way. And if they scream I'll make sure they keep quiet.

He particularly liked the desolate countryside of central France. As he drove through the region on the way back to his adopted home of London in the summer of 1990, he decided it was time once more to wreak havoc. The excitement was building so fast that he feared for the safety of his next victim. He wasn't sure if just having sex with her would be enough any more.

Joanna Parrish, a small, attractive brunette with almond-shaped eyes and clear white skin, was another British girl living in France. She put an advertisement in the local newspaper offering English lessons. A strange man answered it and told her on the phone in a strong foreign accent that he was keen to improve his English before returning to London. The 20-year-old Leeds Universtiy graduate left her two flatmates in Auxerre to meet the man on Wednesday, 16 May 1990. She was never seen alive again.

A couple of days later, Joanna's battered, raped and strangled body was discovered floating in a river near Auxerre. Police believe she was only killed because she put up such a fierce struggle. Her killer knew that the police would try much harder to catch him after she died. Now he'd stepped over that invisible line and become an out-and-out murderer. There was no turning back.

He had often wondered if any of the hard-working policemen of Europe were aware of his activities. But he wasn't unduly worried, since it seemed that none of them had bothered to communicate with one another to intensify the search for him. In any case, he was supremely confident of his ability to talk his way out of trouble if caught.

In short, he believed he was brighter and faster than the police. His experiences in Germany in the 1980s had taught him how to keep one step ahead of them. He was sure that, just so long as he kept moving from country to country and part-time job to part-time job, he would be able to continue his quest to find the perfect replacement for Christine, the mother of his beloved son.

He didn't even bother to change his appearance much. His bushy eyebrows remained his most striking facial feature, although his deep-set, cold-blue eyes and hooked nose were also difficult to miss. His victims all agreed that he resembled a wolf, albeit one in sheep's clothing.

Tonight he was driving around the centre of the Welsh city of Swansea, where he'd just started working as a waiter in a hotel. As he drove through the busy city centre, he drew a perverse strength and sustenance from the sight of so many young women out drinking in the local hostelries. To him, they were all just filthy whores who drank too much and had sex with virtual strangers. They were not pure enough for him. He wanted virgins, unsullied by other men.

He actually believed he was making history through his murderous journeys across Europe. In his fantasies, he imagined travelling even farther afield for sexual satisfaction. One day he'd make it across the Atlantic, where North and South America were beckoning. By continually criss-crossing borders, he was sure he could get away with his catalogue of crimes for a long time yet. Besides, if the police were on his trail, they would never think of looking for him in a place like Swansea. So here he was, in 1992, on new territory, hunting for prey a long way from the scenes of his many other attacks, fatal or otherwise.

He threw back a handful of pills and grabbed the whisky bottle from the passenger seat next to him and took a long gulp. City centres were not his favourite places. He preferred the peace and quiet of the countryside, so he drove his car out of Swansea to the well-known local beauty spot of Oxwich Bay, on the Gower Peninsula. To him this was much more familiar-looking territory. It was a beautiful area, popular with walkers who enjoyed strolling through dense woodlands to the bluffs and sand dunes of the deserted beaches that fringed the bay.

Lush, grassy hills stretched into the distance as he slowed down on a narrow country lane close to the sea. He knew it would take just one young girl out alone and his appetite would be satisfied. The drink and drugs were peaking. He needed to find his prey sooner rather than later. But that night the lanes seemed deserted. Eventually, he pulled up in a lay-by beside a small stream and contemplated what to do next. His hands were shaking with expectation but, for the moment, there was no sign of anyone, let alone a young girl to capture.

He downed another handful of pills and more whisky and fired up the engine once more. Just as he was about to pull away, a police panda car slowed down on the road ahead. His heart seemed to rise and lodge in his throat, but he stayed calm and waited for the patrol car to pass. Then he took a left towards the rolling hills.

The pills and booze were making his senses even more acute as his eyes scanned both ends of the road for a sign of anyone, constantly checking in his rear-view mirror in case that police car returned. Just then his headlights lit up a bus stop. He squinted as the beam caught the shadow of someone. Looking harder, he realised it was a teenage girl on her own. He couldn't believe his luck. His hands trembled with excitement as he slowed down to take a closer look. She glanced across at him as his car approached and he convinced himself she had smiled in his direction. She was very pretty and looked foreign.

He stopped just past her, rolled down the window and offered her a lift into Swansea. She didn't reply, so he tried in French. The girl – a 15-year-old French school student on an exchange trip to Wales – was relieved when the stranger said something she understood. Without hesitation, she got in beside him.

Minutes later, he turned down an isolated lane. When the girl asked what he was doing, he pretended not to understand her French. Then he stopped the car and leaned across to her. She saw the drooling look on his face and knew immediately what was about to happen. She screamed and, using all her strength, pushed open the door as he tried to hold it shut. Annoyed that she had dared not to co-operate, he grappled with her, but she pushed him off and ran down the lane. He was about to give chase when he saw her illuminated by the headlights of the panda car from earlier. He killed his own lights and drove away at high speed in the opposite direction. At the far end of the lane, he found his way on to a main road and sped off.

The police in Swansea recorded three other incidents for

which they felt the man with the wolf-like face was almost certainly responsible. In the late spring of 1993, a 13-year-old girl guide from Hull was accosted in precisely the same way as the young French girl but also managed to escape. A few weeks later, the same man tried but failed to drag a girl into woods, and then another victim was forced into nearby sand dunes but broke free. A photofit produced with the help of all the man's suspected victims showed it to be almost certainly the same predator who had already carried out attacks in Holland, Germany, France, Britain and Spain. Yet no match was attempted with Interpol and not one of the police forces concerned had any idea that they had a killer and rapist in their midst.

Back in his favourite killing fields of France, the tall, dark stranger had yet again been rejected by his ex-lover Christine Le Menes, who refused to let him see their son. Soon his hatred of her was boosted by yet more drink and drugs and he was now hunting fervently for a victim. This time he was in Nancy, where he had lived for a while with Christine. It was May 1993 and, unusually for him, he'd been cruising the city centre looking for the perfect girl rather than scouring the countryside.

Helene, a 21-year-old student, looked at least three years younger than her age. He had targeted her after seeing her walking along a small street after dark. Within minutes, he'd dragged her into his car and raped her at knifepoint before dumping her in another side street. Afterwards, Helene told the police that the man who attacked her looked like 'a caveman'. That was one of the many cruel nicknames he had been called during his childhood.

The stranger spent as little time as possible in his home town of Gijon, in northern Spain. But occasionally he returned to try to get more money from his father, who owned a thriving local business. The family dreaded and felt ashamed of his visits, especially the way he always drove a foreign-registered car, which meant all their neighbours knew he was back home.

In a sense, the cash payouts his elderly father made to him were intended to guarantee that he stayed away from them all. They didn't want to be linked to such a strange person with such unpleasant personal habits.

Later he would claim that the stress of being with his family made him want to hit the booze and pills even more. And it was this, in turn, that led him on to the streets of Gijon, prowling for a victim in the late spring of 1994. So it was that he found himself hiding in a doorway, watching a pretty dark-haired student named Elena get off a bus not far from his family's home in Gijon. The teenager then began the short walk to her own home, carrying a small bag containing a couple of books for her studies at college in the nearby city of Oviedo.

Within seconds, the stranger was following her along the darkened streets. 'When I got nearer to my parents' home, I realised the man behind me was a problem, so I started running,' Elena recalled. But he began running faster to try to catch her up. Soon he was only a few feet from her. 'Now I was running for my life,' Elena explained. 'I thought I'd have time to open the front door to my apartment block and get in before he reached me.'

But, as she dashed into the doorway, the man reached out in front of her and pulled the glass door open enough to get in behind her. He pushed her into the lobby, his eyes darting in all directions, looking for a place to take her. The girl tried to break free and escape up the stairs, but he grabbed her and pulled her to the floor.

'Don't move again or I'll kill you,' he said in a soft, almost feminine voice.

Elena recalled, 'The strange thing was that he didn't even sound angry with me personally. That made him seem even more crazy. It was like he was fighting some kind of demon inside himself. The only stupid thing I did was to run to my flat. I should have gone into a bar and then he would have stopped. But I wanted to deal with it myself.'

The man then dragged his victim towards the open door of the lift. As he pushed her in, he pressed the button for the basement. 'But I told him it wouldn't work without a key,' Elena recalled. She realised she had to play for time. 'So I asked him what he wanted and stuff like that. I knew it would be stupid to use violence against him because that would just make it worse.'

'What's your name?' she asked him. 'Where do you live?'

The girl's attacker looked confused by her relaxed-sounding questions and didn't answer. As he squeezed her in a stranglehold inside the lift, she even asked for his phone number and suggested they go on a date. 'I knew I had to get him talking.'

Then he produced a knife from his jacket pocket and dragged her back out into the lobby, desperately looking around for a corner or a darkened area where he could assault her. The lift door slid shut behind them.

The girl continued trying to talk to her attacker. 'I could see he was confused. It's difficult to explain. He looked at me strangely as I spoke.'

Both of them heard the lift coming down. The man looked surprised. The girl saw her chance. 'That's probably my father and he's a policeman,' she told him. 'He's a big, violent man and he'll kill you if he finds you here.'

The man glanced nervously at the lift lights as they flickered down the floor numbers. Then he looked back at the girl. 'Now he was the one who was scared and confused,' Elena recalled.

Suddenly, in one jerky movement, the man ripped off the girl's earrings. 'He must have thought they were gold,' Elena explained. Then the stranger pulled open the front door and ran down the street as fast as he could, not once looking back. The girl was in tears when her father really did appear seconds later. He sent her upstairs to her mother and grandmother and went out to search for the man, but after failing to find him he returned to the family apartment and no one bothered to report the incident to the police. Elena kept a constant eye out for her attacker for many months. 'Stupidly, I still walked home the same route despite what happened, but fortunately I never saw him again.'

Looking back on what happened, she says she believes her calmness helped prevent her being sexually assaulted or killed. 'I remember he seemed so confused much of the time. He was obviously a very mixed-up person.'

The tall, dark stranger with the wolfish face drove out of Gijon the following morning with his sexual appetite unsatisfied, determined to find another victim on the drive back to his bedsit in London, more than 1,500 kilometres away.

4

As he drove eastwards out of Gijon on the Autovia de Cantavrico, he was surrounded by the awesome Picos de Europa, a range of jagged peaks which locals call 'the Devil's teeth'. He was soon passing small *pueblos* filled with scatterings of red-roofed houses which recalled rural Switzerland more than Spain. He felt a surge of relief every time he left his hometown, and all those bad memories of his childhood, to drive along the main coastal road towards Santander and beyond.

The numerous communities dotted along that ragged northern coastline perfectly reflected the changes that Spain had been undergoing since the death of the dictator General Franco in 1975. Old churches flourished next to modern housing estates and new holiday complexes. As the main road swept down close to the raging Atlantic, waves crashed into the deep sand dunes edging the beaches. Next to them were high white cliffs crowned by small clumps of forest. And throughout the drive those massive snow-capped mountains, which

31

separate the region of Asturias from the rest of Spain, looked down on him with their 'teeth' bared in seeming anger.

After the E78 motorway turned back into a normal road, it snaked for more than 60 kilometres before becoming a motorway once again. All that now separated the road from the ocean was a railway track. In some seaside villages, natural fjords had been formed by the fierce Atlantic as it battered the coastline over countless years. These places had names like Paned, Pot and Unkera. The terrain was more like Wales than most people's idea of Spain. And at this time no budget airlines served the area, leaving only two choices of transport – car or train.

The only time the stranger stopped was to refuel his car. He'd always wait patiently for the attendant to fill the car with petrol rather than dirty his own hands. He rarely stopped to enjoy a tasty cut-price lunch from the *menu del dia* at one of the many bars and inns scattered along the old coast road because he preferred not to eat other people's food. How could he be certain it was clean? Instead, he often ate sandwiches which he had carefully made himself at the family home in Gijon before setting off.

By contrast with some Spanish men, his obsession with cleanliness had also stopped him from satisfying his sexual urges in the popular roadside brothels, or 'clubs', as they were called. One such club stood out like a beacon just beyond the spectacular bridge that crossed a massive inlet on the road between Bilbao and the border with France. But the stranger detested brothels because the girls were second-hand goods, soiled by filthy, smelly men who paid for sex. As far as he was concerned, they had to be untouched. He had more chance of finding such pure creatures in youth hostels or by picking up hitchhikers on the roads of Europe.

Just then, he caught his first glimpse of the Pyrenees, which meant the border was close. Once he got past the crossing he would stick to the quieter roads, where there were no expensive tolls to pay and lots of small hotels and hostels filled with young girls to lust after. He had long ago discovered the pleasures of staying in youth hostels, which charged little money. Increasing his speed, he could feel the excitement surging through his veins. He knew this road like the back of his hand and he'd soon be out of Spain and away from all those reminders of his unhappy past.

Crossing into France was relatively easy, for the Spanish border guards took little interest in traffic leaving their country. They also tended to be especially lenient to cars with UK number plates, like the ones the stranger was driving at this time. He always felt more relaxed as he drove through the thick woodland lining the main road between the frontier and Bordeaux. He liked forests. They were scary, secretive places where you could get away with doing really sick things. The road to Bordeaux was straight and easy to handle. It was also dotted with campsites hidden deep in the woods.

The stranger often stopped at one of the isolated little parking areas, or *aires*, nestled in the forest, where he could sit in his car undisturbed for hours. Sometimes he would masturbate while watching couples having sex in cars. One of his favourite *aires* was at La Cote d'Anise, where once he watched a couple for hours without being noticed. He liked the feeling of being surrounded by darkness, even though it had scared him since childhood. But being in the safety of a car, knowing that no one could see him, made him feel protected.

On the Bordeaux road, weather conditions could often change in a matter of minutes. With few street lights and many large trucks coming in the opposite direction with full headlight beams on, a sudden heavy rainfall brought with it all sorts of problems, although at least they drove more slowly in France.

That night the stranger ignored all the temptations of campsites and forests because he was on a mission and he still had hundreds of kilometres to go. He turned on to the 606 road towards Angouleme, which he liked because it was always much quieter than the main roads. In his pocket was a wallet filled with youth hostel cards.

The thick mist which often descended on the road between Bordeaux and Angouleme tended to need a heavy rainfall to wash it away. Sometimes he stopped his car at a huge lorry park when the mist was too thick to drive in. Dozens of trucks from Britain, Spain, Holland, Portugal and Poland were always parked there and sometimes he watched as drivers clambered into the back of their cabs with fat, red-faced junkie hookers.

As a teenager back in Gijon, he had often dreamed of becoming a truck driver because that would have given him the freedom to keep moving. But he couldn't get a licence to drive heavy-goods vehicles because of the medical problems that had haunted his teens and early twenties. He would have loved to be a lorry driver.

Driving on determinedly, he fantasised about what he planned to do when he got to his final destination. His mind was so focused on his next attack that he felt no fear. He was invincible. As he drove, he shivered with excitement and clutched the steering wheel tightly. He didn't care whom he hurt. Why should he care? They didn't care about him.

No one knew his real identity as he passed all those other cars on the road. He'd never told a soul the truth about what he'd done. That was the key to not being apprehended. Murder and rape were his secrets and he guarded them very carefully. Rattling along the roads of central France, he reached 120 kilometres per hour. His grip on the steering wheel tightened even more as manic images raced through his head.

Occasionally he stopped and catnapped for a few minutes. Then he would wake up with a start, wipe the sleep from his eyes and continue the journey. As he approached the Loire Valley, the road began twisting and turning, switching between dual carriageway and two-lane road. He stuck to the old N10 because he liked to avoid the tolls.

On missions like this, he often looked at the clock in his car and noticed how slowly time seemed to move. His mind would wander back to what might have been; to that girl Christine who had given birth to his only child and how they could so easily have brought up the child together. They would have had a happy life, surely? Why did it have to end up like that? That was when he got angry and snapped back to the cold reality of the task that lay ahead.

When he reached Tours, he decided to find a park in the centre and look for young girls. Who knows, maybe he would spot another Christine?

5

An hour later, 14-year-old Irish schoolgirl Valerie Jacques noticed a strange-looking middle-aged man with a wolf-like face staring straight at her in a park near the middle of Tours, which she was visiting with a group from her school.

'It was very busy,' she recalled. 'There were women out walking their dogs, couples with children. That's why he stood out – he was on his own. He was sitting legs akimbo about 20 feet away and staring at our party. He looked rough – very dishevelled and unshaven. His hair was unkempt and he was wearing army combat shorts, army boots, and looked like a backpacker. It even struck us that he might be a bit of a dirty old man. We nudged each other and said, "Look at him, he looks a bit rough." But, even though we were laughing and looking at him, he still continued staring. He didn't show any embarrassment.'

The killer couldn't take his eyes off the happy-looking schoolgirl with dark hair, who seemed to be staring right back at him. That smile convinced him she would be his next one.

Valerie and her friends on the school trip thought nothing of it at the time. They didn't even notice the strange man later watching them from behind a tree as they boarded their coach to go to their hostel in the village of Blere, 25 kilometres away. Minutes later – unknown to them – the scruffy figure in the park was following them in his car.

As he tailed the school coach on a narrow D road out of Tours, an unlikely mix of typical French houses, chateaux and tawdry campsites lined the road on one side as it followed the Loire. Then they came to the beautiful old eight-arched double bridge that crossed the river into the picturesque ancient stone-built town of Amboise.

He followed the coach as it drove over the bridge and on to the narrow D31, which ran through a thick forest towards Blere. The first signpost for Blere informed visitors that it was twinned with the German town of Garrel. A vast hayloft on top of a grey stone tower greeted motorists entering the narrow cobbled streets.

The stranger kept his distance as the coach turned left along an even quieter country lane on the outskirts of the village. He immediately recognised the sign to L'Heresie youth hostel because he had been there the previous year. That knowledge sent a surge of excitement through his body. Fate had stepped in and that beautiful young schoolgirl was destined to be his. As the coach headed up the hill, passing a handful of expensive detached single-storey houses, he crawled slowly up the hill behind it.

The coach driver eventually parked outside the main building of the youth hostel – a venerable old chateau built of grey stone. It looked just as serene and imposing as it had done when he had visited the place the previous year. He slowed down to peer through the trees at the hostel, although he already knew the outbuildings, which housed the dormitories, would be of most interest to him. He shivered at the prospect of taking her into the dense wood behind the hostel.

As he sat a safe distance away in his car watching the schoolgirls getting off the coach, two black crows pecked at the remains of a rabbit on the road in front of him. That was another sign, he believed. A sign that he could strike here with ease and ensure that he satisfied every deranged urge within him. It was meant to be.

Valerie Jacques and the rest of her group ate supper at the hostel and then went upstairs to bed at midnight, blissfully unaware that a strange man had been stalking them since their visit to the park in Tours earlier that day. Valerie and four of her friends were sharing a room that had no key, although that didn't seem to worry any of them. All memories of that 'creepy wolf-man' in the park had long since gone and the five girls soon fell asleep after their exhausting day sightseeing.

It was almost 2am on a steaming July night in 1994 and the heat in the Loire Valley was intense, making even walking uncomfortable. But not even the severe heat could stop the tall, dark stranger from continuing his work. He was sure the police hadn't yet connected any of his attacks, let alone worked out who he was. He parked just off the road next to L'Heresie hostel before making his way silently on the balls of his feet towards the outhouses, now bathed in darkness.

Moments later, he found the front door to the hostel unlocked – like most rural youth hostels across Europe – and silently turned the knob. He slipped quietly into the lobby and then headed for a wooden stairway which, he knew from his previous visit, led to the girls' bedrooms. The stairs creaked and each time he made a noise he stopped for a few seconds in case anyone had heard him.

He reached the first floor, where the first door he tried led into a shower room. After hesitating for a moment, he decided to take a shower. True, he was a lot scruffier now than he used to be, but he was still obsessed with cleanliness and the opportunity to shower was taken gratefully. It was essential to be completely clean before he caught his prey. How could he expect her to stand being touched by him unless he was immaculate?

Having quietly showered, he dressed again and edged his way out into the darkness. He slowly turned the knob of the first door and found the girls fast asleep in their room. On the floor he spotted a school backpack next to the sleeping form of brunette Valerie, whom he immediately recognised. He bent down, pulled one of the schoolbooks from her bag and slipped back out of the room with it into the dimly lit hallway. He could just make out the name 'Valerie Jacques' on the cover. That was enough for him.

He crept silently back into the bedroom.

Around 2am, Valerie Jacques stirred from her deep sleep to find herself lying on her face with her sheets around her ankles. Later she recalled, 'I don't know what first disturbed me but I can remember him stroking me on my ankles. I turned over to prop myself up and there was a shadow, a dark figure sitting on the bed leaning over me. I didn't know then if it was a male or female. I asked who it was and he spoke in a foreign language, very softly. Fear set in. Time slowed down. I remember looking around and thinking, Why is no one else awake?'

The stranger switched to clear fluent English, 'Valerie, I want you to come out with me and help me with my car.'

Valerie was petrified. How did he know her name? But, as she later explained, 'I might have been only 14 but I was very clued up and I knew what he wanted.'

The man didn't feel an ounce of guilt about what he was doing. After all, he'd attacked many young girls in similar circumstances. The fact that they had been raped, molested and even murdered during that process didn't matter to him.

But Valerie Jacques turned out to be not as easy to manipulate as most of the others.

'No, I'm not going with you,' she told the stranger.

He stood up and said, 'Valerie, I'm going to turn the light on.'

She was terrified that if she saw his face she would never be able to get it out of her mind.

'No, just go,' she pleaded.

But to the stranger her response didn't sound like a plea. He believed she was being as compliant as Christine, the mother of his child, had been. He believed that she was saying now wasn't a good time but he could come back and she would give him everything he wanted. He walked out of the room and down the creaky staircase, happy in the knowledge that Valerie wanted him in just the same way as Christine had all those years earlier. He'd be back.

Valerie had absolutely no intention of leaving her bed. She stayed under the covers, shaking with fear in case he returned.

6

The stranger was soon several kilometres away, looking for somewhere to stop his car and have a nap. He was angry with himself and still on a high from the usual cocktail of drink and drugs. He had wanted to satisfy his urges but failed. He decided that he would return the following night because L'Heresie was the perfect hostel for his evil purposes and Valerie seemed so attracted to him. He never even considered that the police might have been called. In any case, the man didn't care about such things. All he wanted was to achieve what he'd set out to do and nothing – and no one – was going to stop him. After all, this was how he'd met the love of his life. Maybe that schoolgirl would fall in love with him, just like Christine had.

He was convinced Valerie was the girl of his dreams. He believed she would come downstairs with him when he came back. Already he had put her on a pedestal, just as he had Christine.

After she'd heard his car pulling away, a petrified Valerie had woken her friends. She went with one pal to report her ordeal to two women helpers belonging to their party. She recalled, 'I was in shock. I went back to my room and found that my backpack had been gone through. I had a phrasebook with my name on it and that's where he got my name from.'

Valerie and a couple of her friends then made a strange discovery. 'The shower floor was wet. None of us had had a shower. And he had opened the window.'

She alerted her teacher, Martin O'Brien, who at first thought it was all a silly overreaction by an excitable 14-year-old. But after speaking to Valerie's friends he realised something very serious had happened.

Somehow, Valerie managed to get back to sleep that night, but later she would reflect that it was a miracle that she put the incident out of her mind so easily.

The following morning her fears returned with a vengeance as she and her school friends joined a tour of a nearby chateau. 'All I was thinking was, I've got to go back to that room tonight and he'd said he would come back and there's no bloody key for our door.'

The stranger spent most of that same day in an elated state of ever-increasing sexual excitement. He had convinced himself that Valerie wanted him and he was going to slip back into her room that night and, who could say, maybe they'd end up running off together, just like he did with Christine Le Menes? He spent much of the day back in Amboise, watching young female tourists wandering around the square. But he didn't approach any of them because he had Valerie to look forward to.

At bedtime that evening, the other girls in Valerie's room

rallied round and told her they would stay awake playing cards and games while she slept. The group propped all their bags and rucksacks against the bedroom door, which was still not locked. Valerie recalled, 'I was so tired I remember falling asleep straight away. But I wasn't asleep for more than an hour when I woke up and heard his voice calling my name. Everyone else was asleep by this time.'

More knocking on the door followed. The man sounded almost pathetic the way he was pleading. Then he started trying to push the door open. The suitcases began wobbling. Valerie feared they might fall over and then he'd come in and get her. She jumped out of bed and stood in the far corner of the room to be as far away as possible if he got in.

'I thought, Oh my God, they're asleep again. He's forcing the door. I pinned myself against the far wall. I was more terrified than the night before. He'd said he would come back and he had.'

Suddenly Valerie and the others heard a commotion outside their room as three gendarmes grabbed the man and held his arms behind his back. They heard him protesting his innocence in French.

Unknown to Valerie, her teachers had tipped off the police. 'The teacher in charge of the trip knocked on my door and said, "Valerie, it's me. I'm coming in." Then he said, "The police have him downstairs. Get dressed, get yourself together and come down."'

Valerie went to the local police station with a female teacher. In a state of shock, the teenager pleaded with the police not to ask her to see the man, telling them, 'I will remember that voice anywhere. Don't show him to me. I'll never be able to get his face out of my mind.'

But eventually they persuaded Valerie that she had to identify the man and moments later took her into a room where she came face to face with the 'wolf-man'. 'He was just sitting there,' she recalled. 'I knew straight away it was him and that it was the same man I had seen in the park.'

Valerie was then obliged by the police and her teachers to sit and listen while the man pleaded his innocence. 'He was looking through me, looking over me, saying, "I wasn't here. I wasn't there." He was making up stupid reasons as to why he was there and being very conciliatory. The police were casual about it. They took a statement from me while he was sitting in front of me denying everything.'

When it suited him, the stranger could turn on the charm in a most convincing way. He looked one of the gendarmes in the eye and said without a flicker of self-doubt, 'I don't know how somebody could think that I would be able to violate anybody. I was just looking for a room to sleep in.'

He referred to the many fiancées he had back in Gijon, to reassure the police that he was a normal, sexually active male. He even told them that one girlfriend lived on the main road into Gijon and they made love together very regularly. Then he went into sordid detail about his sex life, talking about how they 'sometimes do it in my car'.

He added with pride that he and his lover always showered thoroughly before they made love. It was an extraordinary admission but the gendarmes failed to appreciate the significance of that statement in relation to how the man had used the shower in the hostel before trying to attack Valerie Jacques.

When Martin O'Brien challenged him, he was even more evasive. The teacher later explained, 'At one stage he even tried to pretend he didn't know what was being said to him, although it was clear he spoke French and English.'

He also noticed that the stranger seemed very aware of his legal rights and refused point-blank to give an explanation as to why he was in the hostel. 'It was the behaviour of someone who knew exactly what he was doing.' In the teacher's view, 'He was very clever and very shrewd. This was clearly no ordinary man. When he was arrested, he began to behave as if he didn't know what this was all about. He wasn't at all panicked, he was absolutely cool, and I got the impression he had been in this situation before. He wasn't at all worried by the presence of the police. This was obviously not an opportunist or a one-off criminal. He knew the system and he knew how to talk to children to lead them into a false sense of security.'

The manager of the youth hostel, Yves Franquelin, believed he had been in the presence of a 'very dangerous man'. When the police examined the stranger's belongings and discovered dozens of International Youth Hostel Federation membership cards, it sent a chill down the manager's spine. 'When you're 25 it's fine to have all those cards, but when you're 45… It was very sinister,' he explained.

But under French law the man could not be charged with any offence unless he admitted something. The local police later claimed they passed on his details to Interpol, although this has never been confirmed. In fact, the stranger was already on Interpol's wanted list after a number of attacks in various countries in Europe but for some inexplicable reason those warrants did not come to light at that time. They had little choice but to release him.

Martin O'Brien was horrified. 'I felt that surely this man

was an obvious danger and he should be locked up. Our worst nightmare was that he was out and about, able to get away with it.'

Later Valerie Jacques discovered that the police had found rope and a hammer in the stranger's car yet they had still done nothing to take him off the streets. When she heard about it she wondered, Was that intended for me?

That same day, one of Valerie's teachers asked her if she was going to tell her parents what had happened. She replied, 'I'm 14, if I tell them I'll never be allowed to go anywhere again.'

Then the teacher told her, 'If you're not going to tell your parents, then we won't say anything about it.'

Once again the stranger had had an extraordinary stroke of luck. Despite breaking into a youth hostel twice with the apparent intention of kidnapping a young girl to have sex with her, he had not only been freed by the police but it seemed that there was little or no chance of the incidents being followed up.

Years later Valerie said she still couldn't believe how disappointingly the police and the school handled the situation. She says she should never have been used as a sort of bait without her knowledge, and is still amazed the man wasn't charged. However well intentioned they had been, 'The police set me up that night,' she recalled. 'If they had told me they were going to do it I would have gone along with it – but to let me go to sleep and wake up again in fear was wrong. That is not right for a 14-year-old hundreds of miles from home. They left me in the bedroom like a sitting duck. They could have caught him at the front door. They let him come all the way up to the bedroom.'

Later, it was also revealed that the hostel manager, Yves Franquelin even told the police he believed it was the same man who had been at L'Heresie the previous year, on 8 July, when another girl had been approached outside by a man asking her to help him carry a suitcase. The man had even returned to the same hostel 14 days later and used the same suitcase trick to try to lure a 14-year-old French girl outside, but she too ran off. Even though his car registration number was noted, the police failed to follow it up. And when the youth-hostel manager made an official complaint and demanded that the man be arrested, the local prosecutor told the police that there wasn't enough evidence for them to arrest him.

Valerie Jacques remains convinced that if she hadn't woken up the first night she would have been killed. 'I'm sure the girls in the room with me that night might have woken up next morning and found me dead. I'm still appalled that man wasn't dealt with properly after what happened to me.' She added, 'I also have a feeling of guilt. Guilt that I didn't do enough. Guilt that I was fobbed off.'

When Valerie got back to school in Ireland, her ordeal was never mentioned again. It was only many years later that her parents discovered the chilling truth that their beloved daughter had been attacked by a sinister sex killer.

Yves Franquelin was doubly angry because the police had released the man without charge. He later explained, 'Everyone who spoke to me about this man referred to his extraordinary cold-blooded, methodical and practised manner of approaching girls. The girls the previous year said he'd even followed them to Tours on a school trip and quite openly spied on them. He made no obscene gestures, but they were certain he was watching them and they felt afraid.'

The hostel manager summed up the tall, dark stranger by saying, 'We had somebody here who knew how to approach people with a lot of tact. He did not disturb anybody. He did not wake anybody. He inspired trust rather than mistrust. That makes him somebody who is extremely dangerous. We had someone here who was determined, who had set up a strategy, an intelligent person, who, on top of that, was very strong mentally.'

But the police in Blere were plainly out of their depth. It was, Franquelin recalled, 'too big a job for them'. They referred the case to Interpol and told him it would take time. But he wanted charges pressed against the man immediately in the hope it would at least scare him away from his hostel for good. Franquelin was furious. Little did he know that the man had already served time in prison for a triple rape.

His enduring impression of the strange man was chilling: 'He seemed to be relaxed, an ordinary man who would not stand out in a crowd. He also spoke English and French very well. The man was very calm, extremely calm. The first thing he said was: "You have to release me – you have not charged me." I was extremely surprised he was released. For the first time in my life, I heard somebody with a legal argument. "I didn't do anything bad. You cannot keep me. Let me go." That was it. This is terrible, terrible.'

7

By this time, the stranger had murdered at least two women and raped more than a dozen; it was clear that he was an evil person and there was no turning back from the self-destructive path he had chosen to follow. He was now committed to satisfying his twisted urges whenever they took over his body and soul. And undoubtedly he enjoyed the acts of sex and causing pain. For him, to rape or kill a young girl was the ultimate high; it was now the driving force behind everything he did, from his part-time job, which provided enough cash for him to keep on the move, to his addiction to booze and pills. This was now the entire pattern of his life.

In his heart, he believed that the more sexually satisfying those assaults the better it was for him. Why should he care about his victims? He knew what it was like to be a victim and no one had cared about him. He had plans to keep going for the rest of his life, although this time he would try to be careful not to commit any crimes too near to where he lived. He continued to make sure he always had at least two different sets of number plates in the boot of his vehicle, which could be used to help a getaway. He'd learned after his arrest at the German-Dutch border that if he'd switched plates they would never have got him.

He liked hunting. It provided him with a purpose to his life, something which had been sorely missing when he was younger. Now he had real power and it felt good.

Cramped though his bedsit in London was, the killer was reasonably content with his life in England. He had a job as a waiter at a huge luxury hotel, which provided him with a few interesting diversions, like spying on women guests and stealing their underwear whenever it took his fancy. But he was very careful not to overstep the mark at the hotel because he knew that this might lead to another spell in jail and he never wanted to go back behind bars ever again.

He often volunteered for the evening shift at the hotel, which meant working as a room-service waiter. Every night he would come into contact with guests in their rooms. Often these were very spoiled teenage girls, who would order lavish meals, which he would deliver to their rooms with a smile.

Whenever he was about to respond to a room-service order, he would check the names on the register for the room to see if they were young, female and alone. There were some complaints about the 'creepy waiter with the wolf face' but the police were never called, so it's unlikely we will ever know if he actually attacked any of the hotel's guests.

He saved his really destructive urges for the weekends, when he would stock up with enough pills and whisky to keep him going while he drove out of London on hunting expeditions. One such trip found him driving up the M1 towards the

Pennines on Monday, 7 November 1994. Thanks to his shift work at the hotel, he often got two or three days off in the week and on this occasion he completed a day shift and then headed up the motorway to Yorkshire. He liked the Pennines because they were often deserted for mile after mile, especially during the cold winter months. He'd read somewhere about the British killers Ian Brady and Myra Hindley, who had murdered children and then buried some of them at Saddleworth Moor, on the western side of the Pennines. He liked to think about the couple when he was driving across the Pennines hunting for prey. But this time, after hours and hours of circling without any success, he decided to go into Hebden Bridge.

Just after 10pm, the killer spotted 13-year-old schoolgirl Lindsay Rimer from his car, walking out of a supermarket in the town's high street with a box of cornflakes in her hand. She lived with her parents at nearby Cambridge Street and was a pupil at Calder High School. She was perfect for his depraved purposes. He slowed down and lowered the window to ask directions. His foreign-sounding voice was so soft and gentle the young girl didn't think twice about his kind offer of a lift home.

Five months later Lindsay's body was recovered from the nearby Rochdale Canal. Naturally, the murder shocked the community. The police were baffled and failed to round up any suspects, despite interviewing more than 5,000 local people about the schoolgirl's mysterious disappearance. As so often happened when the killer struck, the police believed a local man must have been responsible.

The death of innocent little Lindsay was soon pushed to the back of the killer's mind as he pressed on with his strange, empty life.

After allegedly murdering Lindsay Rimer, the killer slipped ever deeper into dependency on drugs and alcohol. Afranil became his only escape from the reality of his crimes. To get those tablets he needed money, which he routinely secured from either his father or his part-time work as a waiter.

Meanwhile, he would slink in and out of youth hostels across mainland Europe and Britain, leaving few clues, molesting young girls, many of whom were too scared to complain about his attacks. He also attacked hitchhikers and sometimes, when he lost control, these attacks turned into something even more serious. If he was in his car, he would dispose of the body and immediately drive for hours on end, knowing full well that by the time the police found the corpse he would be long gone. He didn't feel in any way that police forces across the continent would ever catch up with him. Despite his obsession with cleanliness, he now resembled a vagrant. Many who encountered him said he had the look of a broken man, drifting through life with little purpose.

He had no friends and had become even more untrusting of other people, which made him a true loner. Just like when he was a teenager in Gijon, he would often stay in his little room in Earl's Court all day and night, trying to get turned on watching porn videos featuring young girls, although he could never quite achieve the right level of excitement because the only female fix that really worked for him was the real thing.

Schoolgirls, usually aged 12 to 14, were now his staple diet. He liked them that age because they would always be as pure as driven snow and usually too physically weak to fight back.

In a welter of pills and booze, his days in London blurred into weeks and months, only occasionally interrupted when the urge to find a new victim took over and forced him to go out and prowl the streets and communities of Britain, usually far from the capital.

The mixture of strong drink and drugs made him prone to mistakes and sparked much of his paranoia, but he didn't care, just as no one seemed to care about him. His mother had ingrained in him the meaning of unforgivingness by the way she had treated him, especially when he most needed help as a deeply troubled teenager. Now, faced with the reality of his appalling crimes, he had slipped into a kind of trance, which enabled him not to have to deal with the consequences of his actions. He could no longer separate fact from fiction, reality from fantasy. It had all merged into one, although he did sometimes wake up at night wondering if his whole life was just a bad dream.

His hangovers had become so painful and depressing that he even tried to kick the pills and booze habit which had long since fuelled his uncontrollable sexual desires. But that would only last a day or two and then he'd be back downing bottles of Scotch and hungrily swallowing any tablets he could lay his hands on.

8

Sex and murder were increasingly dominating the distorted mind of the tall, dark stranger with the wolf-like face as he hunted up and down the continent of Europe, including Britain. He was constantly on the lookout for a situation to exploit.

Then he would deploy nerves of steel, cool control and a total lack of fear, even though he had always been considered rather placid by childhood acquaintances back in his hometown. He was now in his mid-forties, much older than the stereotypical sex attacker. He also had no dormant, boring marriage to run away from. He was the ultimate loner. He knew what it was like to sleep on a mattress on the floor as he'd done it many times as a youngster. He'd wanted a job in a school or a gym or a swimming pool because it would bring him into closer contact with the adolescent girls he so lusted after, but in the end he decided he preferred life on the road, moving from place to place, keeping a low profile but capable of striking at any moment.

In the summer of 1996, the killer was very busy. In June, as he was driving from London to see his family in Gijon, he pounced on a schoolgirl in a youth hostel in Brittany. During the attack, he slipped into an upstairs room of a hostel where three schoolgirls from Manchester were sleeping. Two of them woke up just as he was choking the life out of their friend. All three started screaming and he slipped away before they could get a proper look at him. One of the girls said afterwards, 'I looked across and saw the shape of a man leaning across my friend's bed. She was making choking noises.'

It was a close shave for the stranger. But it didn't deter him in the slightest. After all, he had nothing to lose. Incredibly, the French gendarmes didn't even bother to circulate a warning to youth hostels in the area about the tall, dark sexual predator. And, as usual, there was no attempt to take fingerprints from the scene of the crime.

A few weeks later, on 11 July, the killer was driving his UK-registered Renault 5 out of Gijon, about to start the long trip back to London. An hour later, he stopped off at the holiday resort of Llanes, 80 kilometres east of his hometown. He'd decided to do some 'research work' because he was keen to find a good hunting ground nearer to Gijon.

Pedro Cembranos, director of the Font de Cai youth hostel in Llanes, noted the arrival of a new guest that day who was unusual in that he was in his mid-forties. He noticed the man had joined the Youth Hostels Association in England and was driving a beaten-up car with UK number plates. The man seemed to behave quite normally, so there was no reason to be suspicious of him at the time. It was not until five years later that Cembranos realised the significance of his visit.

Following his one-night stay at the hostel in Llanes, the

stranger took the smaller roads up through France with the aim, on his way back to London, of trying yet again to see his son and ex-lover Christine Le Menes at their home near Rennes. It was to prove a futile detour because Christine once more refused to open the front door of her apartment to him.

So it was that, after yet more rejection, he found himself driving towards one of his favourite haunts, Mont St Michel, a small rocky, tidal island off Normandy, near the border with Brittany. Its Benedictine Abbey and steepled church built between the 11th and 16th centuries made it an immensely popular tourist haunt for parties of schoolchildren from all over the world. The stranger knew that at this time of year a large number of British teenage girls would be enjoying school trips at the famous beauty spot. He liked British girls the best because of their pale complexions and interesting faces.

On 16 July, the stranger was seen in the Breton village of Antrain, some 20 kilometres south of Mont St Michel. A small farming community virtually impenetrable to outsiders, Antrain occupied a hillside deep in the countryside. Two people in the village saw the killer, but they didn't realise the significance of this until years later. One woman working in a creperie was even approached by the stranger, who asked to use her telephone. She was immediately nervous and pointed to a nearby public telephone.

'What's the problem?' he snapped at her. 'Are you afraid to be alone with me? Do you think I'll rape you?'

A male customer in the creperie was so worried by the stranger's behaviour that he rang his wife, who was working in a nearby shop, and told her to call the police if he approached her. The stranger then crossed to the telephone kiosk and spent around 20 minutes making calls, after which he disappeared.

The following day he arrived at Mont St Michel. As usual, he didn't care who spotted him staring and sizing up teenage schoolgirls because he knew he couldn't be arrested just for looking at them. Dressed in denim and driving his beaten-up Renault 5, he looked like a harmless old hippy touring the highways and byways of France.

In the town square, the stranger closely studied a group of schoolgirls from Launceston Community College, in Cornwall. One of the girls he particularly watched was 13-year-old Caroline Dickinson, who was blissfully unaware of the tall, dark stranger with the wolf-like features staring at her from the other side of the square. Caroline was among a party of 40 pupils from her mixed-sex comprehensive school enjoying an end-of-term trip to Brittany and Normandy.

She was writing a postcard to her beloved father, John Dickinson, about her holiday:

'Dear Daddy,

'I'm in France! It's really good here, I'm having a great time! How are you? We've been to loads of cool places, I'll tell you all about it soon. Love you lots and I wish you were here!

'X Caroline X.'

She addressed the postcard to 'Daddy in England' and planned to post it later that day. Not long afterwards, the group boarded a bus for the 15-minute drive back to their hostel in the pretty village of Pleine-Fougeres.

Caroline's trip to France had been planned for a long time. Before she'd left Launceston at 7.45am the previous Sunday, she and her mum had ended up packing enough clothes for a holiday twice as long.

Sue Dickinson recalled her daughter's departure: 'She was very cuddly and treated me to two huge hugs and kisses. When

I waved her goodbye, I missed her immediately, but consoled myself thinking she'd be back in a few days.'

The coach carrying Caroline and her friends from Cornwall followed a familiar itinerary: it boarded the Sunday-morning ferry from Poole to St Malo, then headed for the youth hostel in Pleine-Fougeres, chosen especially for its location away from major towns but close to the region's biggest tourist attractions. The party would be the hostel's only guests throughout the six-day trip, which would involve trips to Bayeux and Mont St Michel, lots of meals in restaurants and constant encouragement from teachers to speak French.

Sue Dickinson described Caroline as 'just an innocent child' when she set off on the school trip. 'She was very small for her age. She was still very much a child and she was in age-11 clothing when she went to France. She was wearing Forever Friends children's underwear, didn't wear a bra and wore size-three shoes. She had not started puberty. She had no experience or interest in love or sexual relationships. She was a quiet girl and very thoughtful. She loved school and was also a homely person. She loved ballet, piano, playing the clarinet, swimming and gymnastics. Caroline was doing French at school and it was decided it would help her confidence to go to France. I was never very keen about it, but she was excited. She even paid for part of it out of her own pocket money. It was the first trip away from home she had been on. She hadn't even walked to school on her own.'

On reaching the hostel in Brittany that Sunday night, Caroline had phoned her mother to say she'd arrived safely.

'What's the hostel like?' Sue asked her daughter.

'It's crappy, Mum, but I enjoyed the boat trip.' Caroline then promised to send her mother a postcard. Just then the phone pips went.

'See you Friday, darling,' said Sue.

After following Caroline Dickinson and the rest of her coach party to the youth hostel in Pleine-Fougeres, the stranger changed his mind and decided to head for the ferry back to Britain from St Malo, 40 minutes' drive north of the village.

But he arrived five minutes after the last ship had departed for Portsmouth. Drowning his sorrows in booze and pills, he decided to head to the nearby resort of St Lunaire, just a few kilometres west of St Malo. The terrain reminded him of northern Spain, especially the huge estuary that he drove over.

St Lunaire nestled in a little cove. It was the stranger's dream location because it had been specifically designed to attract young people there for holidays. He passed the junior school in the village before spotting signs for hotels and the beach. Then he saw what he was looking for. 'Colonie de Vacances,' said the sign. He slammed on the brakes, did a sharp U-turn and headed up a quieter, much narrower road towards the holiday colony.

A massive white crucifix on a street corner alongside a pond startled him. Just then, he saw St Lunaire's youth hostel in the distance. It was the perfect, isolated spot for him to strike. He gently slowed the car down to a halt and sat and contemplated his next move.

It was well after midnight by the time he felt it was safe to enter the hostel. Most of the dormitory lights were out as he walked silently on the balls of his feet towards the red-brick building at the back.

British schoolgirl Kate Wrigley, 13, was on a school trip and it was her last night in France. She and her friends had held a fancy-dress party earlier in the evening, but by this time they were all fast asleep in their room at the holiday colony after an exhausting day.

Kate's friend Jenna Ellis woke up to the sound of banging, choking and panting 'like an animal'. She explained, 'I climbed on to the top of the bunk bed, woke up a friend and looked over the partition wall. We could see a gentleman standing over Kate's bed. He appeared to be leaning over the bed, as if he was half knelt down. I thought it was a teacher and I shouted at him to see what was happening to Kate, to see if she was having an asthma attack. But he would not answer. He stood away from the bed and then exited the room calmly.'

Jenna immediately went over to Kate, who was foaming at the mouth and suffering from a seriously burned face. 'It looked like severe sunburn,' Jenna recalled. She also noticed that her friend's underwear was in the middle of the room. Kate, who remembered nothing of the actual attack, later said she woke up panicking and delirious. She was struggling for air and coughing and wheezing heavily. Her skin was burning from the alcohol that had been smeared all over her by the intruder.

Kate recalled, 'All I remember is waking up and not being able to breathe. My face was all swollen and bruised like really bad sunburn. I had cuts and bruises on my arms and legs. I woke up the other girls. Then the teachers came down and took me to their room to spend the rest of the night with them. It was only the next morning the other girls said that a man had been seen near my bed just before I woke up. They said Jenna had seen a man over my bed. But, at the age of 13,

I was more concerned about my face. I was in pain and I just wanted to get home.'

Jenna later admitted she panicked when she saw the stranger and, after he left, was so scared she and her friends armed themselves with coat-hangers to protect themselves. She also claimed the teachers 'did not take them seriously' until the following day, when they realised the girls must have been telling the truth.

The stranger himself later explained how he went to the hostel and became aroused by the sight of Kate Wrigley in bed. 'I was excited. I wanted to caress her. I think I sat down on her bed and tried to stroke her. Then I felt someone had noticed. I remember I put my hand on her mouth so that she would not scream and I must have attracted someone, so I left the bedroom immediately.'

What he didn't admit was that, in his strange quest for cleanliness, he stole a box of cotton wool from Kate's bedside table because he was intent on finding sexual gratification elsewhere.

He then left the hostel quickly by a back stairway.

9

The killer was not a man to give up easily. Fuelled by drink and drugs, he was now even more obsessed with achieving sexual satisfaction. He remembered the other hostel in Pleine-Fougeres and the British schoolchildren he followed there from Mont St Michel.

As church bells rang two o'clock that moonlit night, the stranger started his battered old Renault 5, determined to continue to his next destination, where he hoped to satisfy his urgent sexual needs.

He knew it was imperative to get away from St Lunaire as quickly as possible. His hands shook as he grabbed the steering wheel unsteadily, desperate to sate his sick desires. He later claimed he first thought about heading for the ferry at Cherbourg, to get back to London as quickly as possible. But the need for sexual gratification was now so strong he instead headed towards the hostel in Pleine-Fougeres, some 40 kilometres away. He drove down the hill, away from the St

Lunaire hostel, to a crossroads where a sign indicated it was straight on for St Malo.

He was feeling a heady mix of fear and excitement after his close shave at the youth hostel and knew he needed to keep his driving steady, otherwise he would be stopped by the police, who were always more alert at this time of night. The road was bordered by cornfields, which shone eerily in the moonlight. One extreme bend almost caused him to lose control of the car as the road swept deceptively to the right. Eventually he got back on to the main road to Rennes, where Christine Le Menes, his ex-lover and the mother of his child, lived. That made him wonder about going back one more time to try to see them. Surely it was worth one last attempt? He had nothing to lose.

But before that he had some important business to attend to.

Now he was heading along a straight road with 70 kilometres to go before he reached Rennes. He was coming down from the drink and drugs but that simply made him more focused on the task in hand. As he swept across the bridge that linked the estuary, he saw the lights of St Malo fade in the distance and knew there was no turning back.

He was very careful to stick to the speed limit of 70 kilometres per hour because he knew he would fail a breath test. He needed more drink and drugs but didn't dare stop in case he drew attention to himself. Pleine-Fougeres was all he cared about. He had to reach the village, find those schoolgirls and satisfy his urge.

Each time he saw another green road sign for Rennes it reminded him of Christine and his son. He was still hoping that one day she would let him back into their lives.

On his left now was a long, empty strip of beach glistening

in moonlight. Then his mind started cutting back to those young girls staying in Pleine-Fougeres. After satisfying himself with them, he might go on and try to see Christine and the boy one last time.

Another urge – to take more pills and alcohol to bring back the earlier buzz – was also raging in his mind. He stopped in a lay-by and, after knocking back his poison, he sat back and waited for the cocktail to kick in. Thoughts of Christine and his son were replaced in an instant by images of sex. He had to appease the desire which had earlier driven him to break into the hostel in St Lunaire.

Visibility that night was not good. A combination of a light mist and his intake of drink and drugs meant it was hard to make everything out in front of him. Surely it couldn't be much further to that hostel at Pleine-Fougeres and those English schoolgirls? He'd already given up the fight with his own conscience.

Then he spotted a sign warning of deer. Good. He now knew he was in the heart of the quiet countryside, which he so preferred to the city. Just then a sign for Pleine-Fougeres appeared. There was no turning back. This was more important than Christine and his son. These urges had to be dealt with. I'll do what the fuck I want, he thought to himself. Why should I care?

Excitement was crashing through his veins. He had no choice but to yield to his cravings. Behind him, the beautifully illuminated spiral of the church on Mount St Michel was backlit by the night sky.

Pleine-Fougeres, a community with a population of just 3,500, was desolate and the stranger felt as if he was driving through an empty national park when he finally reached the outskirts of the village. Little pillar boxes with small red lights looked like cars in the distance and startled him at first, but they turned out to be kilometre markers. A small wood loomed up on the left shaped like a table. Now he was in full hunting mode, eyes flitting in all directions, searching out any familiar buildings.

Just then he saw a sign reading 'Auberge de Jeunesse'. A youth hostel. He was on track. At a T-junction, he entered the village itself and followed the signs like an addict seeking a fix. The car swayed as his excitement mounted. The signposts urged him on. No, there was no turning back. Then another sign for the youth hostel loomed up. 'Come and get me,' it seemed to say. 'Come and get me.'

He smiled when he saw a sign which told him Pleine-Fougeres was twinned with Huerte in Spain. If it had been daylight, he would have noticed the nearby fields with cows grazing. This area also had strong links to apples, cider and calvados. Strange how similar it all was to Gijon, which was another region renowned for its apples. There was even a cider factory and museum in Pleine-Fougeres.

Carefully he followed the sign for the youth hostel, passing a big water tower, a modern house and a large green warehouse. Then he came to the building itself – an old chateau with an even older semi-circular tower in the corner. He pulled his car up gently so as not to make too much noise. His eyes immediately focused on the entrance at the back of the main building. It looked perfect.

In the distance the rumble of a freight train pushing its way along the track on the south side of the village made him realise he should move his car farther away from the hostel to be certain no one connected him to what was about to happen. His night-stalker instincts were kicking in. He ended up parking 200 metres from the hostel, next to a shut-down agricultural college.

His hands were shaking violently as he leaned behind the seat for more pills and alcohol. He was more sexually charged than ever before in his entire life. He blamed it on that 'near miss' at the youth hostel in St Lunaire. He was blinded by the need for sex.

On the evening of 17 July 1996, the party of 39 children and six teachers and helpers had gathered around the long wooden tables in the dining room of the hostel in Pleine-Fougeres for a dinner of tabouleh salad, chicken and green beans. Afterwards, some watched television while others played cards. At 9pm, Gregoire Choleau, 29, the hostel director, left for the night after he and his assistant, 20-year-old Manuela Bernard, had herded the teenagers to their rooms. Two hours later, it would be 'lights out'.

Laughing and joking, 13-year-old Caroline Dickinson could hardly have been happier as she settled down for the night in a room with four of her closest school friends. They chatted playfully about what names they would give their own children when they were adults. Caroline looked forward to another exciting day visiting the sights and sampling French food and practising the language.

Room Four was on the first floor at the front of the chateau. The rooms all had paper-thin walls and were connected to the ground and second floors by two staircases, one of which was narrow and creaked. Caroline had been granted her wish to stay with her friends but ended up sleeping on a mattress between their bunk beds when one of them shouted, 'Last one to a bed's a sissy' and Caroline lost.

Her friend Camilla Percival later explained, 'We were going to swap each night and take it in turns to sleep on the mattress but never got around to doing it.' Caroline lay on a mattress between the two metal-framed bunk beds as they all chatted. With the mattress on the floor, it was difficult for anyone to open the door fully into the 12-foot-square room.

That night Caroline sang herself to sleep with the nursery rhyme 'Twinkle Twinkle, Little Star'. Camilla recalled, 'Caroline drifted off to sleep… looking out of the open window up at the lovely night sky.'

10

Down below, the predator was quietly entering the hostel through the unlocked front door. Despite overflowing with drink and drugs, he was still focused enough to creep through the darkness like a cat burglar. Slipping quietly along the hallway, he headed for the wooden staircase leading to the first floor.

Amy White, another pupil of Launceston Community College, was sleeping in a dormitory opposite Caroline. Later, she remembered seeing a man in his thirties, who looked very unkempt with his long, straggly hair and 'distinctive bushy eyebrows', walking through the hallway.

The killer was sweating profusely, feeling a strange mixture of fear and elation at what he was about to do. Something was driving him on to commit a profoundly evil act. At one stage, he thought he heard footsteps behind him and this, he later claimed, was why he had decided to climb the stairs to the first floor, where Caroline Dickinson and her friends were sleeping.

Seeing the door of the first room he came to slightly open, he nudged it wider and immediately saw the outline of a young girl's body in a sleeping bag between her friends' bunk beds.

He reached into the pocket of his jean-jacket and grabbed a handful of cotton wool, which he had already soaked in alcohol in the car after taking it earlier from the youth hostel in St Lunaire. His breathing unsteady, he waited for his eyes to adjust to the darkness in the room and then pulled back the girl's sleeping bag and began to wipe her with the cotton wool. Even though she was still asleep, he decided to stuff cotton wadding into her mouth just in case she woke up and screamed. This time there could be no half measures. He felt the excitement careering through his body as he prepared her for the ultimate sacrifice. Then he put his hand over her mouth to stop her whimpering. As he bent forward and undid the zip of his trousers, she was already fighting for breath.

Years later a doctor who examined the killer would comment, 'There was an absolute determination and ferocity to succeed. He wanted his pleasure, whatever the cost to his victim. It was imperative that she did not cry out.'

And the killer himself later admitted, 'I went and lay down next to her. I realised it was a young girl. I was aroused and I didn't feel well. I wanted to do what I had done before, so I placed my hand over her mouth.' He added, 'I lifted up the cover and I wanted to stroke her. I was very much aroused and I wanted to do the same thing that I had done in St Lunaire.' He said he took off Caroline's underwear, put his hand over her mouth, masturbated and then assaulted her. Initially, he denied using cotton wool to suffocate her, claiming he had used the cotton wool found at the scene as a bandage because he had burned his hand on his car engine. But the truth was, he came chillingly well prepared for the attack.

'Afterwards I was still aroused,' he added. 'I think I started stroking her again and then I left.' He said his memory was blurred because he had been drinking heavily.

Ann Jasper was one of the other teenage girls sharing the hostel bedroom with Caroline Dickinson. She woke up in the middle of the attack and later said she heard Caroline pleading, 'Mum!' and 'Help!' as she was being raped and murdered by the tall, dark stranger. Ann thought Caroline was 'talking in her sleep'.

'I woke up because I heard a banging noise,' she recalled. 'Then I heard Caroline wriggling in her bed. I could hear her mumbling but I thought she was dreaming. Then I sat up and saw her kicking in her sleeping bag. It sounded funny but I didn't think anything of it. I was awake for about five minutes.'

Caroline's friend Melissa Hutchings was also woken. 'It was the sound of a sleeping bag being undone and coughing noises,' she said. 'I could see kicking movements coming from where Caroline was asleep. It sounded like someone was having breathing difficulties. It lasted a few minutes but I paid little attention to it. The weather was hot and I told myself she was having a nightmare. Then the noises stopped. Then I saw the shape of a body rising and thought it was Caroline.'

Another friend remembered, 'I was woken by the noise of something hitting the wall. I looked down and saw that Caroline was kicking out in her sleeping bag. It appeared a little odd but I thought she was having a nightmare and turned over and fell asleep again.'

None of the three girls who were disturbed had any idea that a strange man had invaded their room and murdered their friend just a few feet from them.

In fact, the killer had decided on the spot that the murder of this little girl would help him cover up the rape he'd just committed. He'd silenced her first with cotton wool and then violated her. Medical experts later said Caroline died in 'tens of seconds and a maximum of two minutes' and that her killer had left her with bruises to her throat and scratches on her face. According to one of the coroners who examined her body, 'It was as if an animal had ravaged her.'

Before he departed, the killer carefully zipped up Caroline's sleeping bag and made sure her head was covered. That surely meant he knew she was dead. Then he slipped quietly back out into the darkness.

Just before 5am, teacher Jacqueline Thorpe was woken by footsteps outside. She went to the window and saw a man dressed in black walking away from the hostel towards the main road. He did not appear to be acting furtively. 'I wondered who it was at this hour. I told myself that I must speak about it the next morning to the person in charge of the inn.' It was probably the killer she saw.

Also inside the hostel, two other schoolgirls heard footsteps on the gravel in front of the hostel. Then a car door opened and closed, followed by an engine starting. He was gone.

The killer was drenched in sweat. He knew she was dead, but now his priority was to get away as quickly as possible. He drove back the same way he'd come, but he had a few problems remembering the route. He was finding it difficult to focus on the road after consuming so much drink and drugs.

Eventually coming to a stop sign, he recognised the name of a small town called Dol-de-Bretagne and took a left in the hope of getting back on the road to Rennes. He picked up speed considerably as he drove between the dimly moonlit cornfields and then up a twisting hill where brightly coloured chevrons warned of dangerous bends. Above him, the rays of the moon outlined the top of a huge hill crowned by a clump of trees. Now he was travelling at 100 kilometres per hour, hoping he would be far away before they discovered what he had done.

He had to keep driving. He'd done wrong and now had to get to Rennes to try to see his son, the only good thing he had ever produced in his entire life. He concentrated hard on the road, determined no one was going to catch him.

In the youth hostel in Pleine-Fougeres, the reality of what had happened to Caroline Dickinson was only just beginning to emerge. When they awoke the following morning none of her friends realised she was dead. Two of the girls were getting dressed when they noticed that Caroline and their friend Camilla Percival were still asleep. One of them yelled out, 'Come on, Milly. Come on, Caroline. Are you going to get up or not?' Camilla later explained, 'I could see Caroline was mainly under her duvet and I asked, "Is she still asleep? Why isn't she getting up?" I shouted at her, but she didn't appear to be listening.' Then, as she looked over the side of her bunk, down at Caroline, Camilla said, 'She doesn't look very well.'

She got out of her bunk and shook Caroline. Still no response, so she repeated, 'Caroline's not well.' She recalled, 'Then I threw back her sleeping bag and saw she wasn't wearing any pyjama bottoms.

'I had been a St John Ambulance cadet and, even though I was only 12, I knew some basic first aid. I noticed her lips were blue. When I touched her, she was cold. I tried her pulse, but couldn't find any. I said to the other girls, "I think she's dead."

They wouldn't believe me. One said, "Don't be horrible", as if I was joking. I tried to stay calm but I rushed out of the room and grabbed another girl in the corridor and quickly fetched a teacher.'

The teacher rushed into the room and shouted, 'Oh my God!' Then all the children were ushered quickly out of the room.

Caroline Dickinson's head was resting on her mattress, by contrast with its position the previous evening. Also, the shutters, opened by the schoolgirls during the night because of the heat, were now closed. None of them remembered having done that.

Teacher Elizabeth Barker, 61, found Caroline lying on her back covered up to her neck by her sleeping bag. Even though the girl's lips were blue, the teacher put her in the recovery position. 'The cover slipped and I could see Caroline had a lot of blood between her thighs, some of which was dry,' she explained. 'Her lips were cold and blue. I couldn't raise her head. I tried to open her mouth without success.'

A school nurse then arrived at the scene and immediately said, 'There's nothing we can do. She's dead.' The nurse recalled, 'I was very shocked. This was a girl who the night before was fit, well and laughing, and now she was unconscious. Caroline was shy and quiet, but during the trip she blossomed. She enjoyed herself and was developing relationships. She was a delight.'

The scene in Room Four on that Thursday morning was one of utter chaos. Caroline lay in her sleeping bag, one bare arm exposed. Near her body was a folded wad of cotton wool. It bore traces of her blood and saliva and was later to prove an important clue. However, on that first day it was put into a plastic bag by gendarmes and dismissed as irrelevant.

In rural France, serious crimes are always investigated by the gendarmerie under the direction of a *juge d'instruction*, a magistrate who tells the police what they must do. There was no such official to be found that day. The man to whom the job was to fall, Gerard Zaug, was on holiday. The gendarme commandant took charge personally. He ordered all available men on to the case, and, within an hour of the discovery of Caroline's body, officers were milling around Room Four. No attempt was made to put a forensic cordon around the scene. Incredibly, the room and the floor around Caroline's sleeping bag were never thoroughly tested for fingerprints.

Caroline Dickinson had apparently been raped and suffocated by a man who had broken into the hostel on the ground floor and crept upstairs to her room while she and her classmates slept. Her murder alarmed teachers, parents and pupils, who regarded school trips abroad as a natural and enjoyable part of growing up. What they didn't know was that her killer was a serial sexual predator, whose victims included other young girls, attacked while supposedly in the safety of their beds in other hostels.

Caroline's mother, Sue Dickinson, was relaxing with a friend by the sea near Bude, in Cornwall, on that Thursday morning. 'My pal and I were talking about our kids when a police car pulled up beside the beach,' she later explained. A policeman and policewoman walked towards her, and she was immediately told, 'Your daughter has been found dead in France.'

She recalled, 'I felt sick. I remember thinking it must be a mistake. I sobbed as they put their arms around me and walked me to the car. I kept saying it couldn't be true.'

Caroline's father was photocopying paperwork at his office

in Cornwall when his boss grabbed him gently by the arm and led him down the corridor. 'John,' he said. 'It's serious.' John Dickinson thought it was about his job but then he saw the police waiting at the end of the corridor. 'I thought my ex-wife had been in an accident,' he later explained. But then an inspector came up and told him, 'Your daughter Caroline is dead, Mr Dickinson.'

'Almost mechanically I asked, how?' John Dickinson recalled. 'They said it was a suspicious death but they didn't know any more.'

As he and his former wife Sue set off for France by ferry that afternoon, his mind was working overtime. He called a cousin in the police force to ask what a suspicious death could mean and was told it was probably either murder or drugs. On a school holiday? At 13. It's not true. It's impossible, he thought to himself. Then he remembered his laughing words to Caroline before she set off: 'Be careful of French boys!'

His mind flashed back to his only trip to France, camping and hitchhiking when he was 16. Now he was on his way back in France again, 25 years later, to collect his dead daughter.

John and Sue Dickinson caught an overnight ferry from Portsmouth to France. The crossing took seven hours, and it was the longest night of their lives. Sue recalled, 'John and I were shown to a cabin and he lay down. But I couldn't rest. I went to the coffee car and spent the whole night talking to two very kind English ladies. I was crying, telling them I was going to France because my daughter had died. I kept thinking it was not me on the ferry that night. I convinced myself Cazzie was still alive.'

On the couple's arrival at the port of Cherbourg, police

officers escorted them to Pleine-Fougeres. And when they reached the village the French police released all the facts to the media. They then told the Dickinsons they couldn't talk about what had happened to Caroline until the detective dealing with the case arrived. As John Dickinson later explained, 'There was an air of unreality about what was happening.'

They waited for more than half an hour before they were ushered into an office by two French police officers, who seemed very open and sympathetic, although quite hardened to such situations. Sue Dickinson recalled, 'They took us into a bare room and told us Caz had been raped and asphyxiated. I couldn't take it in. How on earth could this have happened on a school trip? I wanted to know every single detail – no matter how painful. But John could hardly bear to listen. The police showed me Caroline's broken necklace. That made it so real.'

John Dickinson recalled, 'There are no words that can express how you react when you are told something like that. It is quite devastating.'

Sue added, 'Then the urge came over me to get Caroline and all her things and bring her safely home. I felt a terrible sense of having lost control over my own child.' She demanded to be immediately taken to the morgue in Rennes.

Less than an hour later, she was cuddling her daughter's corpse and talking to her. 'I never wanted to leave her alone again,' she later explained. 'I hugged her close to me. The injuries from the attack and autopsy were horribly visible. But no matter how awful she looked I could only see my lovely Cazzie.'

The French police gave the Dickinsons just 20 minutes with Caroline's body before insisting on taking them back to their hotel. 'As soon as we got to the hotel, I wanted to be back with her,' explained Sue. 'I hated to think of her alone in unfamiliar territory.'

So, later that same night, she returned to the morgue. 'She was in a bare room with nothing child-friendly about it at all. In the corner stood an artificial bunch of flowers and a Bible. I remember thinking Caz shouldn't be in a place like this. She wasn't an old person. She was a child. I reunited her with Snowy, the only fluffy toy she'd ever treasured. She looked so vulnerable. She'd already been violated and I didn't want her with coroners and other people she didn't know.' Over and over again, Sue kept wondering how all this could have happened on a school trip.

The Dickinsons then asked to see the room where their daughter was murdered. 'I wanted to spend a few moments alone there with Susan,' explained John. It was at the top of a creaking staircase, just like Caroline's room in Bodmin. John's feet were heavy and his heart racing as he went towards the room where his daughter had been so brutally murdered. The door had been sealed by the police but he insisted on being allowed in. However, the gendarmes refused his request and said he would have to come back another time, when the inquiry was over.

11

Less than 12 hours after leaving Pleine-Fougeres and the murdered corpse of schoolgirl Caroline Dickinson, the killer was safely back in his little bedsit in Earl's Court. That night he switched on the TV to hear the news about the young English girl found dead in her room at a youth hostel in Brittany. He later admitted, 'At the beginning I didn't attach much importance to the report. Then, later that night, I started to think that perhaps it was me who did that.'

But within days the killer would start to thrive on the attention being sparked by his appalling crime, safe in the knowledge that no one had the faintest idea he was the man who had snuffed out the life of little Caroline Dickinson. For the first time in his sad, lonely life he was *somebody*, even if nobody apart from him knew his darkest secrets.

Although there had been other killings, this one had completely captured the attention of the world's media, because this time he'd left a body where everyone could see it. The tall, dark stranger was pleased.

In Pleine-Fougeres, roadblocks were put up around the hostel by the police and a team of 50 officers began questioning the town's residents. Most investigators presumed that the killer lived locally, so they fully expected to get their man within days, if not hours.

Most of Caroline's school friends hadn't yet been told she was dead. Shortly after the discovery of her body, her four friends from that room had been taken to the Hotel des Voyageurs, opposite the town hall. Here they were looked after by Lionel and Nadine Morin, the owners, and their 14-year-old daughter, Elouise. Madame Morin was startled by an outburst of weeping that afternoon. She ran to her lounge to find the youngsters in tears. 'I asked the teacher what had happened. She said that they had only just been told Caroline was dead. I never realised that they didn't know the truth.'

Meanwhile, the French police assembled all the boys staying in the hostel, among them five from Launceston Community College. One of Caroline's schoolboy friends, Mark Hilton, recalled how he was told of the tragedy: 'There was something wrong, everyone was rushing around and there were people crying. I was thinking, Is she going to be OK?, and we were all very worried.'

The boys were told by their teachers to stay in the hostel in case anyone else became ill, so that they wouldn't have to rush back for a doctor.

Mark added, 'We could see they'd sealed off Caroline's room with yellow tape. We were all thinking this must be something really serious and the girls who were with Caroline in the same room were taken away from the hostel to a hotel. I was thinking this must be a really bad disease.'

When Mark's mother arrived in France to pick up her son, she was told she couldn't talk to the teenager for two and a half days because the police had to interview him. Mrs Ann Hilton later explained, 'I just wanted to hug him close but we weren't allowed to talk for two and a half days. I realised then that my son had been forced to grow up very quickly, before his time.'

On the Thursday evening, all the boys from Caroline's school were brought together and told that she had died. Mark Hilton explained, 'I couldn't cry. I was too shocked. We stayed up for the next two nights, us boys, to look after the girls because we knew Caroline had been raped. What we did was to split it up between us, and we kept going into the different girls' rooms to make sure everyone was OK. We used to leave the door open so that we could hear everything, then take it in turns to keep guard. I had a cuddly monkey with me and the girls asked if they could have it in their room for good luck, so I gave it to them.'

At this stage Mark Hilton and the other boys staying in the hostel were all considered potential suspects by the French police. As Mark's mother later explained, 'I want people to know what these boys went through because I believe the French police could have saved them a great deal of anguish.' The family agreed to let Mark give a DNA sample because it was 'the best way to end nasty speculation surrounding the five boys'. As the detective took a saliva test from Mark, he turned to his mother and said, 'I am very, very sorry. I want you to know there is no way your boy is a suspect.' The detectives later insisted they had destroyed the DNA test results.

Mark then told investigators of a group of French youths

hanging around the hostel on the night Caroline died and said he would definitely recognise them if he saw them again.

When the full post-mortem on Caroline was performed at the hospital in Rennes it was discovered that her stomach was virtually empty. Given that digestion takes up to six hours to complete, and that hers was completed, her death must have occurred at or after 3.30 that morning. That meant the man heard leaving by car at 5am could well have been her attacker.

Every English-speaking gendarme in the district was called in to help and a great many more broke their leave or holidays and volunteered to join the investigation. As time wore on, the formerly peaceful hostel was surrounded by between 60 and 70 armed policemen, while behind the barriers were 30 to 40 journalists. The police felt it was their duty to protect the children at all costs. The last thing they wanted was for the youngsters to be upset by crude, intrusive questioning from reporters. Keeping them out of sight became a priority. Back in Launceston, all the parents of children at Caroline's school just wanted their children home safely.

Caroline's classmates and teachers in Pleine-Fougeres were then ordered to stay another night at the hostel, despite the awful feelings of fear aroused by her murder. 'We cannot say when they will be allowed to leave. It could be some time, though, as they all have to be interviewed through interpreters,' explained one gendarme.

Investigating judge Gerard Zaug finally appeared from his holiday and immediately issued orders refusing the four girls who had shared Caroline's room permission to leave unless he was assured by a psychiatrist that they were in a fit state to travel. They were examined and pronounced fit by an Anglo-Indian psychiatrist named Dr Valayden.

This picture shows clearly the distinctive and terrifying 'wolf-like' features described by so many of Montes' victims.

Above left: According to neighbours, the ten-year-old Montes was shy, effeminate and awkward.

Above right: Montes in his twenties.

Below: Montes attended the Collegio Politecnico when he was a boy.

Above: The Clinica Providencia psychiatric hospital in Gijon, where Montes was committed during his troubled teenage years.

Below: Elena was followed home by Montes and attacked by him in the lobby of a block of flats in Gijon.

Above: Gijon health club manager Tino Diaz, who threw Montes out of the gym for leering at the female customers.

Below left: Housewife Nieves del Castillo caught Montes staring at her as she exercised at the same gym.

Below right: L'Heresie youth hostel in the Loire Valley, where Montes attacked at least three young girls on separate occasions.

This picture of Caroline became a familiar and haunting reminder of her shocking and tragic death.

Above: The room at the Pleine Fougeres hostel in which Caroline was raped and killed.

Below: A view of the back of the youth hostel.

Above left: The photofit picture of the suspect in the hunt for Caroline's killer.

Above right: The flat on the first floor of this house in Earl's Court was where Montes lived during and after the murder of Caroline Dickinson.

Below: Inside the Earl's Court bedsit.

Above: Patrice Pade, who was wrongly accused of the Dickinson murder.

Below: The sign pointing to Villabona Prison where Montes was jailed for another sex attack after he killed Caroline Dickinson, only to be released on bail and flee across the Atlantic.

The British Consul in Rennes, Ron Frankel, also exerted considerable pressure to get them released and by the third day – Saturday, 20 July – voices were being raised and conflict was simmering just beneath the surface. The French police felt they were being rushed and refused to let the children go. Outside the hostel, a forensic team was at last searching the surrounding grounds and making a proper, detailed forensic examination inside.

At 3.30 that afternoon, the children's bus, escorted by police motorcycle outriders, finally left for an undisclosed port. Roads along their route were blocked despite the fact that London tabloids had placed reporters at every possible ferry port in the hope of catching them. The coach trip proved an emotional roller coaster for all the children, and when the ferry reached English soil many of them wept with relief.

In Pleine-Fougeres, there reigned an atmosphere of complete and utter disbelief. In the small square, a few locals stood in silence watching police officers come and go from the youth hostel where Caroline had been murdered. Crime was virtually unknown in the community. As one gendarme noted, 'This is the kind of town where children can play on their own at night. There are no drugs, no trouble.'

Back in Britain, the cold-blooded murder had sparked an ever-growing avalanche of front-page headlines. MURDERED IN HER BED was a classic example in the *Daily Express* on 20 July 1996, which also published the last photo ever taken of Caroline. The paper summed up the story in its first paragraph: 'It was her first trip abroad. But for this carefree 13-year-old there will be no excited homecoming.' The picture had been taken just a day before she left on the trip to France.

The British press were quick to point out that the French

police had previously come under fire over their handling of cases of Britons murdered in France. Friends and relatives of some of the victims had accused them of dragging their feet.

Some British newspapers highlighted similar cases, including that of language student Joanna Parrish, 20, from Newnham, Lancashire, who was sexually assaulted and then strangled in 1990 in Brittany, and the murder of teachers Lorraine Glasby and Paul Bellion from East Anglia, who were killed while cycling in Brittany in 1996. Little did they know that the murder of Joanna Parrish would later be thought by some to possibly be linked to the same sex killer.

The people of Pleine-Fougeres were soon complaining that British journalists were much more aggressive than their French counterparts. 'They arrived in the village and were very open about wanting details and French people were very surprised at this intrusion. They were offended. It was too open and the French are shy and reserved,' commented one gendarme at the time.

In Launceston, as news of the murder began filtering through to Caroline's school, many mothers were near to tears as they collected their children. With memories of the recent shooting massacre at a school in Dunblane, Scotland, still fresh in people's minds, the rape and murder of Caroline Dickinson served as another reminder of the vulnerability of children. One woman picking up her 12-year-old daughter told reporters, 'This really is every parent's nightmare. When you send your children off on these trips abroad, you pray they won't get into any kind of trouble or danger, so it's always a relief when they come back. I just feel so sorry for Caroline's parents. She was so young. It's just terrible to think she won't be coming back alive.'

At Caroline's school, friends of the murdered teenager placed poignant tributes at the gates. One classmate left a furry toy cat with a solitary yellow rose, and a letter which read: 'Dear Caroline, I will always miss you for we have really been best friends even before we were born.'

Flags flew at half-mast in Launceston. A service of remembrance was held at the town's St Mary Magdalene Church, while in Pleine-Fougeres the police began to scale down their investigation, lifting cordons sealing off half the village and closing the incident room in the town hall. A French policeman admitted, 'We have completed the work on the ground but at present we have no suspects. The inquiry will take some time.'

Having returned to London, the killer avidly read all the coverage of Caroline Dickinson's murder with amusement. Clearly, investigators had not connected him to the murder. He thought it unlikely the French police would find out about his record in Spain or that prison sentence in Germany, since it seemed that criminal records didn't travel across international borders.

However, when the killer read what they were saying about him being a 'sick and twisted person', it made him angry. He believed it had taken courage to enter that youth hostel in the middle of the night not knowing who or what he might face. Britain's tabloids had dubbed him a sadistic, paedophile monster, which seemed unfair. In his eyes, he was a victim just as much as Caroline. But the schoolgirl's murder was his secret and it gave him strength every time he read about himself in the papers. Now he was someone for the first time in his life.

After murdering Caroline, her killer was determined to take

what he was doing to a new level – one that would shock and horrify the world in a way never known before. He adored the sensation of knowing that he alone could strike fear into millions. The killing itself and the way that various police forces had completely failed to liaise and exchange notes proved to him that he had the power and mental agility to avoid arrest for ever. Now he felt free to do whatever he pleased, because no one seemed capable of stopping him.

Sue and John Dickinson returned to Cornwall with Caroline's body in a coffin on board a people carrier driven by a teacher. 'After the crossing, Caroline was transferred to a hearse,' Sue recalled. 'I sat in the front and John followed behind in a police car. I vividly remember seeing the sign for Launceston and saying, "You're home now." I felt amazingly relieved.'

The couple were then faced with the heartbreaking task of consoling Caroline's sister, Jenny. 'We hid nothing from her,' explained Sue. 'She slept with me for a long time afterwards. She was so young and terribly brave. And we often talked about her sister.'

Caroline's angelic face haunted John Dickinson's every dream, a spectre of appalling grief that had totally overwhelmed his life. During the day images of his daughter's death played themselves out in his mind like some ghastly video. He tormented himself with thoughts of how, if only Caroline's schoolmates had stirred while she was being suffocated and raped, she might still be alive today. He believed that those images were haunting him because he was never actually allowed into the room where she died.

The following day the postcard sent by Caroline the day before she was murdered arrived on her father's doormat.

Within days of Caroline's murder, the British press were proving more adept at gathering vital evidence than the bumbling gendarmes. The *Mail on Sunday*'s headline CAROLINE: ATTACKS ON THREE MORE GIRLS revealed the inside story of the British girl attacked in a youth hostel in St Lunaire, just hours before Caroline Dickinson was killed. The paper also highlighted two further cases – one before and one just after Caroline's murder – which had fuelled the belief that her attacker was some sort of serial offender.

The report also said that another attack had occurred on 15 July, three days before Caroline's killing, when an 18-year-old Dutch student staying in a hostel in St Malo woke in the early hours to find a man leaning over her bed. Her screams forced him to flee

Later the same newspaper reported that an intruder entered several rooms in another St Malo hostel where a party of German schoolchildren were staying. Francois Mouchel, duty manager at the hostel, which accommodated up to 250 youngsters, said, 'All our rooms have locks, but sometimes the youngsters forget to lock the doors. We tell them to be careful but sometimes they forget. These girls woke up because there was a man in their room and he left straight away.'

In Britain, the murder of Caroline Dickinson had to a certain extent been overshadowed by the killing of mother and daughter Lin and Megan Russell in Kent, just a week earlier, on 9 July 1996. The only witness to that horrific attack was 45-year-old Mrs Russell's nine-year-old daughter, Josie, who miraculously survived the attack on the family as they walked home from school in Chillenden, near Canterbury.

It was only when the parents of St Lunaire victim Kate Wrigley saw TV reports about Caroline's murder that they realised this might be linked to the attack on their daughter and called the police. The two girls were almost exactly the same age. Kate said the grazes on her elbows and knees were like carpet burns and her face became even more swollen the day after the assault. Her injuries took two weeks to heal after she got home. French gendarmes filed her statement away but privately told reporters they did not think there was a connection between what happened to Kate in St Lunaire and the murder of Caroline Dickinson.

On 22 July, Caroline's heartbroken parents released for publication a poem written by the teenager shortly before her death

> *Small child crying, weeping, dying.*
> *Alone on the concrete floor.*
> *No one worries, life full of hurries*
> *Rushing past the concrete floor.*
> *Someone hops, halts, stops,*
> *Standing by the concrete floor*
> *Child looks up, hope, bright luck?*
> *Lying on the concrete floor.*
> *Friendship happens, opens, blossoms.*
> *Away from the concrete floor.*
> *Life is complete, happy, amity.*
> *Through the summer days of life.*

12

In Brittany, people were appalled by the fact that a young girl who came to spend her holiday in the area had been raped in a youth hostel that was supposed to be a friendly place. Everyone wondered how on earth it could have happened. With the murder making headlines around the world, the media – especially in Britain – were clamouring for results, which put a lot more pressure on the gendarmerie. They had little or no experience of such murders and many wondered if they were up to the job. Cynics described the gendarmes as country cops unable to cope with this sort of situation. They made mistakes everywhere and they had even ignored the murder weapon, the wad of cotton wool, which was initially passed off as something left by medical staff who attended the scene after Caroline's body was discovered.

In Pleine-Fougeres itself, there was even more resentment among the locals about the way they were being blamed for the murder. Father Henri Jet, the parish priest, explained,

'There is a lot of bad feeling here. People feel that they are being blamed collectively for the murder. Their reaction is "It's not our fault it hasn't been solved. It's the fault of the judge." At the same time, all we want is to know the truth. Perhaps the killer is living among us. People don't know whether they can trust their neighbours.'

The village lay at one point of a triangle enclosing a few hundred square kilometres of notorious countryside. The other two points were Combourg and Dol-de Bretagne. This triangle was said to be inhabited by a dark, primitive, mysterious and impenetrable people, whose ancestors had been on the same fields for centuries and whose distrust of anyone outside was fierce.

They were curtain-twitchers who were extremely furtive and carried resentments to the grave or beyond, and they forgave nothing. Nor did they tend to tell anyone anything. Local journalists referred to this strange land as the Bermuda Triangle, for 90 per cent of all crimes involving sexual aberration that came before the courts of St Malo originated there. Many of the people in this area were said to be buttoned up, backward and with strange sexual tastes. And the overwhelming feeling in the days following Caroline Dickinson's murder was that the killer came from among them.

Not only was the murderer a local man, claimed most experts, but he was also well acquainted with the geography of the youth hostel where he swooped so cold-bloodedly. He knew his way around. He must have known that the person on night duty would have her door closed and be sleeping.

It was this attitude that gave the real killer an extraordinarily lucky break in the days following the slaying. Gendarmes had quickly released a composite portrait of their suspect: heavily built, with a moustache, shoulder-length brown hair, an earring and a tattoo on his upper arm. They then took it from house to house in the area and eventually were pointed in the direction of a drifter called Patrice Pade.

On 22 July 1996, 'Paco', as Pade was known, found himself walking aimlessly along a road near Sourdeval, 30 kilometres east of Pleine-Fougeres, kicking buds off daffodils and hoping for a life of peace and quiet, when two gendarmes in a dark-blue Renault 4 pulled up alongside him. 'I had no idea there had even been a murder,' Pade recalled. 'I had been in Pleine-Fougeres on 12 July, trying to get some money off the local priest. But I was not surprised to be checked over by the gendarmes. When you're in my game, travelling around the country, you get used to being permanently under suspicion, for everything from a stolen chicken to the horrible killing of a little girl on holiday.

'There are decent gendarmes who give you a lift and sometimes a meal and then there are other bastards who stop you, search you and drive off with your shoes. These guys were like that, only it pretty soon became clear that they did not just want my shoes. They took me to the gendarmerie and I heard them call the Rennes brigade, who are in charge of the investigation. Five guys interrogated me, one in uniform and the others in plain clothes. They took a blood sample for a DNA test, which is supposed to take 12 hours but took 12 days in my case.'

Pade had taken some tranquillisers with a bottle of wine earlier that day. 'They make you feel mellow and give you a bit of confidence. Everyone on the road takes them,' he later explained. By the time he was being interrogated by the gendarmes, he was sweating and could hardly see straight.

'I remember flashes,' he recalled. 'At one point they had me standing up, handcuffed, with my legs far apart. It's very hard to stand that way for long, specially when you're tired and haven't been allowed to sleep. After 20 hours you're allowed a lawyer, but I never got one.'

Eventually a duty judge extended Pade's police custody. 'It felt to me like the gendarmes were trying to prove they were as good as the British police,' Pade later explained.

After Pade was detained, the French police even withdrew their photofit image of Caroline Dickinson's presumed killer. Also, they made no appeals for witnesses because they were convinced Pade was their man. Locals were alarmed to learn that they had radically scaled down their enquiries, as bar owner Lionel Morin explained, 'The villagers are worried because the police are moving out and there might still be a madman out there.'

At his first and only press conference, investigating judge Gerard Zaug said of Pade, 'For this kind of individual, in this kind of situation, right from the moment he had sighted his prey… once he had started nothing could stop him.' Pressed to explain how one man could have raped and suffocated Caroline while four other teenagers slept soundly in the same room, the judge replied, 'After a busy day, young girls of 13 to 15 sleep very deeply.'

Caroline Dickinson's funeral, held on 25 July 1996, had been allowed to go ahead because the French police believed they had arrested her killer. Her sister Jenny even helped to arrange the service. Caroline was eventually buried just 100 yards from her home.

The funeral service was given vast coverage by the British press and the killer read the reports with a tinge of guilt as, for the first time, he began to consider the enormity of his crimes and the appalling consequences for the Dickinson family. The death of a child was always an emotive issue, but it seemed to him that everywhere he turned there were stories about his victim. He started to wonder if she was looking down on him from heaven, haunting him for what he'd done to her. But the feelings of guilt gradually faded, to be replaced by plans for his next big trip to explore the youth hostels of Europe.

The French police had already announced that they had caught their man and this was like an invitation to him to carry on his mission. The idea that there were thousands of schoolgirls away from their families staying in bedrooms without locks was always there in the back of his mind. It just took a glance at a girl out on the streets of London and those overwhelming urges would return, driving him to head off in his car to find new prey.

Detectives in Brittany continued their investigation by searching suspect Patrice Pade's council flat on the Tulipes housing estate in the town of Domfront and questioning his neighbours. They asked if the alleged killer liked porn magazines and whether he had homosexual tendencies.

Two days later, investigating judge Zaug learned that Pade was not in fact his man. His DNA did not match that of the killer. But the Frenchman wasn't released for another ten days in the hope that by that time media interest in the blundering French police might have subsided. After that error, Zaug ordered a complete press blackout and threw a veil of secrecy over the entire investigation team. This attitude led to many inaccurate stories about the case in the days and months following the murder, including one claim that Caroline's body would have to be exhumed after her speedy funeral had been allowed because the police thought they had their man.

On 7 August, Pade was finally released and told reporters outside a Rennes police station, 'I am no rapist. How could I force a girl to have sex, knowing that I myself was born as a result of a rape? As for murder, I just couldn't.'

His arrest was probably the lowest point of the entire French police inquiry. Not only had they got the wrong man but they had also lost valuable time by suspending the investigation at a crucial point, just days after Caroline Dickinson's murder.

Drug addict Pade later claimed that after 46 hours of mental and physical pressure, while he was out of his wits with cold turkey, he muttered to his police interrogators, 'OK, yeah, since you want me to have done it, OK, I did it.'

Following Pade's impromptu press conference on the steps of the police station in Rennes, his lawyer drove him a little way out of the city before ordering him out of his car and telling him to walk the remaining 200 kilometres home.

In Pleine-Fougeres, detectives announced that they were intending to examine all photographs taken by members of the Launceston Community College party during their stay in France in the hope that it might help identify Caroline's killer. 'It all sounded like a desperate case of too little too late,' said one reporter on the scene.

With the investigation reignited by the release of Pade, Franco-British rivalry began to emerge. Insiders noted the slowness of responses between the Brittany law-enforcement officials and their counterparts in the Devon and Cornwall police. Comparisons were drawn with the large-scale and ultimately successful investigation of the rape and murder of 19-year-old French student Celine Figard, who had been hitchhiking in Berkshire, England, the previous Christmas when she was killed. British newspapers also pointed out that, of 23 cases of murder of Britons in France, 19 remained unsolved. Many believed the press and criminal investigators urgently needed to curb their xenophobia.

But for Caroline's parents, relief that the killer had been found had turned to a new sense of horror when Pade was released. John and Sue Dickinson later said they had doubts about Pade from the moment his arrest was proudly announced by the French police. John summed up the feelings of his family at the time. 'The news that someone had been apprehended for this terrible crime was a small consolation. Now it seems that we have been denied even this. We hope that the authorities will redouble their efforts to catch the culprit. Then the man who robbed Caroline of her future and us of a lovely daughter will not be free to commit such a crime again.'

In Cornwall, the murder of Caroline Dickinson had struck so much fear into her school friends that many of them remained convinced the killer would come and get them in their homes in Launceston. Patrice Pade's release simply exacerbated their anguish.

One child's mother told reporters, 'We know logically that they are not at risk, but we are talking about 13-year-old girls who are much more susceptible to such fears. My daughter has lost weight and bitten her nails down to the quick. She has had counselling for which we are grateful, but along with other children she just did not want to think about this any more. She was just beginning to come to terms with things, and start eating properly again, until the news came through that the police had the wrong man.'

Not one of the witnesses had ever mentioned the numerous tattoos that covered both of Pade's arms from wrist to shoulder. And, because the French police hadn't even bothered to re-interview the children themselves, they never learned of their doubts about Pade.

The outspoken British press were now describing the Caroline Dickinson investigation as 'ill-fated' and pointing out that French police bumbling was causing fresh heartbreak for her friends and family. The core of the problem seemed to be France's staid Napoleonic code of law, in which, as we have seen, the *juge d'instruction* controlled the direction of serious crime inquiries. Though French detectives had some discretion in their probes on the ground, all decisions of any significance, including what evidence should be gathered, were taken by this examining magistrate. In Britain, a senior police officer would have run every aspect of such a murder inquiry.

Another problem was the two-tier police structure in France. Crime in large towns and cities was investigated by municipal police while in a rural location such as Pleine-Fougeres it fell to the gendarmerie, a force with semi-military origins and of variable standard. Other differences included the fact that the French police were permitted to interview juveniles without informing their families. Also, alleged confessions were still considered enough for a prosecution in France while in Britain DNA was now an essential piece of evidence.

But what baffled British detectives most about the French inquiry was the way in which the police scaled down the manhunt and searches the moment they had detained Patrice Pade, who turned out to be innocent. In Britain, dozens if not hundreds of officers would have stayed on the case at least until charges were brought.

Meanwhile, more stories about alleged suspects continued to be drip-fed through the British press. One paper revealed police were seeking three French youths who had tried to molest a group of British schoolgirls in a hostel in the fishing port of Grandcap-Maisy, in Normandy, on 19 June, a month before Caroline's death. The girls had been asleep when the youths scaled a drainpipe and climbed through an open window. After stealing a camera and money, one of them attempted to indecently assault one of the girls. The pupils managed to alert a teacher and the youths fled. The girls were among a party of 34 from a school in Milton Keynes, Buckinghamshire.

On 5 August 1996, the French police suggested that Caroline's murderer might have killed her with an accomplice. A Rennes police spokesman told reporters, 'With only two hands, you cannot rape, kill and stop someone from crying out in a room containing four other people.'

British journalists covering the story dismissed the claim as a desperate attempt to save face by the French police. 'All it really did was further delay the investigation moving forward after the mistaken arrest of Patrice Pade,' said one reporter.

Then, on 10 August, police in Plymouth, Devon, asked their French counterparts for DNA results on the semen found on Caroline's body because of fears the killer might have struck there too, after a care worker called Nicola Parsons was found strangled in a disused nursery school in the city. Police suspected that the killer might have taken the local ferry back to Brittany after the murder of Nicola. But the DNA comparison proved inconclusive.

In London, the tall, dark stranger read reports of such incidents with callous amusement, since they simply confirmed just how far from finding him the French police really were.

Over the following few months, as the hunt for Caroline Dickinson's killer faltered, her father began to take a more active role in the investigation. After he engaged a lawyer, the significance of the police's early errors in the inquiry became even more apparent. And he began carrying a knapsack full of ring binders with him whenever he met journalists or police to discuss his daughter's unsolved murder. His neatly kept files contained details of every development and disappointment connected to the inquiry.

There was little time left in John Dickinson's life now to relax. He had even given up drinking alcohol. He explained, 'I would like to feel Caroline is at peace, but I can't − her murderer is still at large and may strike another child. I am envious of those who can believe in God because I don't have that crutch. I have lost my faith. You send your daughter away on a school trip and a few days later you find out that she has been raped and murdered. That makes you question the meaning of life and the existence of God.'

Meanwhile Britain's newspapers continued to splash the French police's blunders across their front pages. These included:

- Failure to immediately DNA-screen men in Pleine-Fougeres, which meant they missed a chance to flush out the killer.
- Not initially linking the St Lunaire attack three hours earlier on another British girl with Caroline's killer.
- The early arrest of innocent Patrice Pade, which then gave the real killer even more time to escape justice.
- Not spreading the inquiry widely enough to cover Europe and link any similar attacks.
- The slowness of the investigation caused mainly by the French system, which meant the investigating judge − not a policeman − was in charge.
- Official secrecy, which hindered the investigation because there were not enough public appeals or widespread publicity initiated by the police.

13

In London, the killer sat back and enjoyed all the attention his appalling crime was creating. At times the sense of power he now felt was almost overwhelming. He wanted to tell someone about his 'night of love' with little Caroline, but knew that would be too dangerous, although later he would break that rule to damning effect.

The arrival of the French police in the autumn of 1996 in Caroline Dickinson's home town of Launceston seemed yet another example of 'too little too late'. After a team of three Rennes detectives spent nearly a month in Britain, grief turned to anger as the officers admitted they had still failed to identify the schoolgirl's killer. Launceston's mayor, Barry Jordan, later told reporters, 'I do not think they have handled the investigation in the best way. It looks as if they did not do it properly. They have kept us in the dark. I would have thought they could have had better results by now.'

The French police investigators had hoped that holding a

second set of interviews with Caroline's friends under less stressful circumstances might produce more evidence for the inquiry. But it seemed that the longer the investigation went on, the more criticism was being aimed at the French police. French policy towards media involvement summed up the difference between the two countries. In Britain, the police issued regularly updated photofit pictures of suspects and put forward the families of the victims at emotional press conferences, whereas the French police shunned most media attention. Back in London, it must have been music to the ears of the killer, as he watched the TV news bulletins and scanned the sensational British tabloids.

Occasionally, word of a new clue in the hunt for Caroline's killer would filter through to the outside world via the British media. One detective admitted to journalists that they wanted to interview a 19-year-old man seen allegedly harassing Caroline shortly before her murder. One newspaper claimed the man had been spotted trying to kiss Caroline outside the hostel, but the killer knew this was all complete nonsense, although at least it further distanced him from the crime.

Then the French police deliberately leaked the fact there was a new suspect list of more than 200 men without mentioning any of the names on it. As French detectives worked through that list, they came across the name of one possible suspect whose last known address had been in Earl's Court. But, according to the Interpol report on this individual, he had long since left Britain and his current address was unknown.

If the French police had followed up this lead themselves, they would have found out that the information was more than five years out of date and the suspect was now in Earl's Court once again. Instead, this particular suspect's name was pushed to the bottom of their list and never properly followed up.

In France, the mother of another teenager murdered in a town near Pleine-Fougeres told reporters, 'The authorities simply don't want to know. They can't be bothered. I don't think they are capable of properly investigating a murder.'

Further pressure followed from John Dickinson, who demanded the removal of certain officers from the inquiry into his daughter's murder. Then suddenly, in March 1997, Gerard Zaug publicly announced that his detectives had flown to Carcassonne, in south-west France, to interview their latest suspect: a travelling salesman believed to have been involved in up to nine sexual assaults. Investigators said they were going to DNA-test a man following his arrest for trying to abduct a ten-year-old girl. Rennes police announced they had first become aware of him after another ten-year-old girl was assaulted the previous November in St Meen, just under 30 kilometres from Pleine-Fougeres. However, three days later, Zaug announced the suspect was not their man.

Meanwhile, the real killer was free to roam the streets in search of more girls to prey on and it was becoming increasingly obvious that the French authorities were nowhere near tracking him down. The French police were proving useless adversaries. It was tempting for him to go back to France to leave them a few more clues and toy with their minds. He was enjoying the power that his crime seemed to have given him.

For the first time in his life, he was having an influence on events outside his own little world. It was a nice feeling to know that so many people were living in fear of him. For too long he had been a failure, someone that few took any notice of. Now he was powerful. But in the end the killer decided not to return to Pleine-Fougeres. Not even he was that reckless. In any case, there were lots of other hostels to prowl about and beautiful young girls to attack.

The arrival of July 1997 – the first anniversary of Caroline Dickinson's murder – seemed to underline the hopelessness of the French police investigation. In London, Caroline's parents met Lady Symons, the Foreign Office minister responsible for the Consular Service, to discuss putting pressure on the gendarmerie. 'I do feel the French system just doesn't seem to listen and, unless we make an issue of it, I fear nothing will be done,' John Dickinson told reporters afterwards.

He also issued a chilling warning to other parents of young children. 'Another summer has come around, more children will be going to Brittany and this person has still to be captured. I would like British parents to stop children going anywhere near the area. I don't want anyone else to suffer as we have.'

In Pleine-Fougeres, security at the 79-bed, three-storey hostel where Caroline was murdered had been stepped up with a security-code entry system on the front door, movement-sensitive floodlights above the windows and locks on every bedroom door. But, despite the new safety measures, many were still afraid in case the tall, dark stranger returned. One student said, 'You never know – maybe he will come back one day. I keep looking at everyone in the street and thinking, Is that him? I'm not sure if any of us will ever be happy staying at the hostel as long as he has not been arrested.'

Many in Brittany were now accusing their own police of

being 'too secretive'. One resident of Pleine-Fougeres said, 'I'm sure they know something. They're still coming round once a month or so to get some paper or some address. The people in the town haven't forgotten what happened either.'

In Britain so-called 'criminal experts' had some interesting theories about the murder of Caroline Dickinson. Greater Manchester's former police chief John Stalker told one newspaper he believed the killer could be British and would almost certainly strike again. Stalker visited the murder scene and afterwards backed up claims that the killer had also attacked another British girl in that youth hostel, in nearby St Lunaire, just a few hours before Caroline's murder. Stalker explained, 'This is a confident man who has raped before and will do so again. He knew what he wanted that night and having failed to get it in one hostel drove to another near by.'

Stalker said that, although the killer could speak fluent French, he could be British because of his choice of British victims. 'In both cases he chose a room full of sleeping girls. He may have killed Caroline by mistake, trying to keep her quiet. If I had been in charge of the case, I would have been extremely optimistic that I could crack it. But vital ground has been lost.'

At times, it seemed that the British press were unintentionally supplying the murderer with the perfect story to tell detectives if they ever did catch up with him. He didn't mean to kill her, did he?

Stalker candidly summed up the French police's performance: 'What I learned of French police investigations astonished me. To describe the inquiry as bungled is to praise it. When Patrick Pade "confessed" to Caroline's murder, further enquiry appeared to stop. Yet any seasoned detective would know almost every high-profile murder investigation is plagued by false confessions. Caroline's family deserve a thorough investigation. Unfortunately, my belief is that the French authorities will retreat behind a barrier of embarrassment.'

Meanwhile, investigating judge Zaug's assistants had taken to putting the phone down on callers, mainly from the media. A siege mentality had overtaken the French police at a time when they needed all the help they could get.

In August 1997, Gerard Zaug was taken off the case to be replaced by Judge Renaud Van Ruymbeke, who had a reputation as one of France's most effective crime fighters. He in turn appointed seasoned detective Jean-Pierre Michel as head of a select squad of investigators in a new incident room called 'Cellule Caroline'.

Van Ruymbeke immediately uncovered hundreds of pages of statements from Caroline's friends and teachers, which had been compiled by the Devon and Cornwall police but never translated into French. Then, 13 months after her murder, the French police finally came up with a new photofit.

Following Ruymbeke's appointment, police agreed to look much more closely at the break-in at the hostel in St Lunaire, just a few hours before the killing in Pleine-Fougeres. Original investigating judge Zaug had continued to play down connections between the two attacks in public because he felt it was unprofessional to reveal the details to the media.

In Salford, Lancashire, where the St Lunaire school party had come from, the mother of one of the girls in the room where the stranger had struck told reporters she was appalled at the way detectives had failed to properly connect the attacks in the weeks following the killing of Caroline.

Judge Ruymbeke also ordered another test of the cotton

wool found close to Caroline's body. Analysis showed it contained fibres only used in the manufacture of cotton wool sold by a British chain of chemists, the type used by the schoolchildren from Salford.

In Britain, more 'expert' analysis was being published in the press. Renowned crime writer Brian Masters pronounced that the killer of Caroline Dickinson was a local man who would eventually be trapped by his own DNA. He told one newspaper, 'It is likely the murderer is known to more than a few people and is being sheltered. At the very least somebody would have noticed his late return.' He also accused the locals of Pleine-Fougeres of having 'a furtive, secretive and deep distrust of all outsiders'.

However, Masters was more insightful about the circumstances behind Caroline's murder itself. 'He may not have realised he was killing Caroline,' he was quoted as saying in an article in the *Sunday People* in August 1997.

In London, the tall, dark stranger read the piece with interest. He'd already decided that, if he was ever arrested, Masters's explanation could provide his excuse for having killed Caroline.

14

The centre of Llanes, a small resort on the breezy Atlantic coast of northern Spain, was never considered a dangerous place. Tens of thousands of young people flocked to the town on the Costa Verde every summer, attracted by the beach with its sand dunes and rolling waves, which were usually big enough to surf on.

This wasn't a place for thieves, crackheads, muggers or junkies. People walked the streets with little fear at all times of day and night. Late bars crammed in the youthful holidaymakers until the early hours. The compact terraces of picturesque old houses and shops, many built more than 200 years ago, gave the resort a quaint, secure atmosphere; a place where no one worried about safety.

It was into this town that the tall, dark stranger came on 22 August 1997, nameless and nocturnal, as silent and deadly as the sharks sometimes found grazing a few kilometres off the local coastline. He now tended to wear denim, usually black, a match for those bushy eyebrows and dark matt eyes that constantly darted in all directions. He preferred to stay back in the shadows, blending in with the young people even though he was, by now, well into his forties. But by wearing casual clothes it was easy to become one of them. And, in any case, he was usually only seen after it was too late.

That day he had swallowed half a bottle of whisky with Afranil tablets he'd bought in a nearby chemist earlier that evening. He'd even taken an unhealthy interest in the pharmacist's assistant. She was slim and young-looking, maybe even still in her teens, and she smiled at him seductively, or so he thought. That happy look on her face had ignited something inside him. As he gave her the money for the tablets, she seemed to brush her hand against his, or was that all his imagination? Whatever the case, it had stirred something in him and now he found himself in the mood for a mission.

On this warm summer's evening, the stranger was driving yet another wreck of a car, a UK-registered white Mazda saloon. However, no one in this tourist trap paid much attention to foreign-registered cars as there were so many in the resort. People walking the streets of Llanes that night were on holiday, enjoying the freedom to explore and that light feeling of relief at not having to work for a couple of weeks. Many of them were floating through the streets on a heady mix of alcohol and happiness. Few noticed the other people wandering around that night or crawling through the busy town centre in their cars. It was an easy place *not* to be noticed, the stranger thought to himself. A perfect killing field.

There were hotels, youth hostels and campsites scattered around the outskirts of the town, most of them signposted. He liked signposts; they had become like fuel for his depraved hunt. When he saw them, he felt his dark urges flow more freely through him. He looked on those signs as an invitation to strike out at someone, to force himself upon someone small, innocent and pure. He preferred it if that person was untouched, as then he wouldn't be disappointed. Now he was coasting along the roads leading in and out of Llanes, those soulless eyes flitting hyperactively in every direction, looking anxiously for somewhere to cure his sexual fever. He was on a quest that could only end when he was satisfied.

The trouble was, after blowing his cash on alcohol and pills he had barely enough money to book into a cheap hostel. He'd gone more than 24 hours without sleeping or eating. Now he was only answerable to his crazed desires.

He feared he might have to sleep in his car unless he could find a building with a window or door open wide enough for him to creep inside. He was heading west, out of Llanes, when he decided it might be better to head back into town. Suddenly he braked hard, did a squealing U-turn and drove into the centre, where he stopped, gulped down another handful of pills with the dregs of a bottle of whisky, and parked his car. He'd already cruised Llanes for long enough to know the clean, well-kept streets and alleyways as well as the lines on his long, battered, bony hands. He knew where he'd head to without anyone noticing him. Soon he was strolling along a dark alley between two old buildings, just off the main square. He was hoping the latest handful of pills would kick in at any second.

It was a clear, hot summer night. He kept well away from the yellow street lamps where mosquitoes lazily buzzed in the heady sea air. As he felt the drugs rushing to his brain, his limbs responded by speeding up his movements. He clenched his fist and took a deep breath of relief that the pharmaceuticals were finally having the desired effect. He felt for the packet of tablets in his jean-jacket pocket because their mere existence reassured him he must continue his mission. The drugs had heightened his senses and diluted his pupils.

Now sweating heavily, he increased his pace. His eyes darted up every time anyone passed by. Most people were in couples or groups, as is the way of holiday resorts. When two teenage girls walked past the tall, dark man in denim, he hesitated for a moment before examining the shapes of their bodies as they strolled along arm in arm. For a split second, he thought about following them and what might happen if he could lure them into a quiet spot. His warped mind conjured up details of the sort of sex he would have with them. He could hear every intake of his own breath as he fantasised. He moved towards them. He couldn't help himself. The home movie running in his head was vivid and featured him with not one but two compliant victims.

His breathing speeded up as he walked even faster. Just then the two girls stopped to greet a couple of youths they knew and the stranger's senses were killed stone dead. But the mere thought of sex had stirred the devil in him even more, so he continued to hunt for easier prey.

Sweating even more, he returned to the car and decided to take another drive. The centre of town wasn't such a good idea, what with all those kids coming in and out of bars. Too many people would see him. But did that really matter? Somewhere deep in his soul he knew that one day it would all come to an end. He knew he deserved to be punished but for the moment he didn't care.

So he began cruising around the town in ever-wider circles. He drove in almost total silence, not wanting anything to distract him from his mission. He'd never liked music much because it gave him a headache. He preferred to create images in his mind. Music was an irritating diversion. He found it difficult to concentrate at the best of times but the repetitive beat of so much pop music sometimes made him want to scream with irritation. In noisy bars he'd put his hands over his ears to cut out the sounds before they made him feel sick with anger. Many times he'd felt like killing people who were playing their music too loud in parks or other public places. How dare they invade his space with their filthy sounds? To him music was like an infection. It was something he had to cleanse himself of.

Eventually, he stopped the car in a quieter corner of the town, swallowed some more tablets and took a mighty swig from the fresh bottle of whisky he'd hidden under the passenger seat. Then he spotted a group of young people drunkenly staggering towards an apartment block, but knew there were too many for him to swoop.

He needed to satisfy that primal urge which kept coming back every time he topped himself up with booze and pills. As he got out of the car, he saw more youngsters walking towards the main square. The home movie in his mind started playing again, but this time it showed him enjoying a clean, perfect sexual act with a girl of complete and utter pureness. She would be grateful to have a real man take her virginity, he thought to himself without a moment of self-doubt. He would later claim these animal urges were completely out of his control. He had no choice but to find a victim as quickly as possible.

The mix of alcohol and drugs made time move very quickly. He found himself starting to come down again. The euphoric rushes were a key element of his feverish search for the perfect victim. The trouble was that they were often replaced by an edgy anxiety which could only be relieved by more pills and booze. He walked back to the car for yet another hit. This time he left the vehicle more quickly and upped his pace, so as to find someone to satisfy those urges all the faster. Soon he was on a street which ran parallel with the main road leading into the centre of Llanes. His dark eyes, now fully adjusted to the night, were scanning the moonlit pavements for any human movement. He knew what he needed. And he knew that unless he had it that feeling wouldn't go away. He couldn't rest until all his urges had been sated.

He stopped on a street corner and shrank back into the shadow of a doorway. He waited and watched, his mind now a blur of pornographic images snapping through his head. Taking another deep breath, he composed himself to strike out. His eyes scanned in all directions, checking that no one was watching him. But it was always a sixth sense that told him when he was unseen. He walked along the pavement, careful to keep close to the houses so that he would be difficult to spot. With long, silent steps, he moved through the shadows.

Above, the moon bathed the town in a cold blue and white light as a mass of stars glistened in the clear sky. As he walked past a small graveyard, he noticed the intense heat was causing slight clouds of steam to rise from the tombstones. The stars continued shining brightly. From a nearby apartment block, he thought he heard the cries of a girl making love. He looked up to see if there were any windows open. Nothing low enough for him to gain access. Then he thought about hiding in nearby bushes and listening to the couple having sex. At least that might help quell his urges.

Just then, a young woman emerged from around the corner,

walking directly towards him. He took another deep breath and stepped back into the shadows to wait until she passed by. Seconds later, he caught a whiff of her scent as she walked just two feet from him, unaware that he was hiding in a doorway. It was as if her perfume was sending out a signal: 'Come and get me, come and get me.'

As she continued to walk away from him, he held back. Then his eyes focused on the back of her body. Her dark hair and slim build suggested a girl in her teens or maybe early twenties. A little old for him but she would do. It was nearly time to strike.

He began walking silently behind her. At first, she continued at the same pace as earlier. Then he noticed her turn her head slightly in his direction. Was that a signal to follow her? he wondered, never once considering that she had felt his presence and was trying desperately to work out what to do next.

He sped up his pace and began to draw closer. She moved faster in response. His breathing got heavier with the excitement of the chase. Now he knew she knew he was following her and that filled him with even more anticipation. His eyes were locked on his prey. Nothing else mattered. He was a man on a deadly mission. He knew he couldn't stop himself: he was already past the point of no return. As he got closer and closer, she suddenly turned into the entrance of an apartment block and scrambled for her keys. He rushed towards her and caught her just as she was opening the street door.

But what he didn't realise was that ten metres behind him a young waiter called Miguel had been watching the strange man walking ahead of him. Llanes was a small place and Miguel knew this guy wasn't a local. He'd seen the teenage girl ahead of them both, and when Miguel saw the stranger running to catch her he broke into a run as well. That was when he heard the first scream.

The glass door swung shut just as Miguel reached it. He could see that the man in denim had grabbed the girl from behind, and was trying to force her to the ground. She was hysterical and screaming. Miguel struggled desperately to open the door, shouting at the man to let the girl go. Inside, the stranger stared incredulously at him through the glass, his eyes glazed in a drug- and alcohol-induced trance. Then he suddenly pushed the girl to the ground and pulled open the door. 'Get out of the way or I'll kill you,' he yelled. It was only then that Miguel noticed the man had pulled out a knife.

'His eyes were what scared me the most,' Miguel recalled. 'They were very big, and wide open, and they were very red, the veins full of blood, with a calm look but at the same time very aggressive. He could have done anything.'

The stranger left unhurriedly, heading back towards his car. He knew that the police would be on the scene in minutes and it would be less noticeable if he walked away at a normal pace.

Inside the apartment block, the girl continued to yell hysterically. By chance, a *policia local* patrol drove past the building at that moment. Miguel hailed them down and told them about the stranger in denim. The police soon spotted a lone figure at the other end of the street, but when they shouted at him he began running. They arrested him in a park a few minutes later. He offered no resistance.

At the police station, the man in denim accused Miguel and the girl of trying to rob him but the police did not believe him and handed him over to the Guardia Civil. A police force with both military and civilian functions, the Guardia Civil is primarily responsible for security at border areas, rural areas and, in some cases, traffic control. The stranger was charged with attempted rape and told he would appear before a judge in Llanes the following day.

A local journalist took a photo of the prisoner being led into the court, but the picture did not even make it into the local newspaper. It was the middle of the busy, lucrative summer season and the police wanted to avoid bad publicity because it would ruin local tourism. To them, he seemed no more than a sad, third-rate pervert. Why would anyone be interested? Not one officer at the police station in Llanes even thought to enter his name into the Interpol computer. Meanwhile, the stranger was remanded in custody and taken off to jail.

15

In October 1997, two sharp-eyed British policemen in Manchester nabbed a Frenchman wanted in connection with a triple killing and his name was immediately linked to the murder of Caroline Dickinson. The man, 39, was recognised by the two bobbies after they had seen an Interpol alert. PCs Trevor Chadwick, 49, and Martin Hamlett, 37, spotted Girardin outside a bank in the Uppermill area. But after he had been returned to France it was quickly established that he was not the man who had killed Caroline Dickinson.

A few days later the French police revealed that only one out of 170 men aged between 15 and 35 resident in Pleine-Fougeres had refused to provide DNA samples, which had at last been taken by investigators. A spokesman for the investigating judge admitted for the first time that Caroline Dickinson's killer probably did not come from the community, as so many had been predicting for more than a year.

In November 1997, having spent three months in prison in Spain, the stranger was given bail after agreeing to live at home in Gijon with his mother. The only record on him that Llanes police could find referred to an incident when he was in his early twenties in Gijon, in addition to three rapes in Germany. They had no idea he was a killer on the run.

Yet in France at that very same time, the killer's real name had been brought to the attention of the French police investigating the murder of Caroline Dickinson. The source was Yves Franquelin, the director of L'Heresie, the youth hostel in the Loire Valley where the tall, dark stranger had struck three times between 1993 and 1994. Franquelin's information was filed by a gendarme, who eventually passed it on to the team hunting for Caroline's killer.

The French police finally got around to asking the Gijon police for information about the man, a Spanish subject. The Spanish authorities told them about his convictions in Germany in the 1980s but failed to mention he was awaiting trial for attempted rape in Llanes.

'His name created immediate interest because there were similar aspects of his behaviour comparable with the crime at Pleine-Fougeres,' Jean-Pierre Michel, the senior officer in charge of the hunt, later explained. 'They said that the man did exist and that he was known to the Spanish authorities for sexual attacks in Tubingen but that was all. Maybe they had not updated their database.'

So, while detectives across Europe were hunting for Caroline Dickinson's killer, Spanish police knew exactly where he was. Every fortnight he was reporting to a judge in his home town of Gijon, although today the relevant authorities insist that no one told them he was suspected of killing the British schoolgirl. There had been a complete communications breakdown between the French police and their counterparts in Spain.

Then, in December 1997, the French police excitedly announced they were interviewing a former hospital porter in connection with Caroline Dickinson's murder and all their interest in the Spaniard died down. This latest suspect, aged 29, was named by police only as 'Jean-Michel' and had been arrested after breaking into a house and raping a ten-year-old girl in Paris. The similarities between the two crimes had led to judge Renaud Van Ruymbeke being tipped off by the Paris police. But a week later DNA tests showed that 'Jean-Michel' was not the man who raped and murdered Caroline. 'It sometimes seemed as if the French police were just going through the motions to keep everyone happy,' explained a reporter who covered the story at the time.

Waiting in Gijon on bail had left the real killer with a lot of spare time on his hands and that could lead to problems. He began visiting the city centre, watching young girls. Then he chanced upon a dream target.

Maria was a petite, elfin-faced, dark-haired girl of 15 with large round eyes and a trim figure. She could have passed for 12, which was why the stranger came to notice her in a park near the centre of Gijon. She was sitting on a bench with her boyfriend, Adam, also 15. The killer watched the couple kissing and giggling, convinced she was too young to have ever had full sex. Maria even glanced across at the stranger and smiled. He believed that was a signal from her that she was interested, so he began following them. If it came to the crunch, he would stab the boyfriend so that he would go away and leave the girl with him. The boy, he believed, would run like a coward when confronted with a knife. As the couple strolled arm in arm away from the park, the stranger shadowed them at a cautious distance.

As they walked hand in hand along the busy street, he even felt a pang of jealousy rising up inside him. How could she smile at him like that and then walk off with that boy? How could she encourage him and then taunt him? Sometimes he followed dozens of girls a week but rarely swooped on them unless they were alone and the circumstances were just right. But there was something about this one that was pulling him towards her despite the presence of the boy.

Maria was in the throes of a deep adolescent love affair with Adam and she loved telling anyone who would listen about her happiness. The schoolgirl was also very pleased with her recent exam results. Maria was one of three children from a close, supportive family who lived in the centre of Gijon. She'd had the sort of happy childhood that her sinister secret shadow would have envied. A sensitive, highly intelligent child, she had an open mind about everything. That was why she had smiled so sweetly at the tall, dark stranger when he looked at her. Maria believed in being nice to everyone. She thought the best of people. Evil had never entered her world – until now.

As they walked into a coffee bar, Maria and Adam were completely unaware that the stranger was still following them on the other side of the street and had become, in the space of a few minutes, so obsessed with Maria that he had decided to have her whatever the consequences. Maybe it was that innocent smile, which he had construed as something more meaningful. More likely, the prospect of having sex with a young girl of 12 or 13 was the real force behind his behaviour.

The two youngsters had just sat down when the man

suddenly appeared alongside them asking for spare change. Adam shook his head, but Maria smiled up at him and he took that as another signal and sat down with them. 'He said he needed some money for a phone call and I felt sorry for him. He seemed very open and friendly,' Maria remembered.

The man didn't need much encouragement to start talking about his life. He explained that although he was from Gijon he had travelled extensively. 'I've seen the world and it's a lot better than Gijon,' he said.

Maria recalled, 'It was as if he felt the need to impress us. It just made me feel more sorry for him.'

Just then, two more of Maria's friends appeared in the coffee bar and the strange middle-aged man retreated. As he walked back out on to the street, he found himself shaking wildly. The young girl's friendliness had thrown him off guard. She seemed such a genuine person, completely oblivious to all the usual prejudices. The stranger had only been in love once in his life but he had a feeling that maybe he had just fallen in love again, in just a few minutes. But the kind of love he was experiencing would never have a happy ending.

Back in the coffee bar, Maria and her friends thought nothing more about the tall, dark stranger, although her friends did comment on his scary, wolf-like face.

The following day he returned to exactly the same spot in the park where he had first met Maria. A few minutes later, he felt a shiver of excitement when he spotted her walking across the road. But his heart sank when he saw Adam alongside her. In his warped mind, Adam was cramping his style. Why couldn't the stupid kid clear off and find another girl to go out with? Maria belonged to him now.

Maria didn't even notice the man until she and Adam saw him in the coffee bar. 'I didn't think there was anything strange about him being there again. You meet lots of people day after day in a place like Gijon,' she explained.

But Maria did wonder why his eyes seemed so blurred. 'It felt like he was looking through me in a way and that perhaps he was thinking of other things as he talked to us. It wasn't necessarily a bad feeling but I knew something was not normal about him.'

The man seemed much more nervous than he had the previous day as he sat down next to the two schoolchildren. He had an overpowering love for the girl but knew in his heart that that love could only be translated into fear in her if it was going to achieve what he wanted.

Maria recalled, 'He watched me intently as we talked and it was weird. It felt like he was a voyeur yet he was sitting there with us, not watching us from afar. He also seemed so nervous. His hands were shaking and once again I felt so sorry for him. He seemed like a lost soul, not an angry, dangerous person. And he spoke so gently about his work in places like London and how it was all much nicer than Gijon. But the way he talked was strange. He came at things from a different angle. He asked questions in such a way that, when he wanted to know something, he didn't ask directly. But I felt there was a vulnerability about him and that made him appealing to me.' The stranger eventually left Maria and Adam in the coffee bar.

But for the following few days he watched and followed them in the hope that Maria would eventually be alone, and then he could pounce. But it never happened. So about a week later he 'accidentally' bumped into the couple once again when they were in the park.

'He was even more chatty this time and seemed more

relaxed,' Maria recalled. 'He started showing off about London again and what a fantastic place it was.'

Then he took a deep breath and announced to her, 'You could come over and stay at my flat in London and get yourself a job. I can get you work through my contacts.'

The teenagers gulped at the man's offer, which had come completely out of the blue. Maria recalled, 'He didn't say how I would get to London but he made it all sound so natural.'

Then the stranger breathed in deeply again before adding, 'If I had any money I'd give it all to you.'

He borrowed a pen and paper and wrote down his name and address in London, just to make sure the young girl knew he was telling the truth. Maria was a little worried now. 'There was no way I would go on my own to London with him and so I started asking him about other things to try to get him to drop the subject,' she recalled.

Maria wasn't to know that the strange man had left London some months earlier and was living with his mother in Gijon while on bail for attempted rape in Llanes.

Later she said that, from that moment on, 'I felt strange when he was around. It is hard to explain. There was an aura around him. The way he talked. But all along he seemed to be hiding what he really wanted to say and I did notice that when I talked to my boyfriend his face would cloud over a bit as if he was maybe jealous.'

To this day Maria finds it hard to accept that the tall, dark stranger was stalking her with a view to hurting her. 'It makes me very emotional to think about what's happened to his victims and how close I came to being one. Yet in many ways he seemed so gentle. His voice was soft, even mellow, but he did seem a little too happy, as if he was hiding something.'

Over the following few days, the stranger continued to keep a close eye on Maria in the hope he might find a chance to strike. A couple of times she even spotted him talking to other teenage girls in the park.

Today she is deeply disturbed by how close she came to being one of his victims. 'I think a lot about what could have happened and that is scary. It could have been me. I was typical of the sort of girl he was looking for. I looked so young back then.'

But she added, 'Now I know what he is, I don't feel sorry for him. It's like he wasn't the same person I met. Thank God, I never went to London with him. If I'd accepted that invitation I would not be alive today.'

In early February 1998, the French investigators announced that the killer may have been driving a white van and they were quizzing six men who all matched their latest photofit and drove a white van. But, as was so often the case with the French police team, these lines of enquiry soon faded out.

Then, on the 14th – Valentine's Day – the *Sun* newspaper offered a £10,000 reward for information that would lead to the arrest of Caroline Dickinson's killer. It even published a poster in French that promised a reward of 100,000 francs, giving the paper's telephone number and one for the investigating police team in France. The paper also splashed a huge picture of the latest e-fit photo of the suspect across its page 3 and when the killer saw a report on the article in a Spanish newspaper he chuckled to himself because, apart from the bushy eyebrows, there was little or no obvious resemblance to him.

The *Sun* also ran the following incisive verdict on the French police from a senior detective with the Devon and Cornwall force: 'They have acted like Inspector Clouseau. Their investigation has been flawed from start to finish. Let's simply hope that this photofit starts the ball rolling again.'

Chief detective Jean-Pierre Michel admitted his office was flooded with calls after the *Sun* offered its reward. But the fact that the French police needed a British tabloid appeal in order to take the case further seemed to sum up the hopeless state of their investigation.

M. Michel tried to look positive. 'There have been major problems but we are now confident that we are getting things right. All evidence is being looked at with fresh eyes and there are many rediscovered clues for us to look at.'

16

In July 1998, a new suspect was arrested in the hunt for Caroline Dickinson's killer. Frenchman Bruno Tete was arrested after confessing to raping a 12-year-old girl at a campsite, but then a DNA test ruled him out as the British schoolgirl's killer. The news was yet another blow for Caroline's family, although her father John intended to keep up the pressure on the French police by visiting Pleine-Fougeres once again and provoking more newspaper headlines to ensure that the hunt for his daughter's killer did not simply fade away.

Then it was revealed that chief investigating judge Van Ruymbeke would be leaving the inquiry to take up a senior position in Paris that autumn. He even admitted publicly that it was unlikely he would have found Caroline's killer by then. In St Malo, Robert Baffert, the state prosecutor responsible for appointing Van Ruymbeke's successor, insisted there would be no let-up in the inquiry. 'We have a full-time team of 15 detectives on this case. They are very motivated and the file will not be closed.'

The Dickinsons' lawyer, Herve Rouzaud-Le Boeuf, told British reporters, 'It was always a difficult case. But the incompetence that marked the beginning was infuriating. To be frank, I'm pessimistic. Unprecedented resources have been put into this investigation and really not much more can be done. The police are all over France taking DNA samples from every sex crime and sending them to St Malo. I don't like to think it, but the best chance we have now may be if this man strikes again.'

In Cornwall, John Dickinson was appalled that the man who killed his daughter was still walking free. He believed the net should be spread much wider and he insisted he would never give up the hunt for the murderer.

British newspapers then highlighted yet more elementary mistakes by the gendarmes, such as: a failure to consider vital forensic evidence; a refusal to carry out DNA tests on suspects because they were 'too expensive'; a bar on door-to-door questioning for fear of disturbing the local community; and a reluctance to publicise photofits of the killer 'in case it scared him off'.

Luck, it seemed, shone brightly on the real killer. Not only were the French police blundering in spectacular fashion but also other vital witnesses had been extremely slow in coming forward. Nearly two years after Caroline Dickinson's murder, one of her teachers on the trip to France admitted for the first time that he had seen a strange man loitering near the teenager's bedroom on the night she died. French police sources said that Nick Ward had been 'tormented with guilt' for keeping the sighting a secret. One policeman explained, 'He saw a man on a landing on the night Caroline died, thought he was a little odd and then went to bed. When her body was discovered the next morning, he felt dreadful. He was frightened of saying anything for fear of the consequences, but, as the inquiry drew on with no sign of a suspect, he felt compelled to confess.'

Lawyer Herve Rouzaud-Le Boeuf summed up the situation: 'It is very difficult for us to understand why this teacher took so long to come forward. The fact that he saw this man on the night of Caroline's murder and did not alert colleagues is one thing. He could not have imagined what would happen. But we find it hugely regrettable that it took him 18 months to tell police what he had seen. Perhaps if the police had had his description earlier they may have caught the killer by now. Who knows? Nevertheless, we are pleased that he has become very useful to police, albeit at this late stage.'

French investigators then accepted an offer of help from Britain's renowned National Crime Faculty, an elite independent unit set up in Bramhall, Hampshire, to provide instant expertise in large-scale murder investigations. Four detectives from the faculty, together with Dr Adrian West, a leading criminal psychologist, spent three days at the scene of the crime drawing up a psychological profile of Caroline Dickinson's killer.

Then, in the early winter of 1998, French investigators secretly visited Britain to interview an English drifter who matched the description of Caroline's killer. The 'caveman-like' suspect, also thought to have raped a student in 1993, left a sleeping bag at an address in Calais, where he was staying at the time of the murder in Pleine-Fougeres, and apparently it had been closely examined by police. The man was said to have sisters living in Kent and the north of England, and a mother in America. The alert had been sparked when the man – who spoke good French – asked an undertaker to prepare a will for him in the village of Oignies, near Calais. But within days the French police were once again forced to admit that yet another so-called suspect was not their man.

During the winter of 1998, the killer grew increasingly restless as he awaited trial for the attempted rape in Llanes. He knew he stood little chance of avoiding prison if found guilty of the attack and had just been given £16,000 by his family as his share of his dead father's inheritance.

On 15 December, the killer failed to report to police in Gijon in accordance with his bail conditions. However, an arrest warrant was not issued by the court in Llanes until the beginning of January 1999, by which time the killer had gone.

Aware that the highways and byways of western Europe were no longer safe for him, he had headed to Chile. Within months, he had moved on to Buenos Aires, Argentina, then Venezuela and other countries in South America. He never stayed long and afterwards law-enforcement officials discovered a spate of sex attacks on women – and at least half a dozen unsolved murders – in his wake.

17

In April 1999, it seemed that the killer of Caroline Dickinson had struck again. In a village 80 kilometres from Pleine-Fougeres, a masked man forced an 11-year-old girl from her bed as her parents slept in the next room. He then took her to nearby woods and raped her repeatedly before abandoning her. The French police also linked the same attacker to the rape of a ten-year-old girl in Nantes a year before Caroline's murder. The suspect – a man in his thirties – was arrested days later.

But publicly connecting these attacks before matching DNA samples was to prove a dispiriting move by chief police investigator Jean-Pierre Michel. He had already admitted to journalists at the time that their inquiry 'needs fresh impetus', but now he seemed to be clutching at every available straw. Few were surprised when the DNA tests proved 'inconclusive', leaving the French police nowhere nearer catching the murderer.

By the summer of 1999, the police themselves were admitting that their best chance of success was if the killer struck again. The frustrating hunt for the tall, dark stranger with the bushy eyebrows had been punctuated by police blunders and the odds against finding the perpetrator were increasing all the time.

On a wider scale, the killing of Caroline Dickinson continued to put the majority of British families off even stopping for a night in Brittany while on their way to other holiday destinations. 'It has been the kiss of death for our tourist industry,' said one youth-hostel owner in the area.

Yet again chief investigator Michel was left to explain away his team's failings. 'There are no more policemen in France than in Britain, but France has twice as many murders,' he said by way of an excuse. 'But we are all praying the case of Caroline will be solved as soon as possible.'

Then, in October 1999, the *News of the World* published 'seven vital clues' which it said pointed to a British sex offender named Clive Barwell being Caroline's killer. The tabloid announced that 'following our ground-breaking investigation, detectives in France and Britain, working with Interpol, will try and discover if he killed the teenager'.

The piece referred to e-fit pictures that seemed to resemble lorry driver Barwell, his movements at the time of the murder and a host of other so-called clues. Barwell, of Wortley, near Leeds, had just received eight life sentences at Teesside Crown Court for four kidnaps, three rapes and an attempted murder between 1982 and 1995. He was also given seven years for two other sex attacks and an assault. The story was given such huge prominence in the *News of the World* that other newspapers around the world ran excerpts, which the killer could not have failed to notice even though he was by this time on the other side of the Atlantic. No doubt, it further fuelled his persistent conviction that he would never be caught.

Also, in October 1999, Britain's National Crime Faculty completed a secret report on the Caroline Dickinson murder. This included a psychological profile of the killer as well as more significant details about the incident and the other break-in on the same night in nearby St Lunaire. It referred to the earlier victim's statement that she had woken up to find herself coughing, her nose running and her skin feeling very tight – as if a chemical had been used to either knock her out or kill her.

The report went on to state that, because the 'stupefying matter' had not worked in the St Lunaire attack, the killer had possibly changed his mind about using it on Caroline Dickinson. It stated, 'Having failed at St Lunaire, he was not sated and carried on to Pleine-Fougeres. He decided that the next victim must not wake up.' According to the report, the attacker's motive was to experience the victim's powerlessness rather than see her fear. He may, therefore, have had tendencies towards necrophilia. In other words, he might have been unable to get his sexual thrill without killing his victims.

The report clearly implied that, if this was the case, Caroline's death was not the 'accident' that had frequently been suggested since her murder. John Dickinson had always been convinced the man meant to kill his daughter.

In January 2000, the hunt for the killer was wound down when the 15-strong French investigating team was reduced to just two. New investigating judge Francois Debons admitted, 'The time when our hopes were highest is coming to a close, which might lead to fears that the Dickinson case will gradually slip from memory.' Incredibly, Debons claimed that it was now up to 'fate' whether or not Caroline's killer would be caught.

Many thousands of kilometres away, the real killer was back in Argentina, where he began a relationship with a 17-year-old Buenos Aires college student he had first met when he lived in London. Entry stamps for Chile, Argentina, Peru, Venezuela and at least three other South and Central American countries were in his three passports over the previous year.

The tall, dark stranger was using the £16,000 inheritance from his wealthy father to travel the globe and seek out new, safer territory where he could attack – and in some cases kill – more young girls. The authorities in all these countries now believe the killer murdered and raped at least a dozen young girls while he was visiting their nations.

During 1999, the killer also travelled in and out of Miami, Florida, at least three times. His tentacles were, it seemed, reaching out far and wide.

18

Sliding across the rainbow from erotic pink to lizard green, the art-deco structures on Miami Beach's Ocean Drive were originally built to uplift the spirits of Americans and offer a distraction from the Great Depression. Seventy years later, they helped turn the beach area into a gaudy, head-turning district filled with architectural eye-candy – tacky, faddish and showy. Collectively, they helped Ocean earn the local nickname 'Deco Drive'.

Less than a quarter of a century earlier, the district had been better known for its derelict buildings, hookers and crack dealers. But, by the eve of the new millennium, it had been transformed into South Beach, the art-deco darling of the world and a mecca for college students and Florida's vast gay population.

The bronzed and beautiful thronged the district. They rollerbladed and strolled by the tables of places like the popular News Cafe on Ocean Drive, along the sidewalks amid the early-morning traffic, past the wedding-cake-deco hotels and beneath the palm trees and the sparkling golden sun.

The arrival of celebrities like Sylvester Stallone, Jennifer Lopez, Madonna and a galaxy of others confirmed the revival of Miami Beach to its glory days of the Roaring Twenties, when the police department had to put up boards on the sand to remind the bathing belles: 'Warning. Law Requires Full Bathing Suit.'

The News Cafe had become a regular start-of-the-day haunt for the tall, dark stranger with the wolfish looks. He would sit at a table inspecting the young girls walking past in skimpy bikinis on their way to the beach. He also liked to scrutinise the British newspapers to see if they were still covering the death of Caroline Dickinson.

The killer needed to keep one step ahead of the law, so Spanish-speaking Miami seemed the perfect spot in 1999. Initially, he stayed in a small youth hostel but soon got himself into trouble by annoying other guests with his 'creepy behaviour'. But then he had few so-called people skills. He would take food off other guests' plates and complain constantly about the quality of the hygiene in general. And he couldn't resist talking to the younger, more naive girls on vacation.

Just before he was evicted from that first youth hostel for not paying his rent, security guards started getting fresh complaints from other guests. Some said they found him in their room or watching them through gaps in the curtains. When confronted, he always pretended he didn't speak either English or Spanish and claimed he thought it was his room.

His next port of call was Miami Beach's 9th Street hostel. Two weeks after checking in, the stranger turned up – 'looking crazy', according to staff – at 2.30 in the morning. The manager confronted him and a vicious argument flared up. Eventually, the police were called after the stranger ran out of the hotel. A Miami-Dade County police cruiser picked him up a few streets away but they couldn't charge him with anything, so he was held overnight and released the following day.

In March 2000, a man who looked like the 'caveman' photofit of Caroline Dickinson's killer was arrested in Seine-St Denis, north of Paris, after a drunken brawl. During a routine cross-check, police found he was wanted for questioning by detectives investigating the Dickinson case. The arrest sparked some positive publicity for beleaguered Commandant Jean-Pierre Michel. But this time the French chief investigator tried to play it down, insisting to reporters, 'I am not immediately going to label this man a suspect, even if there are elements which could strongly point in that direction. But obviously, I would not be taking such an interest in him if I did not have a pretty good idea of what I was looking for.' However, within days this latest 'suspect' had also been cleared of involvement as a result of DNA testing.

Around the same time that yet another suspect for the Caroline Dickinson murder had been released without charge, the real killer flew back to Spain, bought himself a cheap second-hand car and headed for Germany once more. En route, he 'raided' a Swiss girls' school to which Britain's Prince Andrew intended to send his daughters. Two girls, aged 14 and 16, were anaesthetised, stripped and sexually assaulted at Aiglon College, in Villars.

This assault meant he had now struck in at least ten countries around the world. In Germany, where he had been jailed for three rapes in 1989, he was still wanted for questioning in relation to other assaults. In Spain, the Llanes warrant was still outstanding and in South America he had been connected to a number of outstanding sex crimes, including murder. In Belgium, the killer had also allegedly raped three teenagers in 1996 (his DNA was later recovered from the scene of the attacks). Also, he was eventually connected to the murder of a 16-year-old Portuguese girl in Geneva in 1988. Yet neither the Caroline Dickinson investigators nor any of these other police forces across the globe realised their suspect had committed so many serious offences.

After a two-month visit to Europe in the late spring of 2000, the killer took off once again for sunny Florida. He had decided not to return to South America after almost being caught by the father of a girl he raped in Buenos Aires. He already knew that Miami Beach was the ideal place to get a part-time job and hunt down some of the fresh, young college girls who flocked to the resort every summer.

As the fourth anniversary of Caroline Dickinson's murder approached, the French police tried to prove they were still actively hunting her killer by announcing to the press in July 2000 that they had widened their net by interviewing seasonal farm workers in Brittany. Extra officers were deployed to the depleted squad to question these casual farm workers in the hope they might know the killer. 'We believe he is a drifter and this is the type of work he would do,' said one gendarme.

By this time, investigators had questioned more than 7,500 people across Europe and 3,800 DNA tests had been carried out, including 425 men in Pleine-Fougeres. Yet detectives openly admitted they were no closer to finding their man.

Having left behind a trail of death and rape in Europe and South America, the killer began to feel virtually invincible. And now, back in Miami, he was soon consuming copious amounts of booze and pills on his days off from his work as a waiter, which meant that his urges to attack and kill young women were once again in the forefront of his mind.

In October 2000, the tall, dark stranger broke into a women's dormitory-style room at Miami's Clay Hotel, an international youth hostel. He was chased through the darkness by police and security guards and arrested in possession of a torch and a small pair of scissors. He insisted he was innocent, sticking rigidly to his guns. For some reason he was charged only with trespass and once again released after being held overnight in the county jail, even though his tourist visa had expired. The Miami police later said they had no cause to hold him because when detectives made a request to Interpol for more information on him they were told he had no criminal record.

The killer loved Miami and interpreted his latest release as further evidence that he should make it his permanent home. By now, he was familiar with all the darkened alleyways and dimly lit streets near the beach. And, with young female students on every street, it was the perfect stalking ground for the predator.

Towards the end of 2000, the French police admitted that the two-man permanent team searching for Caroline Dickinson's killer had been taken off active duty because the trail had gone completely cold. A spokesman said, 'Now we're running out of leads. We can only be patient and await fate's helping hand. Time is not on our side. But we will never forget our obligation to Caroline.'

Back in Miami Beach, in March 2001 two Scottish brothers were walking back to their hotel when they spotted an odd-looking man with wolf-like features trying to climb into the open window of a youth hostel. Michael and Graham Boyle immediately snapped a photo of the man with staring eyes as he was putting his arm through the open window of the hostel. 'When he saw our camera, he gave us a load of abuse. But he was foreign, so I didn't know what he was saying,' Michael Boyle recalled.

The 24-year-old salesman from Paisley had been to Miami to visit his 22-year-old brother, Graham, who was living in the US as part of a four-year soccer scholarship. Michael remembered, 'He looked as if he might have been breaking in. We only took the photo for the sense of humour value because he was so strange-looking. We take lots of pictures, so it wasn't unusual for us.'

But neither brother reported the man's activities to the police. Michael Boyle explained, 'A lot of the residents used to get into their rooms by reaching through the window for their keys, so we thought nothing more of it.'

That photo had been taken at a Miami Beach hostel right next to another hostel called the Banana Bungalow, which was especially popular with young women and one of the cheapest places to stay, at $17 a night. Attached to this was another youth hostel, where people paid even less to share a dormitory filled with single beds.

It was this easygoing atmosphere which attracted six pretty, teenage Irish students to stay at the Banana Bungalow a few days after that photo of the killer was taken, on 11 March 2001. They had just turned up for the weekend after enduring an 18-hour Greyhound bus drive from Washington State on the other side of the United States. After a long walk on the beach, the girls all flopped into their bunk beds to sleep.

Later that evening, the killer entered the hostel through an open window. Fuelled by his usual intake of drink and drugs, he was in a forceful, twisted mood and moved swiftly towards the stairs that led to all the rooms. As he crept up the steps, he experienced that familiar surge of fearlessness, which became stronger after every attack.

He gently pushed open the bedroom door and immediately focused on one of the Irish girls asleep on the bottom bunk. He moved alongside her silently, leaned down and gently pulled back the covers to find she was dressed only in a T-shirt and panties. He then took out a pair of small, silver-coloured scissors and cut off her panties, snipping carefully through the narrowest part, on the hips. He had brought scissors this time because he was convinced his victims would be less likely to wake up if he used them to remove their underwear. Then he folded a towel and spread it across the girl's hips before standing up, unzipping himself and masturbating over the towel. Incredibly, none of the other girls awoke. Once satisfied, he quietly left the room.

Next morning, the victim woke up and realised something was wrong when she noticed the towel neatly laid over her hips. 'I realised my underwear had been torn and then that something awful had happened during the night,' she recalled. 'I had slept right through it and in a way that was the worst thing about it. I slept through it and didn't know what was happening.'

The distressed girl told the hotel management, who called the Miami-Dade County police. Their initial response was complete disbelief. One officer later explained, 'We couldn't believe that someone would break into the room, cut this girl's panties and masturbate while she was asleep.' The police thought there was something more to it. Maybe drink or drugs were involved? But when investigators found semen stains on the victim's bed sheets and the towel they realised she was telling the truth. From this, they extracted DNA, a forensic aid the killer knew little or nothing about.

But Miami police had no eyewitnesses, apart from one guest from another room who thought she'd seen a strange man leaving the hotel in a hurry. So there was little or no chance of catching him unless the police could match that DNA to information on their databases.

In fact, the killer had presumed he had completely got away with his latest crime and, unaware of the police's involvement, convinced himself there were more potential victims at the Banana Bungalow and decided to definitely return there. Some experts would say he wanted to get caught, while others might insist it was pure stupidity or arrogance. The truth was, the killer simply didn't care. He never had, so why change the habit of a lifetime?

Two days later, on 13 March, he returned to the Banana Bungalow earlier in the evening to check out the guests and try to hand-pick the perfect next victim. But that female guest who had seen him leaving two nights earlier spotted him in the grill area. She immediately contacted the manager, who called the police. Meanwhile, the killer was calmly eyeing up young girls as he casually sipped a cocktail through a straw at the poolside bar.

Even after four burly Miami-Dade County police officers frog-marched him away from the grill, he remained completely cool. 'I was only looking for a room,' he insisted calmly in immaculate English. When officers referred to the sexual assault two nights previously he even conceded, 'Perhaps I was drunk so I don't remember committing a sex act upon her.' They were astounded at his calmness. How could he tell police this and think he could get away with it?

One of the policemen later explained, 'Initially we didn't think anything of him. He seemed a middle-aged man who stayed at youth hostels.' But, as the interview at the local police station progressed, it became evident that the Spaniard was some type of pervert. He was eventually charged with two felony counts of burglary and one misdemeanour count of lewd and lascivious conduct. In the days ahead, the Miami-Dade police would discover that the man was more than just a pervert.

Back in Britain at the end of March 2001, John Dickinson renewed his appeal for help in solving his daughter's murder at an inquest which was to rule on whether or not the teenager's death was the result of unlawful killing. The British inquest into Caroline's murder helped spark yet more headlines about the case, but it did little to reassure people that the French police were still hot on the heels of her killer.

19

On 1 April – in the middle of the British inquest into Caroline Dickinson's murder – the *Sunday Times* published a story headlined 'HUNT FOR SCHOOLGIRL'S KILLER MOVES TO BRITAIN', which some readers might have been forgiven for momentarily believing was some kind of bad-taste April Fool's stunt by the newspaper. Reporters Maurice Chittenden and Edith Coron revealed that the French police had asked Scotland Yard to help them locate a new suspect, a Spanish restaurant worker known to have been living in London before the killing.

The article referred to the photofit of Caroline's attacker which showed a 'caveman'-type character, and named 50-year-old Francisco Arce Montes as the suspect. He had, it said, a history of complaints against him for allegedly sexually harassing girls at youth hostels in the Loire Valley. Francois Debons, the latest investigating judge leading the Caroline Dickinson murder inquiry, had named Montes in a list of possible suspects.

Debons and two police officers, Captain Yvon Jezekel and Gendarme Marie-Jean Luc, were due to give evidence in Britain at the inquest into Caroline's death, which was expected to record a verdict of unlawful death. Debons told the *Sunday Times* that the French police particularly wanted to trace Montes from a list of outstanding suspects. 'It is his modus operandi that interests us,' said Debons. 'If the killer is dead or has disappeared, then we are clearly looking for a ghost. However, we cling to the hope of finding him.' Debons admitted the murder squad investigating Caroline's death had been virtually closed down and the overall thrust of the article was that naming Montes was nothing more than a last, desperate throw of the dice.

The inquest had at least brought the case right back into the public spotlight in Britain. 'FRIENDS WATCHED THROUGH A HAZE AS CAROLINE FOUGHT KILLER' was one headline in the *Daily Mail*. This was a reference to emotional written evidence from two of the murdered schoolgirl's friends as they lay in bed in the room where she was killed.

Across the Atlantic, the killer –known to Miami police only as 'Francisco Arce' after he showed them one of his three passports, which bore that name – was still in a Dade County lock-up, blissfully unaware that he'd been named in a British newspaper as the chief suspect in the hunt for the murderer of Caroline Dickinson.

BOOK 2

'JAVI'

———

'WE USUALLY FIND IN THE HISTORY OF SCHIZOPHRENICS THAT
BOTH PARENTS HAVE FAILED THE CHILD, OFTEN FOR DIFFERENT
REASONS. FREQUENTLY THE COMBINATION IS AS FOLLOWS:
A DOMINEERING, NAGGING AND HOSTILE MOTHER, WHO GIVES
THE CHILD NO CHANCE TO ASSERT HIMSELF IS MARRIED TO A
DEPENDENT, WEAK MAN, TOO WEAK TO HELP THE CHILD.
A FATHER WHO DARES NOT PROTECT THE CHILD BECAUSE HE IS
NOT ABLE TO OPPOSE HER STRONG PERSONALITY IS JUST AS
CRIPPLING TO THE CHILD AS THE MOTHER IS.'

Silvano Arieti, Interpretation of Schizophrenia

20

But it should have been so different. Francisco Javier Arce Montes – or 'Javi', as his family called him from the start – was born on 14 March 1950 in Gijon, on the northern coast of Spain in the province of Asturias. The city had been a Roman settlement formed between the hills of two small fishing communities called Santa Catalina and Cimadevilla.

Now, with a population of around 300,000, Gijon had become a major industrial and commercial centre exporting vast quantities of coal and iron, as well as a manufacturing centre for steel, chemicals, petroleum, glass, food and tobacco. Back in the 8th century it was one of the first places recaptured from the Moors following their invasion of the Iberian peninsula. The city then flourished under the first Asturian kings. In 1588, the defeated Spanish Armada took refuge in its harbour.

But the overwhelmingly dominant force for the people of Gijon throughout all these wars and many centuries was the impetuous Bay of Biscay – or the Cantabrian Sea, as it is known locally – which embraced the city and has marked its history for over 5,000 years.

By the time little Javi came into the world, Gijon was a busy industrial centre, a highly traditional port and a summer holiday resort all in one. The main San Lorenzo Beach, with its five-kilometre promenade, boasted deep, rich-golden sands. Behind the beach lay historical attractions, including Roman baths and medieval palaces, as well as the baroque Revillagigedo Palace, which dated back to the 18th century. All this brought a steady stream of visitors to Gijon from other parts of Spain.

The city centre was the envy of many in the rest of the country thanks to its picturesque, narrow cobbled streets overshadowed by Spanish Gothic architecture, evidence of centuries of construction designed to withstand the power of the often ferocious Atlantic Ocean.

The Spanish Civil War of 1936–9 had a profound effect on every family in Gijon, not least little Javi's father, Gerardo Montes, whose parents owned a busy grocery store in the working-class neighbourhood of El Coto. The nationwide military uprising had originated in Morocco and was headed by General Francisco Franco. It spread rapidly all over Spain, sparking the 20th century's most bloody civil war in mainland Europe. A number of battles took place in and around Gijon as fortunes changed from one side to the other. Franco's 'nacionales' finally prevailed and made a victorious entry into Madrid on 28 March 1939.

Gijon had, by the 1950s, taken on a serene calmness that was the envy of many other communities in Spain. By this time, the harbour of El Musel, located next to the city, in

Cimadevilla, was one of the busiest ports in Europe and held up by Franco as a brilliant example of the progressive modernisation of his country.

With the vast Asturian mountains overshadowing the city, Gijon was supposed to represent the acceptable face of successful, modern Spain, possessing many of the country's appealing features but few of its bad habits.

Eclipsed by Oviedo in the race to become the capital of Asturias, Gijon was believed by many outside the region to be inhabited by short, stocky, fiercely independent mountain folk. However, by the time Javi was born in 1950, it had assumed a comfortable mantle all of its own.

But unlike, for example, Andalusia – where communities basked in Mediterranean sunshine almost all year round – Gijon's weather was tempered by its close proximity to the unpredictable Atlantic, which meant cold, wet, often snowy winters, followed by crisp, clear summers. As Javi grew up, Gijon earned itself a reputation as a healthy, affluent and largely conservative city proud of its independence from much of the rest of Spain. And for the first few years of his life, he probably could not have wished for a better place to be raised.

The Montes family were well off compared with many in El Coto because Javi's father had inherited his own father's very successful grocery. Casa Gerardo, he called the corner shop, which nowadays would be described as a mini-market. Gerardo was often so busy running his thriving business, it was left to his wife Benigna to bring up their shy, retiring skinny little only son. Geraldo and Benigna Moro had married just after the end of the Civil War in 1940 and first had a daughter Blanca. Javi – born nine years after his sister – had virtually been an afterthought.

Having no brothers or sisters close to his own age seems to have had a detrimental effect on Javi's childhood. His only other companion much of the time in the family's dusty, dark apartment above Casa Gerardo at 1 Calle Zorilla was Javi's elderly grandmother, whom he adored in many ways much more than his parents. Visitors to the home noted that little Javi seemed withdrawn and shy and was in the habit of running to his grandmother every time anything happened which upset him. Meanwhile, his mother Benigna would stand near by, stony-faced and with her arms folded. When his grandmother wasn't around, Javi would sometimes rush to his mother's side, but she would push him away and tell him to stop behaving like a little girl. He would then dash to his bedroom in floods of tears.

As Javi developed into an increasingly shy, withdrawn, slow-learning child, so his mother became even harsher on him. Benigna's temper often flared up as her frustration with Javi grew. Some in El Coto speculated that perhaps she was afraid to admit that her small son was a tad effeminate and oversensitive, in case they labelled him a homosexual, which back in the late 1950s and early 1960s was a stigma few could recover from, especially in macho Spain under Franco's dictatorship.

Javi quickly developed some classic childhood phobias, including a fear of the dark brought on by his mother's habit of insisting the lights were switched off in his bedroom from the moment he went to bed to save electricity. 'It's something I've never recovered from,' he told one psychiatrist many years later.

As a result of this fear of the dark, Javi sometimes persuaded his beloved grandmother to let him sleep in her bed rather than lie terrified and alone in his room in pitch darkness. But at times when she wasn't around, he had no choice and would stay awake in fear of what life held for him when she died. Then tears would well up in his eyes as he contemplated a life without her.

Soon after Javi began attending elementary school, he told teachers that bruises on his body were from beatings he'd received from his father. Gerardo Montes took the attitude that children – especially boys – needed strong parental discipline and any hint of his son being gay had to be beaten out of him. Yet, strangely, in later life Javi said he felt no real bitterness towards his father. It was his mother he would blame for most of his problems.

At school, other kids picked up on this vulnerability by chasing Javi in the playground and calling him a 'Jupi', a Jew. 'They used to call him that because he was a cheap person, never seemed to have any money even though his family were wealthy compared with most of us,' explained a classmate named Julio.

In his early childhood, Javi's parents did at least feel a degree of guilt about what their son was going through and pampered him when he was at home because they felt sorry for him. But, it later emerged, they were only reacting to Javi's grandmother, who regularly lectured the couple about being more loving to their little boy.

Many years later, when Javi was asked about his parents, he broke down in tears and said, 'My mother never liked me, unlike my father. Mother always said I was lazy and too slow.' He added, sobbing, 'I don't consider I had a happy childhood. My friends made fun of me and beat me. I don't know why.'

A school photo of little Javi shows a shy, feminine-looking little boy with prominent ears and a smooth complexion. The only clue to his later life were the eyes, which seemed sad and droopy, almost lifeless. It was one of the only photos ever taken of Javi during his childhood because cameras were considered a luxury in Spain back then, even for a relatively well-off family like the Montes.

Javi was so unhappy at school that when he was still only five his parents decided to pay fees to send him to the Colegio Politecnico Asturias, on Calle Ramon y Cajal, a street named after one of Gijon's most famous doctors. Javi's parents hoped he might learn a proper trade since the teachers at his first school had already predicted that he would struggle to pass any exams. It was even suggested by some that he might be in some way retarded. In public, Benigna and Gerardo refused to even consider such a possibility, although Benigna continued to call Javi 'slow' whenever he annoyed her. The answer to any doubts about their son was to sweep the subject under the carpet and simply make sure he had some kind of trade when he left school at 14 or 15.

Javi's sister Blanca seemed unsympathetic when asked about her baby brother many years later: 'He was mollycoddled as a boy. Private school, special attention. It didn't do him much good, did it?'

If Javi had been more encouraged to communicate, maybe he would have told his parents that what he really needed was some patience and understanding, because the child was undoubtedly very different from most of his contemporaries.

Within months of arriving at the Colegio Politecnico, Javi was skipping classes and handing in homework late, and most teachers had labelled him a moody troublemaker with little future. Javi himself was growing ever more resentful. He had quickly realised that he would be left to his own devices by both teachers and classmates if he acted weirdly. In many ways he was the exact opposite of the pupil who realises he can get absolutely anything by being charming. He wanted absolutely nothing except to be left alone to live in his own strange world.

These days it's likely that a moody, withdrawn pupil like Javi would be given counselling to help him work through all the bitterness and resentment. At school, he was bullied and teased, so his behaviour became a round-the-clock reaction to his own unhappiness. And it was no better at home, where he was either ignored or beaten.

By the time Javi reached seven or eight, he was a pale, gangly boy who had become the butt of most other children's jokes. His face was thin and well defined, with strong eyebrows and a hooked nose. Many commented at the time that he already looked like an adult. It was as if his childhood never happened.

Javi possessed a perverse and very determined streak which made him seem much more uncooperative than other children. He enjoyed watching his classmates squirm when he pulled the wings off a butterfly because it was the only time he got a proper reaction from other people. He craved attention.

The boy also had a photographic memory, although none of his teachers spotted this potential in him when he was a child. If they had, perhaps he would have been given more of a chance at school. But Javi's problem was that he only bothered to learn what he found interesting. In other words, if the subject didn't appeal to him, he just switched off and retreated into his own little world.

Back then, Javi and his classmates didn't have much use for any foreign languages, so, even though he would prove in later years to be incredibly adept at speaking other languages, he didn't even excel at French, which was then the main language taught in Spanish schools.

The only thing Javi excelled at was football. Sports teachers reported that he was an excellent defender and predicted that he would one day make the senior-school first team. For Javi, football was the only escape from the tedium of life, although he had to almost beg his father to pay for a second-hand pair of football boots, sparking even more resentment between him and his parents.

Almost 50 years later, this author was given unprecedented access to Javi's school records. In September 1962, aged 12, Javi took his exam for secondary education two years later than most, which implies he had severe learning difficulties. His school report named him as 'Francisco-Javier Arce Montes' and his parents even had to re-register his birth in March 1962 because they had lost the original certificate, which they had to provide in order for him to take the exam. They also had to supply a medical certificate to prove Javi had no diseases.

This turned out to be the only official exam Javi ever took, although there were others later, at 14 and 16, he should have been obliged to sit. His handwriting was neat and upright but he failed a number of the subjects within the exam and had to re-sit some subjects twice more over the following year. This resulted in him being labelled as having borderline intelligence.

A copy of the exam paper shows that in school year 1961–2, when Javi had to fill in his mother's full name he scribbled it almost illegibly, as if his hatred of her was so intense he couldn't stand to even think about her. At the age of 12, he announced to his friends and family that he would prefer to be known as Francisco because it made him feel more grown up and even signed the exam paper 'Francisco J Arce'. However, his parents continued calling him 'Javi'.

In his early teens, Javi began working occasionally for his father in the grocery store beneath their apartment.

Former classmates recall little about Javi, except that he read a lot of books and magazines. Javi particularly adored reading the true-crime magazines that were popular at the time and often featured reports of notorious American killers who had become legendary names in the United States through their appalling crimes. One classmate later claimed Javi also regularly read from a dictionary he kept on the table besides his bed.

At school, Javi sat one language test in which he recited an old Spanish text which seemed to sum up the way he was feeling about his childhood at the time. The piece read: 'The pigeon for no reasonable motive had many enemies in the village. Some openly, others hidden, and these, since they hadn't found a way of fighting him openly, were fighting him on the sly, insidiously.' This quote has led many to speculate that Javi considered himself to be that pigeon. He identified so closely with the passage that he couldn't get it out of his head.

Meanwhile, Javi's handwriting began deteriorating, instead of improving, as he grew older. As one of his school teachers in Gijon later commented, 'There is something quite interesting about his handwriting because it starts off good and straight and then gets worse and worse, almost as if his life was becoming increasingly stressful. He also used accent marks instead of dots on 'i's. It is very confusing because he marks all of them with a stroke as if it is an accent.'

Sometimes Javi got so nervous writing out school exercises that he would both misspell his own name and make it run off the edge of the paper.

In El Coto there were obvious signs of Javi's difficult childhood. When he walked into the local fruit and vegetable shop with his mother, she shouted at him about what size of oranges he should pick for her. 'He was very edgy and nervous around his mother as she was always picking on him. It was sad to see,' explained the shop owner many years later.

This feeling of helplessness was compounded when his beloved grandmother died. Javi, now 14, was so distressed that when he went to school next day he stuffed his wooden desk with newspapers and set fire to it. Staff felt so sorry for him when they heard he was reacting to his granny's death that they did not discipline him.

Ultimately, Javi was the child of a mother whom he found overbearing and insufficiently loving. She had made it clear to him from a very early age that he would be a failure in life. Javi later attributed his inability to hold conversations with strangers or even to look people directly in the eye to his mother's influence. He also blamed her for his complete and utter ignorance about sex.

From an early age, Javi had been confused about his emotions towards the other boys in his all-male class at school. Some girls, including his big sister, scared him even more than the boys because they seemed so pushy and inquisitive. Back then, Blanca felt it was her duty to be a second mother to her baby brother but all that did was confuse him even further.

She recognised that Javi was a deeply unhappy, somewhat disturbed individual and she tried hard to bring some warmth into his life but it wasn't easy. Javi did not react to situations in the same way as a 'normal' child. In fact, he didn't respond at all. It was almost as if he was dead inside. Either that, or he was simply afraid to say anything in case it sparked another beating or a shouting match.

Deep inside, Javi saw everyone else as he saw his mother and presumed that they all were just as full of hatred for him. Initially, it made him resentful but then a mood of sheer apathy prevailed and he found the best way to cope was to cut himself off emotionally and not react to other people. That way, at least most of them would leave him alone.

21

Javi had created his own little world inhabited only by him. Everyone else was an outsider who threatened his peace and stability. In the end he would resort to anything, even murder, to ensure no one entered his world. But back then, when he was bullied at school and home – which was still frequently – he'd take the beating and then just walk away without uttering a word. The only other children he felt attracted to were the weaker, quieter ones like himself.

At home, Javi had gone from being openly resentful to running into his room the moment he got back to the family's apartment above the grocery store. Many of his relatives were bemused by how little they saw of the boy. His relationship with his mother was so bad he refused to come out of his room, even at mealtimes.

Javi summed up his own miserable existence in an interview many years later: 'My mother would lie to me about everything. At 14 I had no friends and I used to lock myself away and not see anyone.'

Already he was looked on as the black sheep of the family, even though he hadn't actually done anything wrong. His painful and unhappy childhood was about to become an impossible adolescence. He was deeply immature, shy and awkward in front of strangers. What chance would he stand in the outside world?

Other strange characteristics soon began to emerge, including an obsession with keeping clean. He began by cleaning his hands five or six times a day after announcing to his mother that he didn't like being dirty. She ignored his behaviour, even when he eventually started going to the bathroom at least 20 times a day just to wash his hands. This weird habit soon became like a metaphor for his life at that time. He was already so far removed from reality that he actually believed his health could be at risk if he didn't keep washing his hands. He had also got into the habit of refusing to take responsibility for anything – even his inability to turn up for classes. 'He'd always have some excuse and it was *never* his fault,' one teacher recalled many years later.

By the end of the 1965–6 school year, Javi was performing so badly that he was asked to leave the school and from that moment his formal education ceased. His handwriting had worsened alarmingly and many at the school noticed that he seemed to be under even more stress. His hands shook almost constantly and he barely spoke a word to anyone.

Yet it should all have been so different. After all, he'd been born to a financially comfortable couple with a successful business. He'd been sent to a private school but still ended up being regarded by most as a loner and a misfit. So, as he grew up, his strange behaviour took on a more sinister air. Some neighbours reported finding him leaning against walls for hours in complete silence watching children walking past. Rumours about a hygiene obsession, including how he opened doors with a handkerchief, were also spreading around El Coto. Soon neighbours were stopping their children going anywhere near him.

And Javi's hatred of his mother had become so intense that he convinced himself she was trying to poison him. He began insisting on cooking all his own food at home and would get into vicious slanging matches with his mother if she tried to interfere when he was in the kitchen. No one to this day knows who taught Javi to cook, but by all accounts he was quite good at it.

Psychiatrist Arnaud Martorell later described Javi as a nervous child, bad at exams. 'As he entered adolescence, he became obsessed not only with cleanliness, but also with cooking his own food because of a chronic fear of germs.'

At least, as he got older, Javi began to get on better with his father, despite the beatings that he'd regularly received as a child. In some ways, Javi blamed himself for the punishments handed out by Gerardo. He knew his father was working incredibly long hours in the grocery store and desperately didn't want to cause any friction between his parents. Helping out in the shop meant spending quite long periods of time with his father and they actually began having a few conversations. As a child, Javi felt a strange sense of guilt, which constantly ate away at him because he was desperate for his father's love and approval since his mother had already made it clear she didn't care whether he lived or died.

But helping out in the family store didn't exactly make him any more popular in El Coto. Javi was nicknamed 'Chupa pollo', or 'Chicken-licker', by many local kids because he was in the habit of licking other children's ice-cream cones before passing them over. One contemporary explained years later, 'That was horrible and he deserved the nickname because he would always do it with a sick and twisted grin on his face.'

Javi was also called a '*maricon*' by other kids: a queer. Some even teased him that he looked like a caveman with his bushy eyebrows, hooked nose and messy hairstyle.

The beatings earlier inflicted on little Javi by his father had already turned him into a classically self-destructive personality. As a child, he simply did not receive the emotional response he required from his family and increasingly found it difficult to establish a boundary between himself and the world beyond his largely uninterested parents. He was becoming an all-encompassing individual, seeing things from his own perspective and no one else's.

Other family members noticed how fearless Javi became and the way he would try to manipulate situations to suit himself and no one else. He had also become incapable of appreciating when he hurt others' feelings. When Javi did something bad, he felt little remorse and certainly showed no sympathy for his victim. For beneath the strange, troubled exterior lay an inner sadness caused primarily by the fact that he found it incredibly difficult to enjoy any of the usual childhood interests.

For most people, childhood is a pleasurable experience in which the developing individual learns how to be happy and derive happiness from as many situations as possible. But Javi's sister was much older and he had virtually no friends, so he had no one to bounce his feelings off. His family were forever telling him he was 'not normal' and that made him feel even more detached.

Javi's quietness was construed as shyness and others would presume he was daydreaming a lot of the time. And they were right to a certain degree, although his dreams were often filled with chilling, horrific images which made him distrust the world even more. Death and destruction dominated his dreams and there was one overriding character in these nightmares – his mother. Yet in some ways Javi found the dreams to be as pleasurable as they were fearful. They had their own deranged symbology, steeped in his terror of appalling memories that were incised in his mind.

But, he revealed many years later, the most disturbing aspect of all this was that sometimes he found himself in a half-dreaming, half-waking state that combined all those nightmare images with the reality of his miserable childhood. This meant that drawing a line between reality and fantasy was already proving difficult. Sometimes, without warning, he found himself living through the fear that he was experiencing in his dreams. People's true identities and sexuality became confused as Javi became more and more locked inside his own weird world, where he set his own moral agenda. Death was normal. Fear nothing special. Happiness non-existent. No wonder he exploded with venom in later life.

Overall, Javi was growing bitter and filled with hatred at a time in his young life when he should have been filled with happiness and hope. He'd grown increasingly disillusioned about families because he presumed they were all as unhappy as his. So, wandering around in this strange netherworld meant that he missed out on many enjoyable aspects of life. His experience of so-called normal things was virtually non-existent.

While many of his classmates at the Colegio Politecnico Asturias had bragged about their sexual experiences, Javi found himself unable to relate to any of their words because, even at 14, he hadn't yet really thought about girls. For him, it wasn't a matter of feeling any shame about sex. He just didn't know what the word meant. His parents hadn't even bothered to tell him about the birds and the bees and because he had no friends there was no one else in his life to talk over subjects like sex, drugs and everything else encountered by teenagers, even back then.

Eventually, Javi realised that in order to relate to his classmates at all he would have to make up stories about his sexual conquests. One of his classmates later explained, 'Javi came out with some really weird stories and he wasn't inhibited about describing what he did with girls. We were shocked by what he was saying but I don't think he even realised how rude he sounded.'

Javi simply didn't know when he had crossed the line. He thought that by bragging about his imaginary exploits he might actually make himself more popular. But all he did was make all his classmates even more wary of him. As one explained, 'We all thought he was a creep and used to cross the street to avoid talking to him if we saw him outside school.'

Back at home, Javi continued to use his room as a refuge from the rest of the world. By now he was insisting on doing both his cooking and cleaning because of his fear that his mother was still trying to poison him. Blanca had long since left home, and whenever Javi went out at night his mother would demand to know where he was going and who with.

Most of the time he was just walking the streets of Gijon alone. In the end, it became easier just to stay in his room and read books and those gruesome crime magazines.

By now, Javi had concluded that he was very different from most people, and why fight that? In many ways, it made him feel superior to other people because they were just like everyone else while he was something special. Well, at least that was what he thought.

His room had become his only refuge from all the unhappiness he was suffering. Sometimes he stayed there for days, just to give himself time to think about his life and what the future held for him. Javi was sufficiently self-reflective to not particularly like what he had become at such a young age, but he didn't know how to change things and he wasn't even sure if he really needed to.

The atmosphere at home had become increasingly tense since Blanca had moved out. Every time Javi encountered his parents, he believed from the expressions on their faces that they loathed him. When they tried to talk to him about anything he would shut down altogether and refuse to say a word. It seemed to them that their son was like an alien. Later, Javi said he didn't get any of the love and attention that a child can expect from his mother.

Javi's father was now a lot easier to talk to but he clearly had suspicions about his son's strange behaviour. However, he was far too remote a personality to tackle his son directly. Javi was already so isolated that his sense of right and wrong was practically absent. He was heading in a very dangerous direction.

His mother looked at things very differently. Many years later, Benigna said, 'Something like an allergy stopped me going into his room. I always felt a certain repulsion there. I didn't want to risk going in there.'

In later life, Javi claimed the breakdown of his relationship with his mother was caused by the way she spoiled Blanca. 'The bad feeling I got from my family had a definite negative impact on my studies at school,' he said, typically seeking to blame others for all his problems.

22

By now, Javi was in the habit of wearing his trousers belted high above his waist and spoke in a soft, effeminate manner, as if his voice hadn't properly broken. Many El Coto residents noticed him hanging around street corners ogling girls as they walked by. One time another teenage boy, Martin, was shocked to hear him pronounce, 'All women are whores' under his breath, as he hung about near the gates of one of two local girls' schools.

One of his mother's best friends recounted, 'Javi began to have mental problems and became very problematic in his mid-teens. He could change mood in the blink of an eye. One minute he would say hello in the street, the next he would be in his own world. And he became more and more convinced his mother was trying to poison him.'

The same woman claimed that Javi began hitting his mother as 'punishment' for trying to kill him. She said, 'Benigna would never talk about it but we could all see the results of his violence. She was frightened of him, and the family would do anything to get him out of the house. God only knows how Javi got these things into his head. It is dreadful what they had to put up with.'

A local butcher commented, 'He had no friends and was uncommunicative and would walk around not looking people in the eye and seemed very distrustful of people.'

Javi began spending time alone at the local beaches, where he would stare in adolescent wonderment for hours on end at young girls in swimming costumes. These were the moments of his first, real sexual awakening. Not the ludicrous fantasies he recalled to school friends earlier. He would examine every detail of the bodies of those girls on the beach, without ever being aware he was making them feel uncomfortable.

One day, Javi walked into a bar near his home called the Bodega Moreno and got talking to a young girl of about 12 sitting in the corner. The owner, Sergio Figuar, recalled, 'He asked her if she wanted to go for a walk with him, which I'd seen him try and do on a number of occasions with other young girls. The kid became nervous because she was only 12, so she asked her brother, who was sitting near by, and he warned Javi off immediately.'

After this incident, many of the youths of El Coto began calling Javi '*el pervertido*'.

Years later Javi himself claimed to a psychiatrist that he had a brief relationship with a local girl, Felli, in Gijon when he was a teenager. Javi had met her because she was related to one of his sister's friends. But the relationship failed after he found it impossible to have sex with her. 'Something made it impossible. Maybe it was my obsession with cleanliness,' Javi later wrote in a questionnaire for his psychiatrist. The relationship was frowned upon by his family, who tried to make him stop seeing Felli because she came from such a poor background.

In their cramped apartment above the shop, Javi's father shouted down his son when he tried to explain he was going out with Felli. As one neighbour explained many years later, 'Gerardo was a very tall, strong man and very indifferent to most people, including his own son. We would all hear him shouting at poor Javi because they hated his girlfriend.'

Gerardo had a very loud voice and as he got older he developed a mild form of Alzheimer's, which manifested itself in his regularly annoying people in the lift of the apartment block where he lived. One neighbour later said she'd never go in the lift when Gerardo was in it because he was always trying to grab her breasts. Some El Coto residents believe to this day that Javi inherited a lot of his attitudes towards women from his father.

It was no surprise that, eventually, as a reaction to his many emotional problems, Javi turned to alcohol. He later wrote to his psychiatrist, 'I started to drink and argued with my parents even more.' He also admitted fantasising about women and claimed that many of them wanted to sleep with him. 'Women always wanted to make love to me but I pushed them away,' he wrote.

By the age of 17, Javi had evolved into a withdrawn, introverted teenager with a slightly warped interest in sex and an obsession that his mother was trying to poison him, which had led to his manic cleanliness and cooking all his own meals. His parents eventually lost patience with him and persuaded him to visit a well-known Gijon psychiatrist called Dr Rubero Prieto Rodriguez Ponga at his Clinica Salas, near the bull ring on the eastern edge of the city. Outspoken Dr Ponga recalled, 'I don't remember that much about him but I know he was in need of immediate help. I thought he had schizophrenia.'

The psychiatrist told Javi's parents that their son should be admitted to his clinic for a proper examination. 'He was pretty sick for me to recommend that,' he recalled. 'He needed to go into hospital so I could supervise him and find out what was really wrong with him.'

When questioned by Dr Ponga in the clinic, Javi admitted being deeply depressed and said that football was the only enjoyable aspect of his life. He even told the doctor he had hopes of making it as a professional one day. By all accounts, Dr Ponga administered some medical treatment on Javi during his stay in the clinic. Then, after just three days, the now deeply disturbed teenager checked out.

Javi's parents were disappointed that he had left the clinic. But they knew he hadn't got on well with Dr Ponga, so they persuaded him to visit another psychiatrist, Dr Felix Margolyes, whose practice was in the busy centre of Gijon. Javi was immediately put more at ease by Dr Margolyes.

Margolyes's office, where he still works today, seemed welcoming. It had immaculate parquet flooring and walls lined with bookshelves, and he insisted Javi sat on a sofa in the corner of the huge office while he addressed him from a big wooden desk opposite.

The trim, short psychiatrist immediately struck some kind of chord with the shy Javi, who poured out his life story. Margolyes later told this author, 'In all the 50 years I have been a psychiatrist, this is the most extreme case I have ever seen, although I have to emphasise that during my personal interaction with Montes he came over as a perfectly normal person.'

Javi told the doctor he couldn't get an erection with his girlfriend and that had worried him because he wanted to have children. As Dr Margolyes later explained, 'He was first brought to me because of his problems with obsession but then he talked about his sex life openly.' Javi later said that Dr Margolyes was the first person he had ever spoken to on such personal terms in his entire life.

Dr Margolyes added, 'You must remember that we were still under Franco back then and people were severely inhibited from talking openly about sex. He was talking to me about having sex with a girl when he was not married to her. He was also living at home and the girl was as well. This was a big issue and it was brave of him to bring it up.' Javi also claimed to Margolyes that he had tried to have sex in several different places with his girlfriend, including a field and in the sea, but to no avail, which had left him feeling even less confident about women.

Javi also told the psychiatrist that his girlfriend had complained constantly about the pain he might cause her if they even attempted to have sex and that was the other reason why he couldn't keep an erection. It seems certain now that his obsession with young girls was fuelled by these experiences when he was a teenager growing up in Gijon. He never wanted to feel that sense of rejection ever again from a woman.

Dr Margolyes recalled, 'Montes had an "erotic history" and I remember that interview with him was strange. I noted that he was "a boy with many sexual feelings and other influences". He was also very sadistic and had psychopathic tendencies in relation to various parts of his life. But most of all he was obsessive. In many ways that made him a textbook psychotic.'

Javi told Margolyes that his 'girlfriend' made him feel it was all his fault he couldn't have sex with her. He was already starting to wonder if all sexual relations caused pain both emotionally and physically. This had another bizarre spin-off in later life when he found he actually felt more aroused if a sexual partner was not conscious, because then she couldn't stop him from having sex with her.

Javi also confessed to the psychiatrist that he had insisted Felli wash her breasts and body with alcohol before they attempted sex, because he was so obsessed with cleanliness. As Dr Margolyes commented many years later, 'No wonder the relationship didn't last long.'

Javi's older neighbours still looked on him as little Javi, the harmless yet simple teenage son of Gerardo, owner of the locals' favourite grocery store. 'We thought he never caused any actual trouble in the neighbourhood,' said one many years later.

Yet the atmosphere in the Montes household was going from bad to worse.

Javi constantly cried alone in his bedroom, especially when his mother shouted at him and told him how repulsed she was by his 'filthy habits'. Benigna would often accuse her son of being an animal with whom she didn't wish to share her life. 'I would rather sleep rough than share a house with you,' she shouted one day at her highly sensitive only son.

Even as an adult, the memories of those clashes with his strong-willed mother often reduced Javi to tears. He felt shame about many things, but he couldn't understand why his own mother despised him so much. Javi was clearly suffering a form of nervous breakdown after years of unhappiness both at home and at school.

23

At 17, Javi was, by his own admission to Dr Felix Margolyes, 'in a constant state of fear about food and cleanliness'. He told the psychiatrist, 'I refused to let my mother cook any food for me or anyone else for that matter. I was washing my hands many times a day. I didn't even like touching doorknobs or things like that.'

Dr Margolyes today describes Javi's case as 'the most classic case of obsession I have seen in 50 years as a psychiatrist'. He added, 'He used mineral water, no salt and boiled all his food carefully. He didn't want anyone in his room at home and spent most of his time locked in that room refusing to see anyone. He even washed his own clothes and rarely left the house. By this stage, he was washing his hands at least 20 times a day. He even used paper to avoid touching light switches and would use his feet to open doors. He wouldn't allow anyone to iron his clothes either.'

Years later, Javi claimed that he knew his behaviour was

bizarre and he was desperate to change and become normal. His obsessions were interfering with every aspect of his life. He couldn't even hold down a part-time job. But his parents refused steadfastly to blame themselves for their son's obvious emotional problems. They still hoped that one day he would simply wake up and become a 'normal person'.

Dr Margolyes never forgot the way Javi referred to himself and his psychiatric problems. 'He wrote about himself very gently and even claimed that his first-ever memory was of taking first communion when he was six, although that seems a little too convenient to me. However, his actual handwriting at the age of 17 was childlike and his spelling was poor. It was almost as if he had gone backwards in his development as an adult.'

Javi was clearly an extremely mixed-up teenager, so it was hardly surprising that he was by now drowning his sorrows by swallowing back whole bottles of whisky and brandy. He combined this with the anti-depressant Afranil – newly prescribed by psychiatrist Dr Margolyes – to produce a powerful cocktail which dissolved all the tension in his body, dulled his senses and loosened his inhibitions.

Gerardo had paid out a considerable sum of money for psychiatric help for his son. He and Benigna even filled in a questionnaire for Dr Margolyes, in which they described all Javi's problems, including the fact that he was a complete hypochondriac.

Many years later, Dr Margolyes explained, 'In medical terms he felt obsessed to go against things. I prescribed him Afranil and Valium to begin with. I had no idea that Afranil would later become his drug of choice.' However, he was equally concerned about the attitude of Javi's parents, and later recalled, 'The parents wanted him to be locked away for ever. It was not a healthy attitude to have.'

Javi felt rejected. His behaviour was a cry for help but it had fallen on deaf ears. His mother and father had already decided they had had enough of their son's weird behaviour and they wanted him put away forever so they could get back to their safe, comfortable lives.

The sexual obsessiveness that was to mark his future out so terrifyingly had not yet fully risen to the surface of Javi's personality. At Clinica La Providencia on the outskirts of Gijon, where he stayed for a few days while being examined by Dr Margolyes, there wasn't one complaint about his behaviour towards the nurses. As the eminent psychiatrist later recalled, 'And there were many pretty nurses working there at that time. But he didn't cause us any trouble whatsoever.'

By contrast, once back home, Javi began getting fixations on girls he encountered on the streets of El Coto. He would also spend hours each night peering through the curtains at the apartment block facing his room to see if he could spot any women undressing in front of a window. He soon progressed from merely watching women undressing to trying to get their attention by standing naked at his own window in the hope that one of them might spot him and invite him into their home for sex. It was a twisted pipe dream, but, when he had swallowed enough Afranil and booze, he became fixated on the idea that all the world's women wanted him.

Around this time, Javi's parents received a number of complaints about their son's behaviour. Benigna believed he was turning into some kind of sexual pervert. In Catholic Spain, dominated for so many years by the ultra-right-wing Franco, sex remained an unspoken word, which made it even more difficult for Benigna to cope with her son's behaviour.

She was already being hit by Javi when they argued but his behaviour soon grew so much worse that she told her husband she was terrified of him. She told friends she suspected he was going insane. She wanted him to leave the family home and was infuriated that he hadn't been admitted full-time to Dr Margolyes's clinic after his visits to the psychiatrist. She believed her son was, at the very least, an exhibitionist, who was bringing shame to the family.

It seems clear now that Javi was doing all this because he didn't want to leave the safe, clean environment of the family apartment to risk having sex. He didn't know or care about his victims. Their plight never entered his head. He just had one mission in life and that was sexual satisfaction without rejection.

He had long since stopped helping his father in his shop because he couldn't bear to risk 'infection' from all the goods and the people who shopped there every day. His father thought his son was being ridiculous, but Javi's behaviour in the store had become so bizarre that Gerardo had concluded he was better off without him there.

Javi felt a deep sense of desperation at his own plight. He knew that what he was doing, flashing at those women in the flats opposite, was wrong but he felt compelled to do so. In any case, there was no longer anyone in his home who cared, so why should it bother him? His beloved grandmother had been the only person he could talk to. Yet in one way he was glad she was dead, for he knew she would have been shocked by his behaviour.

Javi's obsession with cleanliness meant that he hardly ever dared set foot in any of the shops in the neighbourhood. The owner of a local fruit and vegetable store recalled, 'We all knew

Caroline's sister Jenny is comforted after Caroline's funeral.

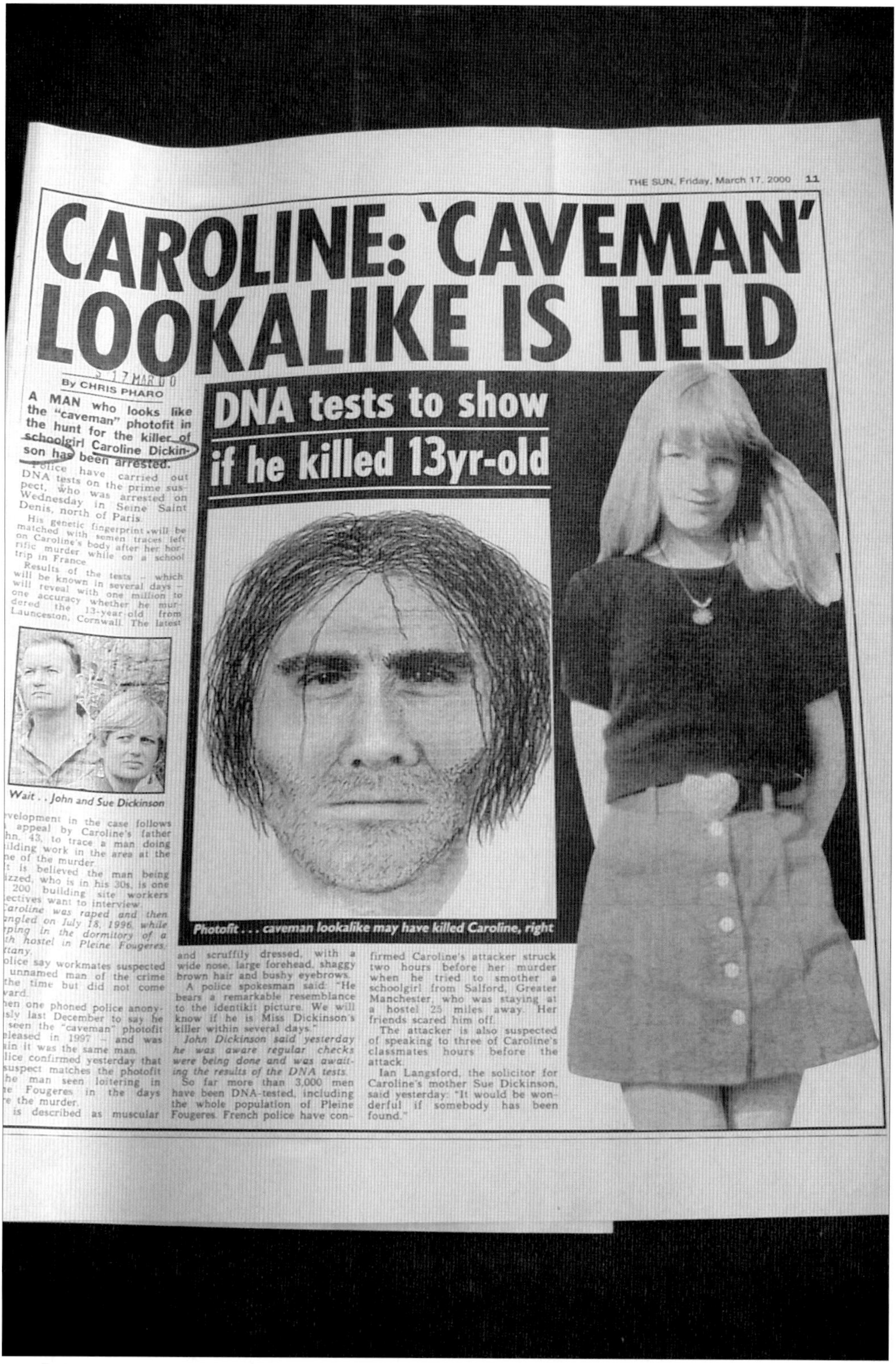
THE SUN, Friday, March 17, 2000 11

CAROLINE: 'CAVEMAN' LOOKALIKE IS HELD

S 17 MAR 00

By CHRIS PHARO

A MAN who looks like the "caveman" photofit in the hunt for the killer of schoolgirl Caroline Dickinson has been arrested.

Police have carried out DNA tests on the prime suspect, who was arrested on Wednesday in Seine Saint Denis, north of Paris.

His genetic fingerprint will be matched with semen traces left on Caroline's body after her horrific murder while on a school trip in France.

Results of the tests – which will be known in several days – will reveal with one million to one accuracy whether he murdered the 13-year-old from Launceston, Cornwall. The latest

Wait . . John and Sue Dickinson

velopment in the case follows appeal by Caroline's father hn, 43, to trace a man doing ilding work in the area at the ne of the murder.

t is believed the man being izzed, who is in his 30s, is one 200 building site workers ectives want to interview.

aroline was raped and then angled on July 18, 1996 while ping in the dormitory of a th hostel in Pleine Fougeres, ttany.

olice say workmates suspected unnamed man of the crime the time but did not come vard.

hen one phoned police anonysly last December to say he seen the "caveman" photofit eleased in 1997 – and was in it was the same man.

lice confirmed yesterday that suspect matches the photofit he man seen loitering in e Fougeres in the days e the murder.

is described as muscular and scruffily dressed, with a wide nose, large forehead, shaggy brown hair and bushy eyebrows.

A police spokesman said: "He bears a remarkable resemblance to the identikit picture. We will know if he is Miss Dickinson's killer within several days."

John Dickinson said yesterday he was aware regular checks were being done and was awaiting the results of the DNA tests.

So far more than 3,000 men have been DNA-tested, including the whole population of Pleine Fougeres. French police have confirmed Caroline's attacker struck two hours before her murder when he tried to smother a schoolgirl from Salford, Greater Manchester, who was staying at a hostel 25 miles away. Her friends scared him off.

The attacker is also suspected of speaking to three of Caroline's classmates hours before the attack.

Ian Langsford, the solicitor for Caroline's mother Sue Dickinson, said yesterday: "It would be wonderful if somebody has been found."

DNA tests to show if he killed 13yr-old

Photofit . . . caveman lookalike may have killed Caroline, right

One of many newspaper reports that appeared in the UK during the hunt for Caroline's killer. The British Press seemed to become frustrated that French police were not making sufficient progress on the case.

Above left: The headstone at Caroline's grave.

Above right: The entrance to the flats where Montes pounced on an intended victim in the seaside resort of Llanes, after killing Caroline.

Below left: Maria, who was stalked by Montes in Gijon.

Below right: The interior of the youth hostel in Florida where Montes assaulted an Irish girl.

Above: US immigration official Tommy Ontko, who read an article in
The Sunday Times about Caroline's murder, and was able to provide information
on the whereabouts of Montes.

Below: Miami Beach Police Detective Angel Vasquez holding the British
newspaper article.

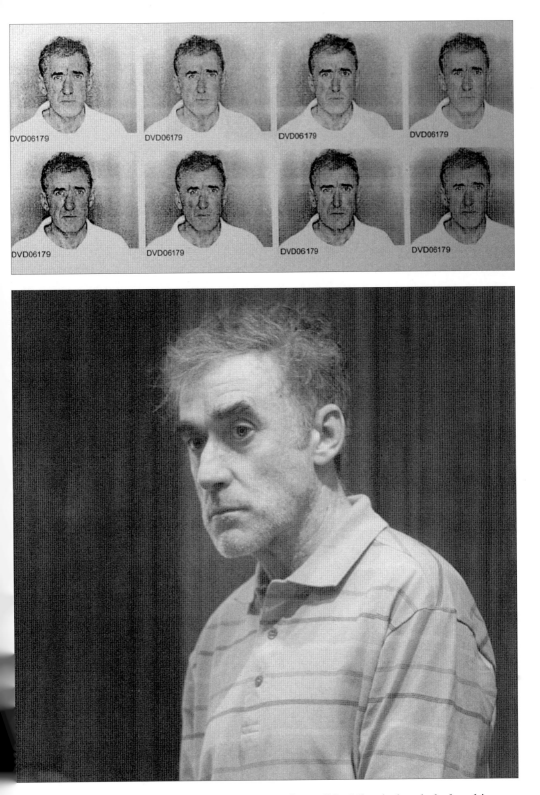

Above: The photographs of Montes hanging on the wall in Miami, shortly before his arrest for Caroline's murder.

Below: Montes in court in Miami.

Above: The extradition documents for Montes' deportment to France to be tried for Caroline's murder.

Inset: Montes' signature.

Below: Gijon journalist Octavio Villa.

Above left: Montes' lawyer, Patrick Elghozi.

Above right: The lawyer for the prosecution, Herve Rouzaud-Le Boeuf

Below right: Montes, finally in the dock.

Below right: Eduardo Suarez, after giving evidence at the trial. He spoke of how Montes showed him a photo of the schoolgirl and bragged about having sex with her.

Above: Caroline's parents, Sue and John, speak to the press after Montes is sentenced for 30 years.

Below: Fresnes Prison, where Montes is serving his sentence today.

about his cleanliness obsession. I had never met anyone like that so I watched him closely. He was really strange about touching things. When I gave him a piece of fruit he looked disgusted.'

Not long after this, Javi exposed his naked body to a woman living opposite his home who took the case to the police. They were reluctant to prosecute because there was no evidence, but officers visited the Monteses' home and warned Gerardo that his son was liable to be arrested if there were any more complaints.

'We did a special report on him and spoke to his neighbours and decided that, while he was mentally disturbed in some way, he was not a potential criminal,' explained one of those Guardia Civil officers many years later. 'He wasn't considered dangerous.'

Minutes after the police departed, Gerardo had a massive row with his son and hit him. Javi ran to his room in tears and once he was in there his tears turned to anger as he realised that the '*puta*', or whore, opposite had caused him all this trouble. He then plotted out a plan of revenge to make sure that everyone in the neighbourhood got the message not to inform on Javi ever again. The following night the woman's husband's car was torched and reduced to ashes after an arson attack that the police were never able to pin on anyone. Rumours that Javi was responsible were followed up by the police, but in the absence of evidence of his involvement, the crime went unpunished. Javi's message to the community was short and simple: Do not come near me and expect to survive.

Amid all this, Javi's hatred of women seemed to be growing by the day. He now called them all '*putas*' and openly blamed all his problems on his mother and sister.

Today, Dr Margolyes says he knew all along what sort of person Javi was, although no one could have predicted what he would do later in life.'He was a psychopath and very dangerous. He was a conflicted person at school and then developed into this monster. In my opinion nothing specific triggered what happened to him. It was just a personality which developed.'

The psychiatrist added, 'You must remember that this was the worst case of obsession I have ever seen because he'd allowed the obsession to take over his entire life. He wouldn't leave the house because he was obsessed with washing and ironing his clothes. He hated it outside the house because he could not control all these elements. The outside world had become an evil place and his cleanliness was an attempt to rub off that evil.'

At one stage, Dr Margolyes even persuaded Javi to undergo 'flower therapy' to help him overcome his emotional problems. The treatment was based on the discoveries of British specialist Dr Edward Bach, who claimed that there was a specific flower – a crab apple – which indicated an obsession with cleanliness. This was particularly credible as Asturias and especially Gijon was obsessed with apples and known throughout Spain as the cider capital of the country.

It was in 1969 that Javi began to plot his escape from Gijon. He knew the only way he could turn his life around was to get away from all the gossip-mongers and troublemakers who had been haunting him ever since certain details about his behaviour had become common knowledge in El Coto.

He knew that a car was the key to his plan, so he worked hard to pass his driving test first time in the nearby city of Oviedo. Years later, he described that success as in many ways the best day of his life. It marked a new beginning for Javi. He'd already decided he would eventually head for London.

It had always looked very appealing on the television and he'd noticed that many girls there wore very short skirts.

Driving was to become the most important pastime in Javi's life. He eventually persuaded his father to help finance the purchase of a car once he got to London. Both his parents were happy to oblige because they were desperate for him to leave Gijon. By now, people on the streets of El Coto were openly calling their son a '*pervertido*'.

Within days of passing his driving test, Javi took off for Bilbao, a large port and industrial city on the coast four hours' drive east of Gijon, for a part-time job as a waiter while he waited for his passport application to be processed. Back then, during Franco's dictatorship, it usually took a couple of months for an application to be processed, so, rather than wait in Gijon, Javi decided to make Bilbao his first stop on the way to Britain.

He was going to stay away from Spain for as long as possible. He hated Gijon and everyone who lived there. He had new seeds to sow and couldn't wait to get his hands on those easygoing English girls.

24

In reality, 'little Javi' had morphed into the sinister Montes, a drifter who worked only when he really had to, a disturbed loner with a penchant for teenage girls, many of whom had not even reached puberty.

A definite pattern was emerging in Montes's life. He didn't care what people thought of him because his family had made him feel so worthless. Once he reached London, he was soon staring obsessively at girls in parks or on the streets without realising how obvious he was being. But then no one during his childhood had taken the time or trouble to sit him down and explain to him the basic rules of reasonable, decent behaviour.

Within weeks of arriving in London, he had bought a tatty, rusting, UK-registered VW Beetle and found part-time work as a waiter. His parents had encouraged him, at the age of 19, to leave Gijon and all the shame he had brought upon them through his strange behaviour. His father had even promised to send him money if he stayed away. Not wanting his problems on their doorstep, they allowed him to take them elsewhere, unaware that Montes's 'condition' would only get worse as he developed into a soulless wanderer, filled with hatred for most people.

In fact, after 18 months in London, something happened to Montes which triggered another nervous breakdown. When he drove home to Gijon, many in his neighbourhood said he looked even more stressed and withdrawn than he had done before he left.

Dr Margolyes still has a file on Montes today. Following his breakdown, Montes was sent to the local Clinica La Providencia in the eastern suburbs of Gijon. Records show he was committed to the clinic twice in three months.

The clinic stood on a cliff overlooking the windswept Atlantic close to a popular local campsite. Montes adored the incredible view of the waves as they crashed on to the grey rocks below. But he also often watched all the young girls who stayed at the campsite. And despite his nervous state, he was allowed out for walks on the nearby rolling hills. The clinic was also close to an expensive suburb filled with large detached villas. The yellow 1960s building looked like a bland prison block compared with the conservative, century-old mansions that surrounded it.

Dr Margolyes prescribed yet more of Montes's favourite drug, Afranil, unaware that he had already started using it as part of a recreational cocktail to overcome his crippling shyness. Margolyes also used other, even stronger chemical compounds in his efforts to treat Montes's depression. Montes completely trusted the psychiatrist and was quite happy to stay at the Clinica Providencia for as long as he prescribed.

Margolyes seriously considered giving Montes electric shock

treatment to counter his obsessive behaviour. He admitted to this author that he had used the controversial treatment on many patients. 'It has been much maligned but I believe it can work much better than drugs sometimes,' he explained more than 30 years later. 'Although I decided in the end not to use it on Montes.' Margolyes continues to defend electrolysis and said, 'It can often work extremely well on certain patients. But I never tried it out on him. Maybe I should have. In many ways Montes was already a textbook example of a psychopath. I am proud from a professional point of view that I had him as a patient.' He had long labelled Javi as 'anacastic', the technical term used to describe an obsessive personality.

Then, on 5 August 1972, Montes's condition took a turn for the worse and he was committed to the state hospital in Oviedo, 50 kilometres south of Gijon. The doctors held him there for three days, until he ran away. Strangely, no effort was made to recapture him.

His family later claimed that Montes disappeared for many months after his 'escape'. It seems their only priority was to ensure he did not come back to Gijon. As usual, the farther away he was the better.

In the summer of 1973, Montes returned once more from his travels, which soon sparked problems within the Montes household. In September, his parents reported to the police that he had run away from the family home. At this time, they had employed a tutor to help him get a basic qualification so that he could work because doctors had said he was better off staying in Gijon.

The family even tried to get Montes legally arrested in a bid to have him readmitted to a mental hospital, but all they managed to do was further alienate him. A neighbour called

Lucia later explained, 'There were rumours that Montes went out at night looking for women in Gijon. Whenever Montes turned up from his travels, there were loud fights and quarrels in the flat. Lots of screams from the mother and sister when she was at the apartment. The mother wanted her son to leave Gijon permanently. Just stay away. We all noticed that by now he was dressing more weirdly. His hair was messier and longer. He looked virtually like a homeless person. Not actually dirty but unkempt.'

Montes knew he had deep psychological problems but later said they were always worsened by his family. It seems that during this latest, difficult stay in Gijon he really did want to get help.

From 20 January to 14 February 1974, Montes booked himself into another mental institution in Gijon, the St Julian Clinic. According to medical records, this visit came after he had more rows with his family and allegedly threatened his mother. The clinic was located in a formerly exclusive suburb east of Gijon, near many picturesque villas in the 18th-century French style. Many had electronic gates, tennis courts and swimming pools, and outside their grounds trees lined the immaculate pavements.

Dr Margolyes visited Montes at the clinic. He recalled, 'He was desperate for help. But I saw no traces of the schizophrenia mentioned by other doctors. He had what we call a residual defect left by a form of psychosis. But, significantly, at that time he was not suffering from hallucinations. His main problem was his long-running obsessiveness. I gave him injections of Afranil in the clinic. Then he became less obsessive and began wearing normal clothes washed in the laundry and started eating the same food as everyone else. He really did seem to be improving.'

Montes himself wrote in his own case-history notes at the time, 'I feel much more positive about life and I want to get work.'

But that feeling of contentment didn't last. A few days after checking himself out of the clinic on 14 February, he returned voluntarily but then left again the following day. Montes's problems seemed to be mounting once more.

Not long afterwards, he was involved in an incident that should have earmarked him as a developing sexual predator for all to see. Within days of his moving back into his parents' apartment, a maid and his sister reported him to the police for indecent exposure. According to a police report filed at the time, Montes appeared behind the maid, naked and masturbating while she was cleaning the floor outside his room.

Yet, when he was questioned by Gijon police, no photos of him were taken. It was considered only a 'flashing incident' and no official record of the incident was ever made. One neighbour explained, 'The police were a little lenient because it was the maid and Montes's sister who came to the police station and they were not taken very seriously.'

At that time, Spain was such a male-dominated society that Montes's parents were able to explain away the incident and blame it on 'a couple of hysterical women'. In reality, the only reason they helped their son wriggle out of trouble was because of the shame that would have been heaped on them if the case had gone to court.

In a later interview with police, Montes said of the maid, 'She was crazy but my parents sorted it out.' He also described his sense of rejection at the time, saying that 'nobody liked me and everyone wanted to hurt me', and called himself 'a wanderer' around Europe.

Gerardo and Benigna Montes put a brave face on the

'shameful' charges but they knew full well about Montes's 'weaknesses'. But it seemed their only priority was to get their son to leave Gijon for good.

Dr Margolyes recalled, 'The parents told me about the cleaner who claimed he exposed himself to her but they thought she was exaggerating. They didn't want to face their son's compulsive sexual inclinations.'

Even though the charges against Montes were withdrawn, the local police did at least open a file on him. It described him as 'a bohemian moving around the country with bad clothes, an unsubstantial person'. The policeman who opened up Montes's file to this author many years later said, 'He was aimless. He had no aspirations. He had no job whatsoever.'

However, Montes's involvement with the police sparked off another problem: he had skipped military service, which was compulsory for every man aged between 18 and 21 in Franco's Spain. He claimed mental illness as an excuse for not signing up, but he was immediately interned at the Santa Teresa private mental hospital in Leganes, near Madrid, 500 kilometres south of Gijon. Before long, he had been evaluated as a genuine psychiatric case. His psychiatrist in Gijon, Dr Margolyes, is certain Montes was not pretending to be ill in order to avoid having to sign up, although there were rumours in El Coto that he had been walking around with a dummy in his mouth for weeks in an attempt to be pronounced mentally unfit for military service.

Montes had an aunt who was a nurse at the hospital in Leganes and she kept a special eye on him. He spent a total of three weeks at the hospital and later said it was a very traumatic experience. But at least he had avoided the dreaded military service.

At Leganes, Montes was once again diagnosed with schizophrenia. Doctors described it in their medical notes as 'residual progressive schizophrenia', although Dr Margolyes has always insisted he saw no evidence of schizophrenia. Whatever the illness, there was little doubt that Francisco Montes suffered from extreme psychological problems.

Dr Margolyes is convinced that Montes was already developing into a psychopath. He explained, 'People with this kind of obsession can still lead a normal life. These terms are very fluid. He could easily have had one of these personality disorders and not necessarily be a dangerous psychopath.'

His stays in various mental institutions did little to help Montes except fuel his insatiable appetite for the anti-depressant Afranil, washed down with huge quantities of booze. He adored the way it helped dissolve all his inhibitions.

A few months later, towards the end of 1974, Montes once again returned to Dr Margolyes's clinic in Gijon for tests following another breakdown but refused to have the brain scan suggested by the doctor, which he believed might discover what was really wrong with his patient. In his notes, Margolyes commented that he was in need of expert treatment and recommended a full set of psychological tests, but Montes never responded to the doctor's letter.

One young resident of the street in El Coto where Montes lived with his family was eight-year-old Juan Rigaldo. He never forgot his neighbour. 'He had eyes like Jack the Ripper,' he remembered. 'He had this stare that he'd fix you with but it was only when I got older I thought anything about it. He was a weirdo but we all thought he was pretty harmless back then.'

Like many others in the close-knit community, Juan

reluctantly talked to this author about Montes in March 2006. He explained, 'We are so worried about the family. I don't want to hurt them and the neighbours around here are like the Gestapo.' Juan claimed that his own parents had warned him he would have his throat cut if he dared to talk openly about Montes. After two days of careful negotiation, he finally agreed to speak on condition we met in a car many blocks from his home so that none of his neighbours saw him.

Juan was six when his family arrived in El Coto in the mid-1970s. 'It was a rough area back then,' he recalled. 'Lots of murders and domestic assaults. It was full of people with no jobs and no money, although Javier's family seemed to have plenty of it.'

Montes made an immediate impact on little Juan, who explained, 'He had this big Afro hairstyle and a beard. And back then it was still Franco's reign, so there weren't many people who dressed and looked like that. His clothes were different. Jeans and T-shirts. Very casual and laidback. I guess it made him a very appealing character in many ways. He also used to drive around in a white VW Beetle with foreign number plates, so we all knew him from his car.

'Looking back on it, I suppose he was a bit strange. He'd turn up for a week or two in El Coto and then disappear again. I got to know him through his nephew, who was his sister's son.' To Juan, Montes 'seemed like this exciting, well-travelled figure who'd ride in and out of town like the Lone Ranger. Back then, El Coto was almost like a separate village from the rest of Gijon. We used to call it a republic because we felt very different from the rest of the city. That meant the foreign licence plates on his cars really stood out. They also told us just how worldly he was.'

But, says Juan, Montes was always alone. 'I don't recall seeing him out with any friends ever. But he was one of the few adults who'd ever stop to talk to us when we were kids. Most of the adults would glare in irritation at us and treat us like we didn't exist, but Javier was different. He always seemed to have time for a chat and a joke.'

Montes made a point of never being aggressive to little Juan and his friends. Juan recalled, 'I remember to this day that he was overwhelmingly soft and gentle, almost feminine in the way he conducted himself, although I didn't think about the significance of that until many years later.'

Then, after a few years in the mid-1970s of just showing up in El Coto unannounced, Montes suddenly stopped coming.

The death of General Franco in 1975 created a profound change in Spain, which would be felt as far away from Madrid as Gijon. Franco's successor was the current Spanish monarch, Juan Carlos, who bravely pledged to restore democracy to the nation and later even helped crush an attempted military coup in 1981.

Attitudes in Spain seemed to change almost overnight. The fiercely Catholic vein that ran through the country would eventually be replaced by a liberal, forward-thinking society. But that in many ways left behind people like Gerardo and Benigna Montes. They were too old to change and would continue thinking 'the old way'. That meant many issues would be swept under the carpet, including the behaviour of their wayward son.

In some ways, however, Montes was extremely adept at looking after himself. Unknown to his family, he had secretly become a forger of passports. From 1973 onwards, he sold at least a dozen forged versions of his own passport after repeatedly applying for renewals, claiming to have lost his. This was one of the reasons for his prolonged stay in Gijon at this time. Later, in 1981, the Office of National Security in Madrid even issued a directive to police in Gijon to look more closely at Montes because of his suspicious activities.

By the late 1970s, Montes was back on the road in continental Europe and Britain. In 1979, he was deported from the French city of Perpignan, near the Spanish border on the Mediterranean side, after being picked up by police as a vagrant. He had no car with him at the time and was said to be in bad physical and mental state, although it is unclear from his criminal file why he was detained. The cost of his transportation to his hometown was charged to Spain's Ministry of Foreign Affairs. One police officer in Gijon recalled, 'It was truly amazing how little was known about him when he got kicked out of France. He came with a French court document asking for official co-operation. That was it.'

The following year Montes was properly investigated by the Gijon police for the first time after an unusual complaint arrived from a branch of the Banco de Espana in the city centre. Images taken by the bank's CCTV cameras showed Montes behaving very oddly, looking around inside the bank, and staff feared he might be planning a robbery. Back then, Francisco Benito of the National Police in Gijon was a member of the police's anti-robbery unit. He recalled, 'We did a report at our station and it was decided that Montes was mentally disturbed. Apart from observation, you ask neighbours, relatives, people who have contact with him, who can say what his character is like, and from that one can deduce that his conduct is not normal.'

Within days of being pulled in for the bank incident, Montes was back gripping the steering wheel of yet another rusting heap bought with money supplied by his long-suffering father. As he drove manically out of Gijon, he sincerely hoped he wouldn't be back for a very long time. He had heard from one family member that there was a lot of casual work in Germany and he was desperate to start a new life somewhere as far away from Gijon as possible. In time he would be back, but only when he had run out of money and needed more from his father.

25

By the early 1980s Montes was travelling widely across Europe. Regularly looking for cheap places to stay, he began using youth hostels, which he had long ago realised were a mecca for pretty young girls. It was around this time that he was in Utrecht, in Holland, and sexually attacked Frenchwoman Christine Le Menes, before falling in love with her.

Montes later said that his affair with Christine was the first time he'd had full sex in his life. In other words, he lost his virginity at 30 years of age. Some time later it was alleged that he tried to recreate that first time with Christine on each occasion he broke into youth hostels over the following 20 years.

There is no doubt that Montes had, in his own distorted way, been in love with Christine, so when she announced she was pregnant he thought he had found some kind of normality in his bizarre life. But within days she had thrown him out of their home and he had moved back to Germany. Within months, he was raping, assaulting and even killing innocent young women.

When he heard that Christine had given birth to their son on 14 March 1982, Montes made a point of telling his family back in Gijon in the hope they might treat him with a little more loving care now that he had produced a grandson for them. Gerardo and Benigna Montes were surprised by the news but then made a point of telling neighbours and friends about the birth as if it in some way showed that their wayward son was a decent person after all. They told him they hoped he would one day bring the child to see them in Spain.

One of the family's oldest neighbours in El Coto recalled, 'We all knew that Javier had a baby and a girlfriend in France. His mother even seemed to think it was a normal relationship. It made Benigna so happy to think that Javier had achieved something at last.'

For the following seven years, Monte's name did not appear on any police records and his specific movements around Europe remain a mystery to this day. Neighbours in El Coto remember seeing him drive in and out of Gijon between trips abroad but no one is exactly sure when those visits occurred.

Then, in 1988, Montes's psychiatrist, Dr Felix Margolyes, received a letter from Inspector Casado of the Gijon police requesting medical background on Montes, who had been arrested in connection with a number of rapes in Germany. Margolyes later recalled, 'I wasn't surprised. Because of Montes's pathological behaviour I had been expecting something like this to happen.' Margolyes told the police all about his patient's problems stemming back to his childhood.

Montes had been arrested at Loerats on the German–Dutch border and charged with three specific rapes committed on 13 December 1985, 2 February 1987 and 22 April 1988. Now it had become clearer what Montes had been doing all those years.

Francisco Benito of the Gijon police later explained, 'The crimes are mentioned. It [the report] says he picked up girls on the road – they must have been hitchhikers – and took them to open land and then raped them.'

The German police report on Montes also said he had been driving a 1600-cc white Toyota Corolla De Luxe registered in his own name in Holland. But inside the car he kept another set of Dutch plates, with the registration number 55RT94, from another Corolla. He had sold the previous car but kept the plates to use on his new version.

Yet, in the middle of all these communications between Gijon and Tubingen, Germany, the Spanish police – despite a standard request from Interpol – never checked if there was any record of Montes having a driving licence in Asturias. Had they done so, this would have provided the authorities with a photo, which might have helped connect him to many subsequent attacks.

Montes's arrest in Germany should have garnered big publicity in Gijon but the local newspapers weren't even notified of his arrest. The Gijon police themselves claimed to know little or nothing about Montes despite their earlier report mentioning his molestation of the maid and other incidents, including the 'problem' at the bank in Gijon city centre.

In Tubingen in 1989, Montes received his first prison sentence: five years and six months for the three rapes.

Back in Gijon, his parents had no idea he had been sent to jail. They were just relieved not to have heard from their problematic son. Then, while Montes was serving his sentence, his father sold his corner shop to a property developer for more than £100,000. Part of the deal was that Gerardo Montes would be given two apartments in a six-storey block that was to be built on the site of Casa Gerardo. 'It was quite a shock when the old man announced he was selling up but he was getting older and no one could blame him for taking the money,' explained a neighbour many years later. Montes remained in a prison cell in Germany, completely unaware of the sale of the property.

Gerardo and Benigna eventually moved into their brand-new luxurious, three-bedroom apartment and their daughter Blanca took up residence in the other one with her husband and children. Once again, Francisco Montes had been marginalised.

In 1992, Montes was released midway through the prison sentence imposed on him in Germany on condition he serve the remainder of it in Spain. However, the authorities in both countries have no record of his going back to jail. It seems as if they simply lost contact with Montes, who was allowed to make his own way back to Spain. But they wouldn't have had to look far because he soon turned up again in Gijon, hoping his father would give him more money.

By all accounts, Montes was made to feel even more of a stranger in his own home. He was furious that he hadn't been consulted about his father's decision to sell the business and was obsessed with finding out how much money he had made out of the deal because he felt he, as the only son in the family, was owed something.

Eventually, the family gave Montes £1,000 on condition he leave Gijon. He happily obliged and headed off back to London, where he soon found accommodation in Earl's Court, a mecca for backpackers from all over the world. It was a perfect setting for him to feed his addiction for young girls. He rented a bedsit in busy Kempsford Gardens. Neighbour Noel O'Sullivan later recalled, 'He was quite nice at first but then after a while he changed and became quite aggressive.'

Gordon Butler, who lived in the flat above Montes, said, 'As time went by it became apparent he was living on another planet. He would attack people on the street outside the house and ask them the time or verbally abuse them. He'd wave at tourists and they would try to avoid him. I'd sometimes get home and he'd be there as I opened the front door. "What de time?" he'd ask me and then walk off. He wasn't someone you wanted to mess with. He had evil eyes. In the daytime he was Francisco the silly eccentric Spaniard, but at night he didn't even acknowledge you in the street. He was like a vampire. You'd see him driving off into the distance.'

Montes's bedsit was cramped, with a single bed alongside the window, an armchair and a sofa pushed against the fireplace, another bed in the recess opposite, a cheap glass coffee table in the middle and a second-hand hi-fi perched on the mantelpiece.

Noel O'Sullivan described Montes as 'a strange, difficult man with a furious temper', adding, 'He was big-built and very aggressive. He would be pushy and rude about the most basic things.'

Gordon Butler said Montes had 'a tenuous grip on reality. I was wary of him. He wasn't the sort you'd want as an enemy. At times he'd stand in the shared bathroom and stare at the backs of the houses in the next street.'

Montes began advertising at Earl's Court Underground Station for girls to rent his bedsit. 'It was all a scam with the young women,' said one tenant in the house. 'He'd hang around by the notice board at Earl's Court station because he could speak lots of languages and entice them in.'

Then Montes would illegally sublet the room by hanging a sheet across it in a pretence of offering privacy. Gordon Butler recalled, 'He'd throw a strong rope across the flat and then chuck a blanket or sheet over it. He'd then say they could have the whole room and he'd disappear. Then he'd come back a few days later and claim half the room back. It was outrageous. He'd try to get in there and give them notice if they were difficult. I think he needed the money to fund his trips abroad.'

'He always insisted on small women as tenants,' said Noel O'Sullivan. 'Most girls would come and take one look at it and run – literally. But some were so desperate for cheap space that they agreed to rent the room after Montes claimed he was going away for three weeks. One day an Australian girl staying there threw a chair out of the window when he tried it on with her.'

O'Sullivan continued, 'It was clear he only ever wanted young girls there. There were lots of them who went to look at the room, mostly backpackers in their teens or early twenties. It was a really small place, and they would have to sleep in the same room as him. But quite a few did stay. They must have been really desperate for somewhere cheap to live.'

Another neighbour, Joaquim Estriga, explained, 'Time after time I would get these girls banging on my door in the middle of the night, terrified and in tears, asking if they could sleep on my floor for the rest of the night because of something that had happened with Montes. He simply saw women as sexual objects. God knows what went on in that room.'

By now Montes was in his early forties, cleanly dressed but always in black jeans and a leather jacket. Noel O'Sullivan helped Montes fix his cars when they broke down, and recalled, 'He'd ask you to do things and if you didn't do them he would shout and scream at you.'

But O'Sullivan also said Montes could be very charming when he wanted something, and his ability to speak many languages was impressive. Through subletting his flat to young women, never paying the rent and working occasionally as a waiter at a nearby hotel, Montes was able to easily raise enough money to go on his sinister 'road trips' out of London. And if he ever got really short of money there was always his father back in Gijon.

'He was always travelling,' O'Sullivan recalled. 'He went to Scotland many times. From Friday night, say, to Sunday night, he'd always be busy.'

If only his neighbours in Earl's Court had realised what was occupying Francisco Montes's every waking minute – an obsessive sexual quest.

And throughout his time in London he continued to drive a variety of cars registered in Spain, Britain and Holland. They were always uninsured and untaxed, because Montes loved outwitting the police. When they stopped him for not wearing a seatbelt, he'd make a point of taking it off immediately after they left. His defiance was almost childlike. It was as if he had decided long ago to do whatever he wanted in every respect.

26

In 1994, Montes drove through France on one of his regular trips home from London to Spain. On this occasion, his name was logged by the French police in connection with an incident which, in retrospect, represents a glaring missed opportunity to have detained him. This was when he broke into the youth hostel in Blere, in the Loire Valley, and tried to kidnap Irish schoolgirl Valerie Jacques.

But, seemingly untouchable, Montes simply grew in confidence. By the early summer of 1995, he even invented his own sick method to guarantee his victims would not 'wake up' when he attacked them. He would not only wipe them clean with alcohol and cotton wool but use the fabric to gag them so that even if they did wake up he wouldn't hear their cries and feel obliged to run away. The fact they might suffocate never entered his warped mind.

In London, Montes's depraved lust for young girls was fed by a fixation on short skirts – one of the things that had drawn him to the city in the first place all those years earlier. Not surprisingly, he'd also long had an obsession with women's tennis. Back in Gijon, bar owner Carmen Figar never forgot how he would sit leering at the TV whenever it showed tennis matches featuring young women in skimpy outfits.

In the summer of 1995, Montes and his neighbour Noel O'Sullivan travelled a few miles across London to the world-famous Wimbledon tennis tournament. Montes said he was determined to get the autograph of top Spanish player Conchita Martinez. When the two men spotted her by the players' entrance to the stadium, Montes pushed himself to the front of a queue of fans, staring down any challenges from the rest of the crowd. He was turned back by a security guard but then, by chance, caught Martinez's eye on her way to one of the courts.

'He ran past the security guard and over to her shouting in Spanish,' recalled O'Sullivan. 'She stopped and looked quite stunned, and he walked up to her with my ticket in his hand and she quickly signed it. I mean, she wasn't going to say no to him. Even the security guys beside her were a bit stunned. He was so quick. I was quite happy to get the autograph, but it wasn't a nice way to do it.'

Conchita Martinez was defending her Wimbledon championship crown that year and she went on to win her semi-final that day. At the time, there were heightened concerns about crazed stalkers after former Wimbledon champion Monica Seles had been stabbed in the back by a spectator at a tournament in Hamburg, Germany. O'Sullivan recalled, 'All that afternoon he kept close to wherever Conchita was and kept giving her the evil eye. She was clearly disturbed by it.'

Back in Earl's Court, Montes discovered yet another easy

way of raising money, claiming unemployment benefit even though he was now working in a large local hotel as a waiter, in addition to subletting his room to young girls and getting cash on demand from his father. As he later told investigators, 'I found it was very easy to get the English government to give me money.' Montes claimed unemployment benefit in Britain between 1993 and 1997, afterwards telling the police, 'I got sciatica so the English government gave me money.'

Whenever Montes let his room, he charged a £500 deposit and at the same time got both unemployment benefit and income support and worked at the local hotel. In total, he was receiving at least £800 a week.

During this time, he continued to make occasional trips to France, telling neighbours he was visiting his wife and son in Paris. Noel O'Sullivan recalled Montes once returning from France in July 1996 without a car and a week earlier than planned.

'He said he'd abandoned his Renault 5 when it broke down but he made no attempt to recover it,' recalled O'Sullivan. This conversation took place the day after Montes killed Caroline Dickinson, in Pleine-Fougeres.

A few months after Caroline's murder, Montes quit his 12-by-10-foot, first-floor room in Kempsford Gardens, after running up £1,000 in unpaid rent, forcing his landlady to get an eviction notice. He then moved to another bedsit around the corner in Nevern Square.

Some months after Caroline Dickinson's murder, Montes turned up unannounced in Gijon and went to visit the family's parish priest Father Fernando Fueyo Garcia, a laidback character who had been working in El Coto since the early 1980s.

Now in his sixties, Father Garcia was the parish priest at the church of San Nicolas on Avenida de Mallada, just a few hundred metres from the Monteses' home. He recalled, 'His mother came to see me and said she was stressed out by Montes because he wouldn't leave the house. He had been back for two or three days and she wanted to get rid of him and didn't know what to do about it. The strange thing is that the following day Montes came to me to ask for pots and pans to cook his food in because he refused to eat what the mother was cooking for him. I think he was high on alcohol and drugs because he was behaving in a very manic and strange way. I think he wanted to talk but he couldn't bring himself to start a conversation.'

Father Garcia had always noticed that Blanca was the favourite child. 'I am afraid it was clear that Montes's sister Blanca was the mother's favourite. When anyone mentioned Montes's name, the parents just rolled their eyes.'

A small, round man with one eye slightly closed, Father Garcia sat at the desk in his office attached to the side of the church as he chatted happily about Montes. He rarely wore a dog collar, he explained, because he liked to integrate with the community. 'Francisco was an odd man. I don't know what happened in his childhood. I never did any confessions with him but it's clear he had some problems,' he added.

Like so many others, he never forgot Montes's soft, almost feminine voice. 'I thought he might be gay. There was something very effeminate about him.'

During that same visit to Gijon, Montes walked into his local butcher's and asked for some chicken and then said that he couldn't pay for it but his father would settle up later. The shopkeeper later commented, 'It seemed strange that a man in his forties had to get his own father to pay for everything.'

Eyewitnesses who met Montes in the second half of 1996 in London or Gijon all say he seemed even more troubled than usual. 'It was as if he had something really terrible on his mind,' said one neighbour in Earl's Court. 'I used to see him staring out into space, standing outside the building alone. He looked like a haunted man.'

In Gijon, one neighbour recalled, 'Francisco's relationship with his mother and father worsened. They'd begun to suspect he was doing bad things, but they had no actual evidence, so never confronted him. But the atmosphere in the family apartment was dreadful whenever Francisco came home for some money.'

Montes's depression may also have worsened because Christine Le Menes continued to refuse to allow him access to their son. So he sought solace in Afranil tablets and a bottle of whisky almost every night. At least the heady cocktail produced an 'agreeable euphoria' and 'psychic exaltation' which helped him forget his troubles.

Meanwhile, Christine Le Menes continued to reject all requests by Montes to see their child. All his trips to France revolved around where primary-school teacher Christine and the boy lived. Every time Montes drove back from his family home in Spain to his tiny rented room in Earl's Court, he made a point of trying to see both mother and son, who were at this time living in Vitre, near Rennes.

Sometimes Montes liked to imagine taking the youngster to the zoo at nearby Fleche. Montes liked zoos, although he felt a bit strange about the way all those animals were locked up. He felt sorry for them because he knew what it was like to be caged.

27

Francisco Montes had turned the countryside of Germany, France and Britain into his own private killing fields and no one seemed capable of stopping him. Every time he found another victim, it was more evidence to him of his superiority over 'normal' people.

Every attack made him feel even more powerful. The best ones were those that didn't wake up, because then they couldn't be horrible to him and stop him satisfying himself. That was why he stuffed cotton wool down Caroline Dickinson's throat. Previously he would have run away when they woke up, because that was when the reality of what he'd done truly dawned on him. But now he was, in his own eyes at least, braver and more forceful.

In Gijon, his father was suffering from prostate cancer and probably didn't have much longer to live. Montes believed he stood to inherit a tidy sum when he died. He had carefully mapped out plans to take off for new pastures, having decided that both South and North America looked ideal for his purposes.

Gerardo Montes had grown much fatter and less healthy since selling his business and tended to sit outside the family's recently built apartment block on the corner of Calle Zorilla doing little more than soaking up the sun. One neighbour couldn't help noticing that when Montes was in town he would make a point of leaving a mattress jamming the lift doors open so that his father was forced to walk up the stairs to his apartment. 'We joked about the fact that Francisco was trying to kill off his father but, looking back on it, maybe that was exactly what he was doing,' recalled a nearby resident called Maria.

Montes returned to Gijon in the late spring of 1997 and decided, to his parents' horror, to stay in El Coto for a while. What no one realised was that, having murdered Caroline Dickinson, he believed he was safer from justice in Gijon than in London. In any case, he wanted to be around when his father died because he suspected his mother and sister would seek to cut him out of any inheritance.

He even got himself a 'normal' job selling battered second-hand cars at a business on the main Oviedo road out of the city. Even more surprising, he made a friend of fellow salesman Eduardo Riesgo Suarez. The two men spent many hours each day chatting about their lives and Montes made it very clear that he had a penchant for young girls. 'He told me the ideal age for a woman was 11 or 12; after 20 he found them too old,' Suarez later recalled.

Montes had broken his golden rule and revealed part, if not all, of his secret life. He was always careful to hold back on the really incriminating details.

During a bragging session at the car dealer's where several men were discussing their sexual prowess, Montes told them, 'You don't know much about women, not like me. I'm going to show you some photos of English girls and French girls, real Miss Worlds.' He produced a scruffy photo from his pocket of a very young-looking girl he called 'Caroline'. He made a point of telling Suarez the girl's full name was Caroline Dickinson, that she was extremely pretty and that she was 'as pure as small porcelain'.

Suarez believes to this day that Montes stole a photograph of Caroline Dickinson from her rucksack and later boasted to him that he had sex with 'a real china doll'.

Montes even told his colleague how he met 'Caroline' in a youth hostel in Brittany after he saw her playing in a park with other schoolgirls. 'He said he made love to her and that the picture was in her bag,' said Suarez, who also claimed he saw Caroline's full name signed on the back of the picture, which showed her kneeling on the ground dressed in her school uniform. Suarez recalled, 'He said she was like a model and was different from other girls. He said she had a particular sort of beauty.'

The mystery of why Montes claimed he stole a photo of Caroline from her rucksack after killing her has never been resolved. Suarez has always insisted he was telling the truth. 'Montes was proud of knowing all the youth hostels in Europe and bragged about spending all his time chasing girls,' he said.

Montes also claimed to Suarez that he had numerous young lovers. Suarez recalled, 'Montes showed me photos of lots of other girls and said he had slept with them all. I thought perhaps he had stolen the pictures or found them.' He also said Montes was known as an 'old pig' – a Spanish expression for mature men who like young girls.

No one will ever know for sure if that photo was of Caroline Dickinson, but Montes certainly relished the fantasy that she was his real lover, not his victim. John-Michel Masson, a psychiatrist who later treated Montes, insisted the Spaniard was 'a normal subject, psychologically speaking, who was in touch with reality. He has free will and does not suffer hallucinations.' Dr Masson explained, 'He can see what is morally right and what is morally wrong. He can see that a rape is not morally allowed.'

In the early summer of 1997, Montes and his new friend Eduardo Suarez drove to Barcelona for a holiday together. Suarez never forgot how Montes went crazy when a pair of shoes and two shirts were stolen from their car. 'He became furious and his hands started trembling and his neck swelled up. He went red and his eyes looked as if they were about to pop.'

Montes turned to his only friend and, according to Suarez, said, 'You're really lucky because I controlled myself then. I'm not like your other friends. I don't care about going to prison. I can kill someone without any problems.'

When he got back to Gijon, Montes looked up his young friend and neighbour Juan Rigaldo, who still lived just across the street from the Monteses' home in El Coto. The fact that there was a 20-year age gap between them did not seem to bother Montes at all.

Juan explained, 'I was friendly with his nephew, who was my age, and whenever Javier came back from abroad he'd try to hang around with us. He certainly liked me. Everyone knew there was something strange about him but no one wanted to say anything openly.'

Later, Juan saw Montes in the street. 'I hoped he wouldn't recognise me. I was on my way to buy a newspaper and ducked into the local shop the moment I saw him.'

Following the teenager inside, Montes asked him, 'Don't you know me? I'm your friend's uncle. We used to run the corner store.' Juan nodded nervously. He later recalled, 'I don't know why but something made me feel uneasy about him that day. Anyway, he kept trying to talk to me even though I kept trying to get away from him.'

A few days later Juan was leaving the local video store when he met Montes in the street. 'He noticed I had a tennis video in my hand and said, "I love tennis, too." Well, then he stopped and talked to me for ages about how he'd been to Wimbledon and got really close to some of the women stars.'

Juan told Montes he was a big fan of Steffi Graf. 'He said he was too, but also mentioned a German woman player. He sounded as if he was virtually in love with her.' Montes also proudly told how he had asked Spanish star Conchita Martinez for her autograph at Wimbledon.

'That's when Montes mentioned he'd been living in London,' Juan recalled. 'He seemed very proud of it. From then on, he'd be out every day when I was on the streets near our apartment. Looking back on it, I suppose he was very lonely because he'd spot me coming out of my flat and then try and catch up with me.'

At that time, Montes usually went to the local library every day to read a newspaper because it was free. 'That shows you how broke he was, I guess,' explained Juan. 'But, to be honest about it, something about him repulsed me even back then. The trouble with Montes was that he had no dignity. He just took what he wanted. He didn't seem to appreciate the subtle things in life. When he started coming round to my home again, my mother used to pretend I was on the phone when he pressed the buzzer. But he didn't care. He'd always say, "I'll wait until he gets off the phone."'

A few days later, the intercom at Juan's family's apartment buzzed and it was Montes asking if he wanted to come round to his flat and watch the Australian tennis open championship. 'My parents were very annoyed that he'd started ringing our buzzer again as he was considered a weirdo in El Coto by this stage. My mother said she had a bad feeling about him. I agreed with her; the guy was annoying me and I didn't want to see him any more.'

The neighbourhood was filled with rumours about Montes, as Juan explained, 'There were so many rumours about Javier. People wondered what he really did for a job. We all wanted to know where he went when he disappeared for days on end. What was he up to? Who was he seeing?'

Juan remembers Montes as being tall and bony. 'But he always seemed very strong and his facial features made him look almost like a wolf,' he explained. 'I also remember he often wore a pair of fancy shoes with pointed toes and a buckle.'

He also recalled how Montes tried to entice him to London: 'Javier started walking alongside me one day and began talking about how wonderful London was because there were girls of all colours, shapes and sizes there.' Montes drooled as he said, 'There's plenty of variety there.' He also mentioned that he was especially keen on two areas in London, Battersea Park and Portobello Road. 'You can get anything you want in Battersea Park and I mean anything,' he told the teenager. The clear implication was that he had attacked women in the park. He then added, 'Gijon is shit. Even the food here is shit. In London you can eat anything you want from any country in the world.'

Young Juan asked Montes, 'Why don't you leave Gijon if you hate it so much here?'

Montes didn't reply and tried to change the subject.

Juan sensed that Montes was for some reason afraid to go back to London. 'It was only later I realised that it must have been because he'd murdered Caroline Dickinson.'

A few days later, Montes was with his young friend yet again. Juan recalled, 'A girl of about 12 or 13 passed by and he pointed at her and said, "Look at her. She must be so tender and sweet to touch." It was horrible to hear him say such things.'

Juan remembered turning to Montes and saying, 'If that was a joke it is in very poor taste. And if you mean what you just said, then you must be crazy.' Montes just laughed. 'He didn't seem to understand the implication of what I was saying. He was trying to make me sympathetic towards him but he was actually having the opposite effect.'

Another time a girl of about 17 walked past them and Montes said he knew her. 'He then made another rude remark about her and sex. I knew then that it was no joke to him. These girls were all potential conquests.'

Not long after this, Benigna Montes upset Juan's mother when she said how happy she was that their two sons were friends. 'My mum was furious and warned me to stay away from him,' recalled Juan. 'She knew there was something really wrong with him.'

But Montes was determined to keep trying to impress his young friend. Juan explained, 'I was around at his nephew's flat one time and Javier produced these photos which he said had been taken in Argentina. He said that a pretty young girl in one photo was his girlfriend from Argentina whom he'd met in London. She looked in her late teens or early twenties and he said she called him "Gallego", the nickname all Spaniards have in Argentina. Maybe this girl was one of his victims. Afterwards, I talked to Montes's nephew about it and he said all the photos were taken in London but then froze and said, "Don't believe a word he says." Even his family knew he was living in a fantasy world.'

Juan then saw Montes when they bumped into each other in a restaurant in Gijon. Juan recalled, 'I couldn't believe my eyes because he was in there with two girls. He introduced the women to me in a very soft, yet proud voice. It was creepy. I just couldn't understand what those women were doing in there with him.'

A few weeks later, Montes was arrested for attempting to rape a girl in the lobby of an apartment block in Llanes. His arrest in the resort was followed by a brief court appearance there, after which he was sent to Villabona Prison, near Gijon. Montes especially loathed that spell in jail since he was treated with disdain by other inmates and staff because he faced charges of sexual assault.

While in Villabona, Montes was obliged to fill out a form so that he could be assessed for possible release on bail at a later court appearance. That was when Montes accidentally revealed his murderous methods. He wrote, 'I do not know how anyone could think I could rape someone. It is all lies from that girl in Llanes and the police. I have had a lot of girlfriends here, they could tell you about me. The last one was A [the rest of the name was deleted] and she loved me a lot. When we made love, she knew that she had to take a shower before. At my request, she always brought with her a bottle of alcohol and some cotton wool to clean her breasts before I would touch her and also to wash myself afterwards. You know how scrupulous I am, how disgusted I am with the food and other things in prison. I know that the bit with the cotton wool was very painful for her but it had to be done.'

If Montes's 'confession' had been more fully analysed at the time, detectives would surely have recognised the similarities between what he was describing and the circumstances of both the murder of Caroline Dickinson and his earlier attack on Kate Wrigley in nearby St Lunaire. But once again there was no communication between police forces. Caroline's killer was languishing in a Spanish jail a few hundred kilometres from where the French police were still searching for him in connection with the murder of the schoolgirl from Cornwall.

Villabona Prison was located in a bleak tract of countryside near a huge forest some 20 kilometres south of Gijon. The route leading to the jail was like a road to nowhere: there were no clearly marked signs, so visitors never knew if they were heading in the right direction.

None of Montes's relatives ever bothered to visit him there and later they said they had hoped he would never be released. Villabona had a tight regime, with towers on each corner of the jail, which was spread over the top of a small mountain that overlooked the valley and the Atlantic Ocean beyond. From his prison cell Montes could see nothing but rolling countryside, a few scattered farmhouses and a nearby motorway flyover which stood on vast, 30-metre-tall legs.

While in jail, Montes also requested an examination by a forensic psychiatrist, who recalled, 'He was very paranoid when he was in there and complained about everything as if the whole world was against him. He said he should not be in there and the prison doctor said he was severely depressed. He also complained bitterly that he could not wash properly in the prison.'

Being incarcerated was like hell for Montes. His obsession with hygiene meant that for him even the offer of a glass of water was rife with doubt. He also believed that, as an alleged sex offender, other inmates were trying to poison his food. Most of his fellow inmates ignored him both because of his strange, manic stare and because they considered him nothing more than a minor '*pervertido*', accused of trying to attack a girl in a crowded street. You'd have to be pretty stupid to do that, most of them thought. No doubt Montes wished he could tell them of his importance and the notoriety of his other crimes, since then they might give him some respect. But he knew only too well that someone inside Villabona might inform the police, so he kept quiet and bided his time. He felt sure that if he kept a low profile he would make bail.

Meanwhile, he continually annoyed prison staff and inmates by complaining that the food was dirty. One prison officer later described him as 'a really weird guy. He had no friends and most of us kept our distance from him because he was so strange.' Montes hated all aspects of prison life and promised himself he would never again serve time in jail if he could help it.

In early December 1997, Montes reapplied for bail on the Llanes charges because his trial was taking so long to prepare. Prosecutors admitted to the judge that the trial would not now take place for at least a year. Then Montes's elderly mother, Benigna, told the judge she was terrified of her son and pleaded with him to keep Montes in prison. The family said they would be appalled if he got out once again. However, the judge ignored the family's plea and released Montes on bail on condition he live at his family home in Gijon. Spanish justice certainly seemed to work in mysterious ways.

It was only after his release from Villabona that Montes learned that his father had died after a long spell in hospital. The family had initially tried to keep the news secret from him, even though he was living with his mother at the family's home under the conditions of his bail.

In one way, Montes was relieved by his father's death, for his biggest fear had always been that one day the French police would catch up with him and it would cause his father no end of shame in Gijon; even more than the charges he faced in Llanes. He didn't care about his mother or sister, but his father had been generous to him, even though he knew that the money was a bribe to make him stay away from Gijon.

But now Montes was determined to remain in Gijon until he was given his fair share of his father's estate. He suspected that his mother and sister would try to cheat him and there was no way he would allow that. In any case, he was desperate for the money so that he could continue hunting victims across Europe and beyond.

A huge row erupted the moment Montes confronted his mother about his inheritance. He even threatened to stay in the town until he got what was due to him from the estate. Montes hoped that this would speed the process, as there was no way his mother and sister wanted him hanging around any longer than necessary.

Despite his arrest in Llanes, there had still been no communication between police forces in France, Germany and Spain linking Montes to the murder of Caroline Dickinson. Part of the problem was that, thanks to the EEC's so-called 'open borders' policy, he had been able to slip in and out of member states without any record of his movements.

In El Coto, Montes's young friend Juan Rigaldo had just arrived back after a trip abroad, when he bumped into a friend who said he had met Montes in Villabona Prison. 'Then I heard how he'd tried to rape that poor girl in Llanes,' recalled Juan. A few weeks later Juan was walking through downtown Gijon when he heard Montes call out his name. He recalled, 'I got the shivers when I heard him because I now knew he was a rapist. I thought he'd be too ashamed to speak to anyone in his old neighbourhood but he wasn't in the slightest bit worried.'

Juan had even stopped buying a newspaper in the local newsagent in an attempt to avoid running into Montes, but he knew it was inevitable he would turn up at his home sooner or later. 'That very night he started ringing my buzzer over and over in a really manic fashion. My mother would pick up the intercom and get pretty angry sometimes. She even told him once, 'Leave him alone and do not call here again'. But he didn't take any notice. He just kept on ringing.'

It was as if Montes had fallen in love with Juan and put him on a pedestal in the hope that somehow their friendship would survive the rape charges he faced in Llanes. Juan explained, 'After those earlier calls he'd just wait until my parents had left the flat and press the buzzer for me. He was almost like my stalker. One day at 5pm my parents had left for a walk and I didn't pick up. I heard him cursing outside and saying, "I know you're in there. I saw them going out."'

Another time Juan was in the street talking to a neighbour when Montes started waving at him and said, 'Don't run off. I need to talk to you.' Juan explained, 'I ignored him and said I had to go and would see him later. By this time he was giving everyone round here the creeps.'

A few days later, Juan found a newspaper clipping in the family's mailbox. It was about Montes's arrest for rape in Llanes. 'It freaked me out. Then I bumped into him yet again and he said coldly, "Apart from tennis, I have other hobbies, you know." He even mentioned the newspaper cutting proudly and it was obvious he had been the one who put it there. He was grinning from ear to ear like the cat who'd got the cream. It was very scary.'

Then Montes turned to his young friend and said, 'A person who understands needs few words.'

When Juan asked him about the case, he snapped back, 'You're wrong. It's not what it seems. I'm going to prove that to everyone. I am innocent.'

A few days later, Juan ran into Montes yet again. 'I was with my father and so I didn't answer when he shouted my name. My father has a bad temper and just the sound of his voice made him furious. Then Javier shouted my name out even louder, so I had to respond. I don't even remember what he wanted but I felt so freaked out by him.'

Juan's lasting memory of his former friend was: 'Montes was in many ways very intelligent, but cold and very calculating.'

It was clear that Montes had great difficulty understanding the difference between fact and fiction. One person who met him just after his release from Villabona explained, 'He'd change his mind all the time and say the opposite of everything he'd just said. It was as if he had two faces. Everywhere he went there had been problems but he just didn't feel able to face up to responsibility. The guy was constantly working on two different levels. On one level, he was very aggressive, but then the moment he was caught he became extremely friendly and like a little lamb, almost like a child. So there was this very violent side to him yet at other times he even had the personality to inspire people to help him because he was so vulnerable and frightened and needed them.'

Also, in those weeks following his release from prison and the death of his father, Montes bumped into his only real friend, Eduardo Suarez, and told him, 'They almost got me. They almost got me.'

When Suarez pointed out that Montes still had to appear before a judge, he replied, 'No way, the police won't catch me.'

28

Montes showed little sadness over his father's death and continued demanding that his mother give him his share of the estate so that he could leave Gijon. His life with his mother under his bail conditions was punctuated by tensions between them. Benigna complained that he was stealing things from her and selling them very cheaply. She also said he invited 'strange' people into the house. One day Benigna came home to find her son trying to sell their TV to a gypsy.

And Montes also angrily clashed with other members of his family about his father's estate. As his brother-in-law, Andres Moro Blanco, later admitted, 'Every family has its black sheep and we regret it, but you do not choose your relatives.'

Montes was confused by his family's reaction to his claim on his inheritance. He was all the more troubled because he desperately needed his inheritance so that he could flee Spain rather than go to court to face the charges in Llanes. He had already earmarked Chile as his first stop on his 'world tour'. Entry to Chile was automatic for all Spanish nationals and it was halfway around the world, so there was little or no chance that the police would find him there. He'd heard too that it was full of pure, innocent young girls.

But friction between mother and son was racking up. On two occasions in March and April 1998, Montes was reported to the police by his mother for mistreatment and injuries that she claimed were sustained at his hands. Officers spoke to Montes but took no further action because of a lack of evidence.

Then, in June, Benigna filed a '*denuncia*' which formally denounced her son for breaking into the family apartment, even though he was still supposed to be living there under the strict bail conditions attached to his release while awaiting his trial for the Llanes offences. The legal instrument of denunciation in Spain had been introduced by General Franco after he won the Civil War. He had encouraged citizens to inform on relatives, friends or neighbours if they thought they were breaking the law. Originally, Franco brought in the system to 'keep an eye on his population' but by this time it was being used for a much wider variety of reasons.

Benigna's *denuncia* stated that her son had threatened to throw her down the stairs. It also claimed that he hit her on several occasions and that she had to go to a nearby hospital for treatment.

She said she had asked Montes to leave the house but he had refused, claiming it belonged to him now that his father was dead. She also wrote in the *denuncia* that Blanca had to stay in the apartment with her because she was so scared of her son. In addition, Montes was alleged to have threatened Blanca and refused to leave the house unless the family got a legal order to get him out; thrown all his sister's clothes into the rubbish bin in the street; and shouted at his mother and sister, 'I will not let you enjoy my father's money.'

Benigna and Blanca sensed that he was hiding some dreadful secret, but they didn't dare contemplate what it might be. They thought he was haunted by something he had done in the recent past. If only they had realised how awful that secret really was. Other family members genuinely feared that Montes might murder his mother. They certainly believed he was capable of it. Incredibly, none of this affected his bail conditions as he awaited trial for the sex attack in Llanes.

Days after an injunction was served on him, Montes threatened his mother that 'something really big is going to happen'. He needed medical help but he had nobody he could trust and inside his head were a thousand ghastly secrets eating away at his conscience. In that same outburst he admitted to his mother for the first time that he had been jailed in Germany and warned her that he didn't mind spending more time behind bars if necessary. In other words, he wasn't afraid to hurt her. His father's death had unleashed even more hatred and bitterness towards his mother.

In the summer of 1998, Benigna became so scared of her son's temper that she and Blanca – a teacher at a nearby school run by nuns – and her son-in-law, Andres Moro Blanco, a builder, moved to a large apartment on the Avenida de Costa, in the more upmarket area of town closer to the main beach. Montes remained in the family flat while his nephew lived in the other apartment owned by his family in that same block.

Shortly after this, a neighbour, Carmen Corujo, denounced Montes, claiming he was stealing electricity from the mains supply. Corujo was president of the local community and said she had received numerous complaints about Montes from his other neighbours. Montes ignored them all. He was living in his own weird world and strangers were not welcome under any circumstances.

In the middle of all this emotional turmoil, Montes began wandering around Gijon looking for outlets for his sexual tension. Armed with a bottle of whisky and his anti-depressant of choice, Afranil, he sought out girls during 'hunting raids' in the city.

Early one evening he turned up at a city-centre gym and told manager Tino Diaz he was waiting for a friend. He then leaned against a wall next to the main gym, where many women were working out. Diaz later recalled, 'He just stood there for more than an hour staring at the women. He came back four or five times over the following month and never once did his so-called friend appear. At first, I thought nothing about it but he had an attitude I didn't like from the start. He was arrogant and would lean on the wall just staring and staring. He always had on the same slightly scruffy leather jacket.'

Diaz eventually confronted Montes. 'He refused to say who his friend was, which made him sound even more suspicious,' the manager recalled.

One customer at the gym, petite blonde housewife Nieves del Castillo, 42, said she was 'completely freaked out' when Montes began staring at her as she went through her exercise regime dressed in a skimpy black leotard. 'I noticed he was especially interested in the under-18 girls who were here. I could tell he was a creep just by the way he kept staring. He didn't seem to care about anyone's reaction to him. He just kept staring.'

On about his fifth visit, Montes, asked by Diaz why he was in the gym again, snapped back, 'Why? I'm doing nothing wrong.'

'I don't like the way you're looking at the girls,' Diaz replied. He then grabbed Montes by the arm and walked him up the stairs and all the way to the exit to make sure he left. The manager recalled, 'He wasn't aggressive at all. I never saw him again. Then I saw his face in the paper later and we all realised who he was.'

Montes was growing increasingly fearful about his fast-approaching trial for the sex attack in Llanes. Initially, he hired a private lawyer, Jose Ricardo Gonzales Fernandez but ditched him in order to save money. He switched to a public defender called Claudio Alvar-Gonzalo Torrerro, who was based in the Asturian capital of Oviedo. Montes visited him repeatedly before his trial was due to begin at the end of 1998. The lawyer later described Montes as 'one of those people who could not accept reality. He insisted he was innocent.' He also recalled that Montes refused to shake his hand when they met. 'I later discovered he had a hygiene obsession,' he added.

Claudio Alvar-Gonzalo Torrerro did not directly ask Montes if he had committed any crimes similar to the attack in Llanes because, as he later said, 'that is not my job'. But he was far from impressed by his client. 'He seemed unbalanced because he was very nervous and not very rational. There was plenty of evidence against him but he was in denial. He was caught red-handed in the house of the girl. But in spite of all the evidence against him he still insisted he was innocent. He was looking for excuses and didn't want to talk about the actual charges. But at least he was very respectful to me.'

One day Montes showed up at Claudio's office without an appointment. 'I told him to go away and make an appointment. He accepted my reaction without any anger.' Afterwards, the lawyer wondered whether Montes had been trying to see him to make a full confession of his crimes. 'But I am afraid we will never know the answer to that one,' he explained.

His overall impression of Montes was: 'He was perfectly polite. There was no trouble with him. He reminded me of Crusty the Clown from *The Simpsons* but his habit of turning up without making an appointment made me a little nervous. I had the feeling he was someone who could have burst into rage at any time.' But throughout their meetings Montes never once specifically talked about his victim or the crime.

The lawyer continued, 'He always talked about how badly the police had treated him. It was as if he was the victim rather than the women he attacked. He seemed very disturbed. His logic was strange. For example, he was always trying to fool me or lie to me, which made him difficult to defend.'

Many years later, Claudio said, 'I had absolutely no doubt Montes had murdered many women when I met him. This was a man hiding so much. I felt all along that he must have murdered girls.'

So Montes certainly had good reason to worry about his trial. None of his friends or family had agreed to give evidence on his behalf. His lawyer then ordered a new psychiatric evaluation even though Montes tried to oppose it. 'I told him it would help him but he did not want to do it,' Claudio explained. 'I think he was scared what the doctors might say about him.'

The date of Montes's trial had been set for the beginning of January 1999. Towards the end of the previous month, a man appeared at Claudio's office in Oviedo with a handwritten letter. 'It was from Montes himself and he said that he didn't have much faith in me defending him and he wanted another lawyer. It was badly spelled and badly constructed and I knew then that he wouldn't be turning up for his trial.' Montes also sent a letter to the judge before the trial saying he was psychologically ill and innocent of the charges. 'It sounded like a classic cry for help to me,' explained the lawyer.

In fact, at exactly the same time he was planning his escape from Spain, Montes had finally secured a £16,000 share of his father's inheritance. It wasn't as much as he had hoped for but it would be enough for him to stay away on his travels for at least a year.

It wasn't until the beginning of 1999 – some weeks after he failed to show up for his court case – that Montes's name was even fed into an Interpol circular about missing prisoners and an international warrant was issued. By that time, he had already settled in Chile, although by all accounts he was still living under his own name.

Montes had run for his life because he had little else to lose. He had been to France while awaiting trial on the Llanes changes and tried yet again to persuade Christine Le Menes to let him see their son, but to no avail. What he didn't realise was that Christine had already concluded that her ex-lover probably was Caroline Dickinson's killer and she was now in a dilemma about whether to go to the police.

While driving back to Spain after trying to see Christine and their son, Montes saw a newspaper article featuring a brand-new photofit of the man suspected of killing Caroline Dickinson. Realising that the suspect bore much more of a resemblance to himself than any of the earlier efforts, he decided it was time to leave Europe.

Over the following 18 months, Montes travelled extensively around South America, as well as flying in and out of the US three times. He was in America for a month in April; he arrived there again on 1 August and left on 8 August; and he returned on 16 August, before leaving on 7 September. He financed his flights with his inheritance and occasional work as a waiter wherever he happened to be.

Whenever he got a chance, he checked the British newspapers and every time he was relieved to see no mention whatsoever of his name in connection with the continuing hunt for Caroline Dickinson's killer.

Montes was helped by the fact that he possessed at least three Spanish passports as he continued moving in and out of the US, Colombia, Costa Rica, Peru, Chile, Venezuela and Argentina, to name just a few of the countries he visited following his decision to flee Spain. Although he had stopped selling forged passports some years earlier, he had retained different versions of his own passport in case of an emergency like this.

In the middle of 2000, he even slipped back into Europe and stayed for two months before returning to Miami.

In France, the judge still investigating the murder of Caroline Dickinson decided he should activate a team of police officers to ask the directors of shelters and youth hostels in France about any similar incidents. Then, after weeks of interviews and requests, investigators compiled a new list of just over 100 possible suspects. The detectives were also finally beginning to realise that in all probability the killer of Caroline Dickinson was the same man who had broken into the youth hostel in Blere in 1993 and 1994. And local police already had a record of his name – Francisco Arce Montes.

Those still investigating Caroline Dickinson's murder could

now, for the first time, plausibly link Montes to the killing and to the fact that he was driving a Mazda car registered in Holland at the time of the attacks in Blere. They also established that Montes carried with him many youth hostel membership cards. However, at that time they believed he was still living in London, as this had been his last known address.

In the autumn of 2000, Montes was arrested in Miami for trying to break into a youth hostel but released without charge, even though he was carrying a torch and a pair of scissors and his tourist visa had long since expired. US police said they had no reason to hold him because after making checks with Interpol in Europe it seemed that he was not a known offender.

It was in March the following year that he was photographed by the two Scottish brothers as he tried to break into a youth hostel in Miami Beach. They later said they took Montes's photo because they thought he looked so 'strange'.

In Gijon, lawyer Jose Ricardo Gonzales Fernandez had not given much thought to his one-time client Francisco Montes since briefly handling his Llanes case back in late 1997. However, Montes never forgot the sympathetic treatment he got from Gonzales, who in March 2001 received a phone call from Montes, calling from Miami.

Montes wanted to know from his former lawyer how much publicity there had been about his disappearance from Spain. He also casually asked whether there had been any press coverage of his name 'in relation to any other crimes'. Gonzales refused to tell this author any more details about his conversation with Montes, claiming it was privileged information between lawyer and client. But he did say he believed Montes was a sad and lonely person for whom he felt deeply sorry. He also recalled that Montes seemed fed up with running and that he got the impression he was going to give himself up.

Pressure was mounting on Montes, but he remained deeply fearful of returning to prison. Was he seriously considering confessing all his crimes? More and more, it seemed, his shattered nerves just made him feel the need to buy more Afranil and whisky to drown out his problems.

A few days after his phone call to his former lawyer in Spain, Montes was arrested for breaking into the Banana Bungalow youth hostel and sexually assaulting the Irish student as she slept in a room with three friends. The scruffy Spaniard arrested by police in Dade County on 11 March gave his name as 'Francisco Arce', the name he had used at the time of his previous arrest in Florida. He even had a passport to show that it was his real name.

Under this name, he was charged with two felony counts of burglary and one misdemeanour count of lewd and lascivious conduct. This time detectives were determined to pursue a case against him because they realised that he was some kind of serial offender. However, when they put the name 'Arce' into the Interpol computer system, once again it failed to match up to Montes. They had no idea they were holding a multiple killer and sex attacker who had struck in various parts of the world over the previous 20 or so years.

In the Dade County lock-up, Montes had a difficult time because he was expected to mix with drug barons, bank robbers and petty crooks, who didn't take kindly to having in their midst an alleged molester of young girls. Montes was eventually switched to solitary confinement at the Miami-Dade Pretrial Detention Center after being repeatedly targeted by other inmates.

On 3 April 2001, American immigration officer Tommy Ontko was halfway through a busy day at Detroit's Metropolitan Airport when he stopped by the British Airways ticket desk to grab a three-day-old copy of London's *Sunday Times*. He later explained, 'I don't eat lunch but I like to read the British papers with a coffee and a doughnut or something from the machine.' Ontko read with curiosity how the hunt for Caroline Dickinson's killer had spread from France to Britain and that for the first time a 'Francisco Arce Montes' had been publicly named as a suspect. Ontko read the report closely and then fed Montes's name into a secure database in his airport computer.

'I just thought that, if this guy was on the move, then he could have come to America,' Ontko explained. 'So, it was around noon and I tapped his name into the immigration service database and immediately found five matches.' After making checks for another 15 minutes Ontko found that someone called 'Francisco Arce' had been detained in Miami just a few days earlier.

To proceed further, Ontko needed an accurate date of birth, so he placed a call to the police in Rennes. The French police telephonist thought Ontko was English and brushed him off with a number for Ron Frankel, the British Consul in the city. 'Which I guess was a mistake, but it turned out to be another big stroke of luck,' Ontko said.

Frankel was intrigued by the unexpected call because it sounded like a possible breakthrough in a case that had closely involved him five years earlier. As British Consul, he had been required to visit the murder scene and offer comfort to Caroline Dickinson's parents.

Also, Frankel's wife's cousin was a translator for the French judiciary and was, at that very moment, in a car with the detective and investigating judge leading the Caroline Dickinson investigation. They were en route to England, first to Portsmouth, then on to Cornwall to attend Caroline Dickinson's inquest. Ontko's enquiries were barely an hour and a half old.

Frankel's wife found a mobile-phone number for her cousin, which Ontko immediately called. The American recalled, 'So they pulled their car over and very excitedly read me Montes's date of birth and lots of other information from the file. I ran his new details through the criminal records database and found it was the same guy who'd been arrested in Miami.'

The French police were startled to learn that Montes was in a Miami prison.

In the middle of all this transatlantic manoeuvring, a verdict of unlawful killing was recorded by the coroner Edward Carlyon at the Caroline Dickinson inquest in Cornwall. Afterwards, John Dickinson said the inquest did not signal the end of the hunt to bring his daughter's killer to justice. 'It is a statutory requirement under English law and should in no way be viewed as the end of the ongoing murder investigation taking place in France.'

Unaware of the current police activity across two continents, he then made a fresh appeal for anyone with information to come forward. He believed a reward could help provide the 'final clue'. He added, 'It is our firm opinion that the identity of the murderer is known or strongly suspected by others.'

The *Daily Mail* report on the inquest ended with the following sentence: 'French police still have officers on the case and currently there are 48 suspects in the frame.'

Back in Detroit, Tommy Ontko contacted Richie Hayward, an old police friend in Florida he knew from his days as an undercover officer investigating biker gangs. Hayward sent him photos and fingerprints of Montes, which Ontko sent to France and Portsmouth. When Ontko returned to work at 7.30am next day, he confirmed it was definitely Montes, who had been arrested for breaking into the Banana Bungalow youth hostel, where he had masturbated while standing over a sleeping teenage girl. More checks were then run in the US and Ontko discovered Montes was wanted in places as far afield as Germany, Belgium, Venezuela, Switzerland and Spain for questioning in connection with similar crimes. The case, said Ontko, was now 'blown open'.

Within hours, Miami police announced to the world they were '99.9 per cent' certain they had arrested the sex killer of the British schoolgirl Caroline Dickinson. Ed Munn, a spokesman for Miami-Dade County police department told reporters, 'Wouldn't like to say anything that would prejudice the legal process and ongoing investigation but we are obviously very happy with the way things are at the present time.

This time there was no way Francisco Montes could talk his way out of trouble, because he was already in custody.

BOOK 3

JUSTICE

———

'I WENT INTO A ROOM. IT WAS VERY DARK BUT I REALISED
THERE WAS SOMEONE SLEEPING ON THE FLOOR. I WENT AND
LAY DOWN NEXT TO HER. IT WAS A YOUNG GIRL. I WAS
AROUSED. I WANTED TO DO WHAT I HAD DONE BEFORE, SO
I PLACED MY HAND OVER HER MOUTH. I COULDN'T
STOP MYSELF...'

*Francisco Arce Montes, describing the night he raped
and murdered schoolgirl Caroline Dickinson*

29

So it was that on 8 April 2001 Francisco Montes found himself standing in the dock of a Miami courthouse with his hands and feet in chains, charged with the Banana Bungalow sexual assault and knowing that the world now believed him to be the man who had murdered Caroline Dickinson.

CAROLINE SUSPECT ARRESTED screamed newspaper headlines in Britain and France. It was the breakthrough many thought would never come.

In court, Montes insisted he was innocent and pledged to start a major court battle to stop being sent back to France. He told his court-appointed lawyers he would appeal against extradition from the US all the way to the Supreme Court if necessary – and prosecutors warned that could take two years. Court documents issued after his arrest in Miami revealed that he had been using at least three Spanish passports.

Montes was remanded in custody for eight days and law-enforcement officials in Florida privately admitted it could well be 'a long time' before he was sent back to France. He would first have to be dealt with for the sex offences in Florida and that hearing might not happen until October at the earliest.

Scottish tourist Michael Boyle had thought little more of the man whose picture he took as he climbed in the open window of a Miami Beach youth hostel until he saw a photo of the same man splashed across the newspapers in connection with Caroline Dickinson's murder. He said, 'I couldn't believe it. I knew right away he was the guy in Miami. When I read he was wanted it sent a shiver down my spine.'

The French police then arrived in Florida to take blood and saliva samples to see if Montes's DNA matched that found at the scene of Caroline's murder. Montes refused to provide the samples, so the testing had to be done on the semen sample found in the room at the Miami youth hostel where he had been arrested.

A few days later, Montes was moved to a top-security psychiatric ward after being seen trying to use his shirt as a noose in his solitary cell, having tied one end to a window bar and the other around his neck.

Miami police explained that Montes had become very depressed after being told that samples of his DNA had been picked up by French investigators for comparison. Montes told a psychiatrist in the prison hospital that he wanted to die.

By this time, Montes was wearing a Ferguson garment, a loose-fitting gown padded at the front and back to prevent him harming himself. 'He is under constant medical supervision,' said a police spokeswoman. 'A doctor checks on him every ten minutes.'

But at this stage Montes was still adamantly refusing to even confirm his full name to investigators. It wasn't in his nature to accept responsibility for his actions. He believed, in his own self-deluded way, that, just so long as he said his name was 'Arce', not 'Montes', they couldn't charge him with Caroline Dickinson's murder.

At the Banana Bungalow, news of Montes's suicide attempt was greeted with anger by the owner of the hostel where he was arrested. 'He is scum,' said Kevin Guillory. 'He frightened the girls here to death. I hope he does commit suicide. It would save the expense of a trial.'

On 14 April 2001, the French authorities began preparing extradition papers to serve on Montes in Miami after they publicly announced that samples of his semen taken in Florida showed 'important similarities' to DNA found where Caroline Dickinson was raped and murdered.

In fact, Montes's DNA sample was a perfect match with that of Caroline's killer. Marie-Helene Cherpin, of the Forensic Science Laboratory in Paris, concluded that 'the chances of a similar DNA profile being found at random in the general population were equal to one out of a total world population'. A second test was also carried out in Bordeaux by another expert, who found that the samples also yielded a match in 14 out of 18 'profile markers'. French law required only nine for a positive identification.

On the basis of these results, a federal judge in Miami granted an international arrest warrant for Montes, a move that paved the way for the formal opening of the extradition proceedings against Montes.

A US Justice Department spokesman explained, 'This looks like a simple case. Montes is not a US citizen, the Miami offence is minor compared to the French case and we have a well-established extradition procedure with the French authorities.'

In Launceston, John Dickinson, with his ex-wife Sue Dickinson beside him, told a press conference, 'Nothing can bring back our dear Caroline, but everything should be done to prevent such a nightmare being visited on another innocent family.' Fighting back his emotions, he went on, 'We have never lost hope. This was such a horrendous crime it could not go unpunished. We would never have given up hope. It is a fantastic fact it has happened – absolutely brilliant.'

Then he graciously thanked the police for bringing his daughter's killer to justice. 'We wish to express our particular thanks to the gendarmes who through their hard work and dedication have bought Montes to justice.' Yet no one knew better than the Dickinson family that the lack of communication between police forces in Europe had allowed Montes to flourish for more than two decades. And this had cost Caroline Dickinson her life.

In France, it was finally beginning to dawn on investigators that Montes might have been involved in many more crimes than the murder of Caroline Dickinson. Commandant Olivier Bouisset, new head of the unit investigating Caroline's murder, admitted to newsmen there were 'at least 30 unsolved incidents revolving around youth hostels in France'. Investigators planned to show Montes's photo to victims.

For almost 30 years, Montes had criss-crossed national borders and continents with minimal interference by the authorities despite a past that included convictions for multiple rapes. Yet it was only now, after he had been arrested in Miami, that police forces across the globe began to trawl through their records and acknowledge the vast scale of his depravity. Police were soon connecting Montes to a string of attacks and killings in Spain, Britain, France, Belgium, Switzerland, Germany, the United States and at least half a dozen South American countries.

In Britain, police began re-examining unsolved sex attacks and murders around the country after it was revealed that the Spaniard had lived in London for many years. His former neighbours in Earl's Court were soon telling reporters how Montes used to try to lure young girls to his bedsit.

Naturally, in the days following Montes's arrest, questions about the French police investigation began to emerge. Many believed he should have been caged years earlier, after the attacks in 1993 and 1994 on schoolgirls in Blere, France. The fact that Montes had been let off with a caution in the Loire Valley town seemed incredible, especially when it was revealed that he had been carrying a rope and hammer in his car. The revelations about Montes's attacks around the world also led to calls for a global database of suspects' names and DNA profiles.

Norman Brennan, director of the Victims of Crime Trust, said, 'We have the most advanced technology in history to catch criminals and it should be used. When someone is arrested, their name should be entered in a computer and if they are wanted in any other country in the world it should show up.'

The revelation that Montes had been arrested for attempted rape in Llanes, Spain – an assault which occurred *after* Caroline Dickinson's murder – also added to the growing controversy. Many were asking why, if he was already a suspect for the killing, French detectives failed to ever hear about the Llanes incident.

The truth was that Francisco Montes had only finally been

trapped by the huge coincidence of Detroit immigration officer Tommy Ontko reading about the case in a newspaper during his lunch break and then checking Montes's name with federal files when he got back to his office.

In his hometown of Gijon, police branded Montes a 'dangerous split personality'. They said that each time he had been arrested he had simply moved on and altered his appearance, although there has never been any evidence to support the claim that he adopted another identity. Newspapers gleefully reported that Montes's graduation from peeping Tom to his current official French status of 'presumed killer' began in Gijon when he would spend his days sitting outside his father's grocery shop watching schoolgirls. One woman was quoted in a Gijon newspaper claiming that he followed her home when, as a young girl, she ran errands for her parents, who lived near by. 'He always made me feel uneasy,' she said. 'Although he was 20 years older he would ask me out. He used to say I had a well-formed body for my age. I hated being near him.'

Newspapers also revealed how Montes – with no educational qualifications and unemployed for years – had decided, while still in his teens, to seek work abroad and later obtained International Youth Hostel Federation membership cards in many countries.

Journalists also dug up references to a 1993 incident in a girl's room in a youth hostel in Tours, France, when Montes fled after his young girl victim started screaming.

Also in France, rumours re-emerged that Montes had an accomplice on the night he killed Caroline Dickinson. Eyewitnesses told how a man left the hostel in Pleine-Fougeres driving a white van with a male passenger beside him.

Commandant Olivier Bouisset told reporters, 'It could be that Montes was just giving the man a lift or that he dropped him off further down the road. Or it may be that the two men hatched a plot. It is one of many hypotheses our men are investigating. We have to look into every possibility. When Montes comes to France to be tried, he may well say that he did not kill Caroline and that another man with him killed her. We have DNA proof that his semen was at the scene of the crime. But what is to stop him attempting to plead guilty to a charge of rape only? We don't want this man to get away with a ten-year prison sentence. We still have a long way to go on this case.'

In Montes's hometown, residents were shocked to discover that a cruel and sick killer had lived among them for so long. Gijon was, the newspapers pointed out, a place where, apart from the occasional killing connected with drugs or domestic troubles, very few murders occurred. At the time of Montes's arrest, the city's annual murder rate was under ten and it seemed likely that he himself had killed at least that number of young women.

Unlike their tabloid counterparts in Britain, Gijon's journalists were told not to harass Montes's friends and relatives for information. Octavio Villa, crime reporter on a local newspaper, covered the story from the moment news of Montes's connection with the Caroline Dickinson case filtered over from Florida. He had hoped to go to France to investigate the background to many of Montes's crimes but his paper couldn't afford to pay for his trip.

Villa explained, 'Gijon as a community was in shock about Montes. They all wanted to get rid of him the moment they heard what he'd done. He is not one of us, they said. People just wanted him to be arrested, sent to jail and never let out again. It was typical of this city in many ways. I suppose you could call it cynical but we were embarrassed by him. We did not want to know him.'

The first thing the reporter did was try to find out where Montes lived. He later recalled, 'I knew nothing at first and used my contacts in the Guardia Civil and they told how he'd been arrested in Llanes two or three years earlier.'

When Villa eventually arrived at the home of Benigna Montes, he found her son-in-law, Andres Moro Blanco, acting as the family spokesman. 'Montes's mother was not well educated and she couldn't cope with all the attention,' explained the journalist. Andres Moro Blanco was 'very normal, quiet and didn't get angry easily', he recalled.

Moro told him that he didn't want to upset his wife or mother-in-law because they were already distressed. He also insisted that he had no idea what Montes was doing in Miami. But, the reporter recalled, 'Moro said that Montes was always calling to ask for money and things like that and then they'd ask where he was.' Moro also told him that Montes never once mentioned South America to his family.

Speaking outside the apartment that the family moved to after the death of Gerardo Montes, Montes's brother-in-law also told Villa, 'Francisco's mother and sister are finding it very difficult to cope with what he has done. They are in a very bad state and are suffering depression. They have hardly eaten since it became clear what he had done. All we can say is that we are sorry for Caroline's family.'

Moro admitted the family gave money to Montes to stay away from Gijon. 'He would ask them for money and they were so ashamed of him they wanted him to stay away,' Villa explained. Moro also told him that Montes was 'always causing the family troubles and that he was a very bad man. He was also very sick. Not really crazy but sick.'

Reporters from British newspapers were more aggressive and soon infuriated the family. 'They offered money for photos of the family,' said Villa. A few days after the reporter spoke to Moro, Montes's elderly mother, now 83, found her Gijon doorstep invaded by dozens of reporters and photographers from London's notorious tabloids. The following day the London-based *Daily Mirror* and *Sun* reported that a 'tearful' Benigna had said, 'I'm not going to delude myself that he might be innocent. I think he's guilty and I have no interest in defending him. As a mother, I'm horrified. I'm so sorry for what I believe my son has done. The way Caroline's family lost her was inhuman. I want them to know I feel their pain. I'm speaking out because I don't want people to think I support someone who has done such terrible things. I disown my son.' The *Daily Mirror* said that Benigna had not left her flat in Gijon since she was told that Montes had been seized in Miami.

The *Sun* reported that Montes's mother had said, 'As a parent, I know what it is to bring up children. And the way those parents lost their daughter was just inhuman – absolutely terrible.

'I am really sorry for all that my son has done. All the family believe he is guilty of everything he has been accused of.'

The *Sun* claimed that Benigna was 'having to come to terms with the fact that she and her late husband Geraldo unknowingly financed his trail of terror across Europe and the US. The couple, who grew wealthy running a grocery store, paid violent Montes to stay away from them because he was such a monster.'

Then the article quoted a 'family friend' as saying, 'Francisco had mental problems and became very problematic when he was a teenager. Benigna would never talk about it but we could all see the results of his violence. She was frightened of him and the family would do anything to get him out of the house. God knows how Francisco got these things into his head. The family are kind, respectable and well-liked. It is dreadful what they had to put up with.'

Shortly after the pieces in the *Mirror* and the *Sun* appeared, another paper claimed that Montes's mother had never spoken to reporters from any of the British tabloids. An article in the media section of London's *Evening Standard* said that the reporters had sought to interview her 'through' her son-in-law Andres Moro Blanco and that he had told them all to get lost. Moro even issued a statement in which he denounced British chequebook journalism and expressed sympathy for the Dickinson family. He said he had not spoken to the papers. 'To do that would be to trade on our sorrow and that of others.'

Britain's tabloids remained obsessed with what had turned Montes into a killer. Octavio Villa explained, 'But in Gijon no one cared about that. They just wanted Montes to be severely punished. Everyone was hoping that he would be put in jail and never allowed out again. Montes's mind and past just wasn't that important to us here.'

When Villa started asking around El Coto about Montes, most people denied even knowing him. 'I talked to many local people about Montes but no one seemed to know him. The most I could get were a few old memories. People would say little. I think they were ashamed to have known him.'

The most surprising thing the local crime reporter ever learned about Montes was his ability to speak many languages. 'That shocked me because people here in Gijon tend not to speak anything other than the local dialect. It made me realise that we were dealing with a highly intelligent killer,' said Villa.

One of the few people in El Coto who recalled Montes from his schooldays described a quiet child, 'but he looked strange, like a wolf with those eyes close together and bushy hair'.

Montes's arrest was greeted with relief by the people of Pleine-Fougeres, the village where Caroline Dickinson was murdered. The mayor, Christian Couet, said, 'We could never accept that this crime could go unsolved.'

And bar worker Corinne Bouzin added, 'We are very happy at the latest news. But there is sadness for Caroline's family.'

30

In London, detectives at Scotland Yard were convinced Montes had committed other rapes and murders while he lived in the city. One admitted to reporters, 'His record clearly suggests the picture of a prolific sex attacker. From what is known about him on the continent it is impossible to believe he would have been a resident in Britain for all those years without carrying out attacks on women.'

In Earl's Court, Montes's former neighbour Gordon Butler told reporters he was terrified of the man. 'He was always causing problems for the landlady and others in the house. Everyone was so glad when he finally left.'

Butler also recalled Montes's movements in and out of London around the time of Caroline Dickinson's death. 'I am certain he said he was in France at the time she was murdered. I remember it so clearly because it was so strange when he came back without his car, saying he had just left it there after it broke down. And at the same time Caroline Dickinson's picture was everywhere in the news – the two just fitted together. Francisco stayed around for a few more months. I remember him going to Amsterdam to get a new car and then in 1997 he disappeared.'

In Gijon, Manuel Ferrero Garcia, Commissioner of the National Police, admitted, 'Looking at Montes's behaviour and psychology, it is probable he has committed other serious crimes. It is not often you catch someone the first time they have committed a crime. If you catch a bank robber, it is likely he has robbed before.'

The city's police admitted they had interviewed Montes three times about threats to his mother after his release on bail for the attack in Llanes. But they claimed she refused to press charges, so he was released. They also confirmed they couldn't trace Montes when he went on the run for the Llanes incident.

In the nearby state capital of Oviedo, lawyer Claudio Alvar-Gonzalo Torrerro told reporters that, had Montes not absconded while on bail, he had planned to seek psychiatric treatment if found guilty, to avoid going to prison for at least ten years.

On 15 April, following Montes's arrest and a mountain of worldwide publicity, his ex-lover Christine Le Menes revealed to the authorities the strange story of their relationship. She told the French police she was living in Vitre, a small town some 50 kilometres from Pleine-Fougeres, when Caroline Dickinson was murdered. She admitted to investigating judge Francois Debons that Montes had been in the area the weekend of Caroline's murder and that she had long suspected he preyed on young girls in hostels. 'I feel mad with shame that I did not say this before,' she told the judge.

Christine said she finally ended all communications with Montes after police released a photofit of the wanted man which bore a striking likeness to her former lover.

Within days of her confession to the judge, Christine Le Menes had barricaded herself inside her tiny apartment in Rennes, where she had moved to in 1997. The blinds were drawn and she turned away all callers. One neighbour explained, 'She's gone to ground because of this. Even a ring on her doorbell terrifies her. It is all very painful for her. This is something she has carried for 20 years and now it is all resurfacing. She has always been frightened that he'll suddenly appear at her door. Then there's her son. It's not as if he had the greatest image of his father, but now…'

Christine's colleagues at the primary school where she taught had noticed how quiet and reclusive she had become, especially since Montes's highly publicised arrest. One later said, 'She was a complete mystery. She didn't even like to tell us her second name.'

Behind the shyness was a terrified woman afraid that if she let slip her identity to anyone, Montes might track her down. It was as if he had come back to haunt her when his picture was flashed around the world. She even had to tell her son who his father really was and how he was wanted for murder and had been captured in Florida.

Meanwhile, Montes remained on suicide watch in Miami's Dade County Jail. He had, according to prison staff, 'gone downhill' ever since being told his DNA matched that found by French investigators at the youth hostel in Pleine-Fougeres. By now he was spending his days and nights naked in a padded 'strip cell' with no sheets or bedding and just an iron bedstead to sleep on. Prison chiefs had taken the drastic precautions after

Montes turned violent and started hurling himself at the walls of his cell. Before that, he had spent the best part of a week banging his head against the same walls.

Montes became even more agitated when Judge David Young ordered him to fill out an affidavit about his finances. When it was produced in court a few days later, it showed Montes had no income, no property in Spain and, he claimed, monthly living expenses of £360. Not satisfied with the affidavit, the judge ordered Montes to be brought back to the court to discuss his finances but was told the prisoner could not be moved because he was still in the strip cell.

In court, it was also revealed that Montes had travelled in and out of the US three times during 1999. The court admitted it had no idea how Montes managed to afford the airline tickets. At that time, none of those present realised he had that £16,000 inheritance following his father's death at the end of 1997.

When Valerie Jacques, who was targeted by Montes at the youth hostel in Blere, saw his picture on the TV after his arrest, she knew immediately it was the man who had attacked her in 1994. She offered to give statements to police and provide evidence at his eventual trial, telling reporters at her home in Ballymorris, Ireland, 'Hopefully there will be some closure now for the Dickinson family – they deserve it after eight years.'

Valerie, who is now 21, admitted she was chilled to the bone when she saw Montes's image: 'I recognised him instantly. It was such a shock, even after seven years I remembered his face. I'm a hundred per cent positive it's the same man.' Her parents told reporters they were dismayed that her school had never informed them of her attempted abduction by a murder suspect when their daughter was 14.

Back in Miami, Montes was taken off suicide watch and returned to the general prison population, much to his horror. He feared the retribution of many inmates and knew what they were calling him behind his back. He shunned both staff and prisoners and quickly earned a reputation as a 'psycho' thanks to his habit of staring at everyone in the prison canteen. Throughout that summer in jail in Miami, Montes suffered numerous attacks by other inmates and his pleas to be returned to solitary confinement were ignored. The authorities felt this was the best way to make him face up to what he had done.

On 25 October 2001, Montes appeared in court and was told that, if he agreed to plead guilty to the charges he faced in Miami, this would finally pave the way for his extradition to France. He had been due to stand trial on the US charges the following June, but the authorities in Miami knew it would be in the interests of justice to return him as soon as possible to face French justice.

Montes entered the court determined not to concede anything. But then he pleaded with Judge David Young to have him moved back into solitary confinement. 'I can't stand that cell I am in any more. They are making my life impossible. Please move me.'

But the judge, who had long since grown impatient with Montes's earlier delaying tactics, said, 'I will move you but only if you tell me you are going to take a plea on Monday.'

'Yes, yes,' Montes replied.

'OK, move him to the tenth floor today,' the judge said. 'Get him out of the general prison population. Put him in solitary if you need to.'

Outside the court, Montes's latest lawyer, Ronaldo Manto, confirmed, 'I am negotiating a plea bargain with the prosecution. The charges are not an issue. We are discussing what the state would see as an acceptable sentence. There will be no trial now, and it is quite possible that Mr Montes will be on his way to France next week. He does not like the American jails because the authorities had not allowed for the nature of the crime he is charged with in France. If he were charged with that crime there, he would be isolated from the general population.'

Now, in a move orchestrated by the US State Attorney, Montes was to be released from state custody and immediately placed under federal detention and extradited to France. 'We hope that today's action can bring justice and closure to a homicide committed by Mr Arce Montes in France,' said Miami-Dade County State Attorney Katherine Fernandez Rundle. 'Our case will remain open pending the completion of judicial proceedings against Mr Arce Montes in Europe.'

She added, 'The victim in the Miami Beach case is willing to forgo a trial here and speed Mr Arce Montes's return to France to be tried on the rape and homicide pending against him. We appreciate and thank everyone for their co-operation and for their desire to see justice quickly served.'

Judge David Young ruled that he would keep the Florida case open. If Montes returned to stand trial on two state counts of burglary and one count of lewd and lascivious conduct and was found guilty, he would face a maximum of 30 years in a state penitentiary. Before confirming that Montes would return to the French authorities, state prosecutors reviewed unsolved criminal cases through the Federal Bureau of Investigation (FBI) and the Florida Department of Law Enforcement (FDLE) to make sure that Montes had not committed any additional crimes in Miami-Dade County or anywhere else in the United

States. They had a number of cases on the file which appeared to have Montes's *modus operandi* stamped all over them, but, owing to lack of evidence, it was decided that justice would be best served by returning him to France for trial.

US marshals were in the courtroom to rearrest Montes the moment he was freed from the original Miami charges. He walked literally from one set of handcuffs into another. He was to be flown to France that afternoon and in the meantime was placed in federal custody and taken to Miami International Airport, where the French authorities took charge of him for the flight to Paris.

31

On 19 November 2001, Francisco Montes was escorted under armed guard on to a plane in Miami scheduled to take off at 5.45pm local time and arrive at Charles de Gaulle airport the following morning.

On touchdown in Paris, Montes, still handcuffed to a French detective, was taken off the plane and transferred to a police car. When press photographers spotted him in the back of the car, he used a sheet of paper to shield his face, which suggested that he did feel some shame about his alleged offences.

Within an hour of landing, Montes appeared before an examining magistrate in Bobigny, a suburb to the north-east of Paris, where he was officially placed under investigation – a step short of being charged. He was accused of raping and suffocating Caroline Dickinson and an application for bail was swiftly rejected.

Next he was taken to the top-security prison at Fleury-Merogis, south of the capital. Under French law, the authorities now had four days to charge him. Officials had already warned it could be at least another year before Montes was brought to trial. On 27 November, Montes was further remanded in custody for up to a year. He was expected to be transferred to prison in Rennes, in Brittany, where he would be held until a date for his trial was set.

A few days after Montes's return to France, two senior detectives investigating the murder of Caroline Dickinson visited their Spanish counterparts in Montes's hometown of Gijon in the hope of piecing together more about his background. One senior Gijon detective recalled, 'It was as if they were just going through the motions but at least we all went out and enjoyed a very pleasant lunch together.'

The two French investigators stayed for three days, during which they tried to visit the Montes family but found they had the wrong address. 'We were shocked that they had so little information about Montes,' added the detective.

It was increasingly obvious that sharp-eyed US immigration officer Tommy Ontko was probably the only law-enforcement official to come out of the Caroline Dickinson inquiry with any outstanding credit. However, Ontko remained modest about his Sherlock Holmes-style detective work, insisting, 'I wouldn't consider myself a hero. It was a group effort and credit must be shared by the detective team in Florida. But it's wonderful that a crime which seemed unsolvable for so long can turn around so dramatically. I hope now there will be some closure for this poor girl's family. Everyone is being very careful to ensure there are no mistakes or slip-ups that might enable this guy to get away.'

In Britain, senior detectives from the National Crime

Faculty requested samples of Montes's DNA. They had compiled a database on unsolved sex crimes and began examining more than 100 files in search of possible links to Montes. One Scotland Yard officer explained, 'It is clear from what is emerging about Montes that he is a night-stalker-type attacker and we do have a number of such cases in Britain for the period he was here. It is important to establish where he was and what his movements were during that four-year period. He is a very good suspect in several cases we are looking at.'

In Swansea, police noticed a startling similarity between the photofit of a suspected sex attacker and Montes. The photofit was issued by police in Wales in 1993 after teenage girls were attacked in separate incidents at a secluded beauty spot on the Gower Peninsula. Detective Inspector Dale Ponting, head of Swansea CID, said, 'We'd like to talk to Mr Montes. There are striking similarities to our photofit and photos we've seen of him. We're liaising with Interpol and making our own enquiries as to where he was and what he was doing at the relevant time.'

There were also other Swansea incidents, including a man trying to drag a girl into woods and an attack on another victim in sand dunes. Detective Sergeant Howard Davies of Swansea CID explained, 'When I saw the pictures of Montes it struck me straight away. It was one of the two best matches to a suspect I ever saw in 30 years as a police officer. I went to get the files and I was sure we had a suspect at last.'

In London, detectives visited the £400-a-night hotel where Montes worked to see if they could link him with any incidents, but the hotel was reluctant to help investigators in case any adverse publicity affected its reputation.

By the time Montes made his first court appearance in Rennes, the eyes of the world were focused firmly on the parents of Caroline Dickinson, who came face to face with their daughter's killer for the first time. In the courthouse, they listened intently to the details of his horrific crimes and also heard why police blunders in Europe had prevented their daughter's killer's arrest for so many years. Montes was then remanded in custody, with law experts still predicting that the trial would not take place for at least another year.

Montes had already made it clear to police that he was not about to admit murdering Caroline, or anyone else for that matter. As usual, he refused to accept any responsibility for his actions. He also knew that he would still stand a chance of an acquittal if he denied everything. The shrewd, cunning mentality that had helped him evade justice for so long was not yet dead and buried. Montes stuck rigidly to his story that he had never intended to even hurt Caroline Dickinson.

32

It wasn't until February 2003 that Montes changed his story and admitted for the first time that he had killed Caroline Dickinson. He told French investigators he raped the 13-year-old and suffocated her 'in error' as he tried to muffle her screams. Until then he had denied even being at the youth hostel in Brittany where Caroline was murdered. Robert Baffert, senior prosecutor, explained, 'This confession is clearly a major breakthrough in our investigation and will be of huge importance to Caroline's family. I understand that his strategy now is to try to minimise the seriousness of the crime.'

Montes provided investigators with a detailed account of how he crept into the hostel and raped the teenager after first smothering her with a wad of cotton wool. As prosecutor Baffert explained, 'He admits killing her but is contesting the circumstances.'

Caroline Dickinson's MP, Paul Tyler, Liberal Democrat member for North Cornwall, who had helped her parents during their campaign for justice, said there 'would be concern and criticism' if Montes used his confession to obtain a shorter sentence. The MP commented, 'Those who have been close to this case are very relieved it is coming to a conclusion after so long. When we see what sort of sentence is passed, that may be a different matter.'

Then, in the early summer of 2003, Montes switched to another tactic by insisting he was insane, although this was immediately rejected by the French examining judge presiding over the case. Medical experts told the judge that they could find no evidence that Montes did not know what he was doing when he killed Caroline Dickinson.

Meanwhile, a top-security watch was mounted on Montes following an attack he carried out on a guard in Rennes Prison. An official from the prison explained, 'He drew a fork across the guard's neck, indicating that, if he wished to, he could cut his throat.'

In prison, Montes was once again regarded as a serious suicide risk. Many believed he would try to take his own life to avoid standing trial for Caroline's murder. He behaved in prison like the ultimate loner, refusing to answer his guards when they addressed him, instead glaring at them with his dark, dull eyes. One guard said at the time, 'We are really scared of him. None of the guards feels at ease close to Montes.'

His fellow inmates called Montes a '*pointeur*', French slang for a child killer. He was considered an animal and treated accordingly. The prison staff said other inmates considered him 'the lowest form of human life', so it was no surprise when, in September 2003, Montes was beaten up by three other inmates.

Then, a few weeks later, Montes tried to imply he was suffering from paranoid delusions in his cell. A guard explained,

'He thinks his cellmates are all undercover police sent to spy on him. He bangs his plate on the table at mealtimes, shouting in Spanish – and seems terrified of going on trial. He appears wide-eyed and nervous and has no friends. He is looked down on as scum by the likes of robbers and fraudsters.'

A former fellow prisoner later explained, 'People kept coming up to him and saying things like: "You killed Caroline and now we are going to kill you."'

Because Montes was an alleged child rapist he was not entitled to any of the privileges that prisoners afforded each other.

In January 2004, Montes was moved to the hospital wing at Fresnes Prison, south of Paris, for his own safety – even the wing holding sex offenders was not considered safe enough for him – and to enable psychiatrists to keep him under closer observation. He was also said to be suffering from anorexia after losing nearly two stone while in Rennes Prison. It seemed that his obsession with hygiene was still haunting him. He told staff he was reluctant to eat prison food because he believed that other inmates were trying to poison him.

At Fresnes, Montes was under 'exceptional protection', placed in a single cell and accompanied by a guard at all times. 'He is never left on his own, wherever he goes,' a French prison source explained.

Many believed Montes was trying to escape justice by pretending he was unfit to stand trial. But his court-appointed lawyer, Olivier Dersoir, insisted his client was 'too disturbed mentally to defend himself'. However, Herve Rouzaud-Le Boeuf, the lawyer who was representing the Dickinson family, remained convinced it was all a clever ruse by Montes. 'I am convinced that Montes is a fraud,' he said. 'I am sure he is completely sane and is merely trying to escape his just deserts.

Of course, Montes is an unstable person, but that does not mean he is crazy. It's all a try-on. He is perfectly fit to stand trial. It would be a disgrace and a blot on French justice if this man were allowed to go untried simply because he is a consummate actor.'

Montes's trial was now scheduled to begin on 2 June 2004. But since admitting a year earlier in a session in closed court that he killed Caroline Dickinson he had been 'attempting to minimise his crime' at subsequent closed-court hearings. Olivier Dersoir continued to insist his client was insane: 'I see this man regularly. It is obvious that he is gradually going out of his mind. He would not be able to give an intelligible account of his behaviour at the time of the crime. He seems to be living in a world of his own. Justice would not be served by putting this deranged person in the dock. His presence in court will not clear up the mystery of this poor girl's tragic fate.'

The lawyers acting for Montes also argued they had not had sufficient access to their client to prepare a defence case because of Montes's removal to the hospital wing at Fresnes. But their request was thrown out by the presiding judge, Fabienne Doroy.

Montes's trial would be regarded with grim satisfaction in the mournful, solidly built houses of Pleine-Fougeres, where Caroline Dickinson was murdered. The village of 1,800 people hoped the trial would signal the end of a period when divisive rumour ran rife; when suspicions were raised that local scores were being settled by supplying police with wrong information. Alain, a man in his fifties, said, 'Until they found him [Montes], there was always a cloud of suspicion over Pleine-Fougeres. You could feel the cloud lift when the Spaniard was arrested. This is a quiet town, an easygoing town, but for five years we lived with the suspicion that there might be a murderer among us or, worse in a way, that other people might suspect you. Since then, people have wanted to forget, to move on, but there is always a great sympathy for the little English girl's family. It is harder for them. They cannot forget.'

A woman in her forties, who called herself Solange, said, 'We lived with a feeling we were being blamed in some way, everyone in the town. I have great sympathy for the Dickinson family, who have behaved with great dignity and courage, but Pleine-Fougeres, in a way, was a victim too. I hope when the trial is ended that we can all start to put this terrible thing behind us.'

33

French officials had been working for weeks to ensure the smooth running of Montes's trial, which would be heard by a presiding judge along with two other judges and nine jurors. But many feared that Montes was still intending to defend himself by claiming he never really intended to kill Caroline. He had admitted molesting and masturbating over her, but swore that he hadn't meant to kill her. He knew only too well that he faced a life sentence if found guilty.

Under French law, the Dickinson family were able to be legally represented and to question Montes when he took the stand. They undoubtedly expected a lot from the trial. Their lawyer, Herve Rouzaud-Le Boeuf, explained, 'First of all, they want to know more about the circumstances of the drama.'

The Dickinsons would be joined by ten British witnesses, including former students from their daughter's school, Launceston Community College, and teachers who oversaw that fateful school trip to Pleine-Fougeres.

So, in a courtroom in Rennes, the events of just one of many destructive nights in the life of Francisco Montes would be recreated, hopefully for the final time. His 27-year history of raping, assaulting and killing girls in Europe and the Americas would finally be coming to an end. Or would it?

Four translators were installed in the courtroom in specially constructed soundproof cabins to provide simultaneous translations of the proceedings in English, French and Spanish. Media from across the world were accredited for the hearing and simultaneous translations via earphones would also be available to the Dickinson family.

On 8 June 2004, a frail-looking Francisco Arce Montes finally entered the packed courtroom at the Cour d'Assises in Rennes and walked to the dock, just ten feet from John Dickinson, 45, his ex-wife Sue, 46, and their daughter, Caroline's sister, Jenny, 19.

On that first day, Montes was dressed in a pink and beige shirt under a scruffy, sandy-coloured pullover and wore glasses. Asked by the judge if he understood French, he replied, 'Non, pas beaucoup' – not a lot. He was then given an earpiece to pick up translation.

Montes couldn't resist one last feeble attempt to delay the trial. Speaking in a weak and high-pitched voice, he told the judges, 'I came back to Rennes too late for my defence to be properly prepared.'

However, after deliberating for 30 minutes, presiding judge Fabienne Doroy ruled that the trial should go ahead.

The only photograph allowed to be taken of Montes in court as the 13-page indictment was read out to him showed a surly, sullen man peering over the top of wire-rimmed glasses. Once his attempt to delay the trial further had been rejected, he became even more crumpled and sat sulking in the dock. He looked on impassively and answered questions slowly, describing himself as 'a waiter' and saying he lived in Spain. He would go on to admit attacking Caroline but, as expected, denied actually intending to murder her.

Prosecutors drew up a damning profile of Montes, describing him as a serial sexual predator of young girls over a 25-year period during which he travelled through Europe and South and North America. They referred to the jail sentence he received after being convicted for three rapes in Germany in the 1980s, and how, in August 1997, he was arrested on suspicion of attempted rape in Spain but later freed on bail. The prosecution also stated that Montes tried to sexually assault a British girl in another youth hostel, in the nearby village of St Lunaire, on the night Caroline was killed.

Sue Dickinson was then invited to speak about her teenage daughter by Judge Doroy. In a composed manner, Sue described how excited Caroline was about the trip to France and recalled the final conversation she had with her daughter.

Montes must have dreaded hearing Sue Dickinson's evidence to the court because it forced him to face the reality of the appalling crime he had committed. Sue stood just yards from Montes as she spoke movingly about Caroline. She described her as 'just a normal 13-year-old girl who had long skinny legs, was not a good eater and adored school. She was a happy child. She loved music. She played the piano and the clarinet and her best friend was her sister. She was a Brownie, a member of the school orchestra and had taken ballet lessons until the age of nine.'

In the dock, Montes looked on with no emotion whatsoever. It was as if he was trying to block out Sue

Dickinson's voice to stop himself feeling guilty. The jury were then shown one of the last pictures taken of Caroline – a photo of her on the steps of Mont St Michel with two school friends. Sue told the court it showed she 'looked younger than her age'. She went on to tell the court that photos of her daughter published in the media tended to make her look older than she really was. 'They were taken at the school fashion show. The family were a bit shocked when they saw them. She only weighed five stone.'

After listening to her, Olivier Dersoir, Montes's lawyer, was asked if he had any questions. He shook his head before saying in a dignified manner: 'We would just like to say how much admiration we have for you and your husband.'

John Dickinson and Caroline's sister, Jenny, were then asked if they would like to speak about Caroline but declined. Herve Rouzaud–Le Boeuf said he was proud of Mrs Dickinson for giving evidence. 'She has been less visible in the course of the inquiry but she felt she had to answer questions immediately after Montes's partial confession,' he said. 'Mr Dickinson told me he thought it was an appropriate time for Sue to talk about Caroline, to talk about the sort of girl she was. She is a loving mother.' John and Sue Dickinson were also praised for urging French investigators to use DNA testing, which eventually led police to Montes's arrest.

After Sue Dickinson's appearance, Rouzaud–Le Boeuf told reporters, 'There is no feeling of revenge in them. They just want an appropriate sentence. It was important for them to hear at least part of the truth being confessed by the defendant.'

Next it was the turn of Christine Le Menes, Montes's former lover. She was allowed to give evidence behind closed doors with neither the defendant nor the media present after an order from the presiding judge. She had argued she would not be able to give an authentic account of their relationship in the presence of Montes.

Christine then told the court how they began their relationship after Montes sexually assaulted her and how he later became violent and they broke up. Her evidence lasted more than three hours.

Back in open court, Judge Doroy transcribed Christine's evidence for Montes and concluded, 'The last sexual intercourse which she didn't want to have with you was in the Paris area in 1983. She felt her life was at risk if she tried to resist your demands.'

Olivier Dersoir claimed the judge had omitted important details from her summary of Christine Le Menes's testimony. He argued, 'I think it is essential to mention that on the night in Holland she said she got some pleasure. She also said for many years she had remembered the loving feelings she had for Arce Montes.'

Montes himself then claimed in court that he was due to marry Christine Le Menes in 1981. 'But her mother was against it and so was I. Her mother went crazy. She threw me out of the house. Christine said she had a child with me but I doubted it was mine. I went to see her twice in Paris but she refused to let me see the child. The last time I saw her was five or six years ago.'

Judge Doroy then pointed out to the court that Montes's evidence greatly differed from Christine Le Menes's account of their relationship. 'She said you walked into her room without her permission – the girls' room in a youth hostel in Holland where she was alone. She had the feeling you didn't know the place. She didn't know how to react because she was nervous.'

But then Montes interrupted: 'I went into Christine Le Menes's room because she allowed me to. If she says the opposite, it's because she read the papers. She might have said I wanted to hurt her but this is her imagination.'

The judge continued, 'You started undoing the zipper on her sleeping bag. You touched her sexually, which she didn't want.'

Montes broke down in tears and the court had to be adjourned.

34

The following day, Montes had to be virtually dragged in handcuffs into court for cross-examination after he feigned illness as he was being brought into the building. Minutes later, the shaken-looking defendant seemed to be trembling as he was asked to explain how he came to murder Caroline. In front of a hushed courtroom, he remained silent, prompting his defence lawyer to intervene in a final attempt to get him to talk.

'Look at me. What happened, M. Montes?' asked Patrick Elghozi. 'Come on. The Dickinsons have come from far away. Their daughter died. They need to know what happened. It is your trial. You've come here to explain yourself.'

But Montes, now 54, refused to tell Caroline's parents, John and Sue, and her sister, Jenny, the events that led to his raping and suffocating 13-year-old Caroline as she slept in the youth hostel in Pleine-Fougeres in 1996.

'I can't,' he said at last in a barely audible voice. 'I want to go. I can't.'

Montes put his head in his hands and started to sob uncontrollably. The Dickinson family stared intently at him.

As Montes continued to weep loudly, Judge Jean-Luc Buckel mockingly told him, 'You are going to answer to them, brave as you are.'

It was then put to the defendant that the injuries to Caroline's private parts were so severe they could only have been caused by her being raped. But Montes denied raping her, saying he had a medical condition which prevented sex. He said he left after masturbating because he was sexually satisfied. Then he added, 'I thought she was asleep, I didn't think she was dead.'

Under further questioning, Montes admitted that he deliberately set out to sexually assault a young girl because he had been disturbed in the middle of another attack two hours earlier. But he still denied deliberately killing Caroline and claimed the schoolgirl must have died 'by herself'.

Cross-examining Montes, the state prosecutor, Francois-Rene Aubry, demanded to know how he could possibly claim that he had left Caroline alive.

'I don't remember, but I don't think she was dead,' Montes answered. 'I would like to say I am not a murderer. I didn't have the intention at all of killing Caroline. I didn't want to kill her. It's true. I am incapable of killing anyone. I'm not a murderer. I just wanted to make a sexual assault.'

Caroline's parents, seated at the front of the court, were concentrating hard on the proceedings. Behind them, a Devon and Cornwall police officer put her arm around Jenny Dickinson.

Speaking quietly and without a hint of emotion in his voice, Montes then described the night Caroline died. He said he had no idea how he ended up in Pleine-Fougeres but claimed he was 'in a bad way' after failing to see his estranged 14-year-old son, who lived nearby with his mother Christine Le Menes. He also admitted that a few hours earlier he had assaulted another girl in St Lunaire, 40 kilometres away, but had fled after being disturbed.

A few yards away, John Dickinson stared at Montes.

Then the court fell silent as the defendant began to recount the events leading up to Caroline's murder.

'I don't know how I arrived in Pleine-Fougeres,' he told the court in Spanish. 'I have no explanation. But I know I was very aroused and I wanted to commit another sex act. I remember there was a fountain or water spout and I wanted a drink, so I stopped in front of the door. I saw a house with a light on and went in. Then I walked into the room. Everything was dark, I couldn't see anything.' Montes said that as his eyes became accustomed to the dark room he could see somebody was asleep on the floor. He said, 'I realised someone was lying on the floor sleeping. I went and lay down next to her. I realised it was a young girl. I was aroused and I didn't feel well. I wanted to do what I had done before, so I placed my hand over her mouth.' He added, 'I lifted up the cover and I wanted to stroke her.'

Montes said he then took off Caroline's underwear, put his hand over her mouth, masturbated and then assaulted her. He denied using cotton wool to suffocate her, claiming he had used the cotton wool found at the scene as a bandage because he had burned his hand on his car engine.

But he admitted, 'Afterwards I was still aroused. I think I

279

started stroking her again and then I left.' He said his memory was blurred because he had been drinking heavily.

Asked if Caroline reacted to the assault, Montes answered, 'I don't think so.'

He said he couldn't remember her kicking her legs or saying anything, but thought she remained asleep during the attack.

But Judge Doroy then asked him, 'You think a young girl on whose mouth you held with your hand for a while as you were masturbating and caressing her and assaulting her can remain asleep?'

'I don't know. I was in a bad way,' replied Montes, who insisted again that Caroline was still alive when he left the hostel. However, when pressed, he was unable to tell the court how he knew she was not dead.

'I didn't try to kill her,' Montes said. 'All I wanted was to have sexual relations with her. I didn't want to kill her.'

But the presiding judge continued to press Montes. 'Were you not aware of the fact that by keeping your hand on her mouth and nose this would automatically lead to suffocation?'

Montes replied, 'No, I didn't know.'

The judge asked again, 'You placed your hand on her mouth sufficiently long for her to die?'

Montes insisted, 'No. She died by herself.'

Then the prosecutor, M. Aubry, approached Montes and said, 'These girls heard panting, heavy breathing, even cries. Would you agree Caroline was waking up and it was necessary to silence her at any cost so you could go on with the rape?'

Montes replied, 'She didn't cry, she was sleeping, she was sleeping.'

M. Aubry then asked, 'So what about the noise the girls heard?'

Montes answered, 'I didn't hear any noise,' before adding, 'I want to specify that I am not an assassin. I did not intend absolutely to kill Caroline, I am unable to kill somebody. I wanted simply to attack her sexually.'

The court was then adjourned because Montes began sobbing once again.

After a 25-minute break, proceedings resumed with Montes apologising for his outburst. He said, 'Excuse me for those tears because in this room I'm not the victim. I understand the seriousness of what I did. I know that the Dickinson family will never forgive me and I know that, from the moment their daughter died, their life was totally different, but I have nothing else to say.'

Next Montes was asked about his family. 'My mother never looked after me,' he said. 'Unlike my father. She gave everything to my sister.' Montes even admitted how as a teenager he was afraid of the dark. 'And I'm still afraid of it,' he told the court.

Then the court heard a reading of testimony by Benigna Montes: 'I would rather have gone out and lived on a doorstep than be with him. The simple act of going into his bedroom disgusted me. Something like an allergy stopped me going into his room. I always felt a certain repulsion there. I didn't want to risk going in there even if he was going away for a week.'

On hearing his mother's cruel words, Montes put his head in his hands and began to sob yet again, at which point the court was once more briefly adjourned.

After returning to the courtroom, Montes even tried to insist that his arrest in Florida in 2001 had been a misunderstanding. He was still clearly in a desperate state of self-denial.

One of Caroline's school friends, Amy White, now 21, then

told the court how she encountered an 'evil' stranger as she and two classmates went to the toilet in the youth hostel in Pleine-Fougeres. The man was aged about 30–40 with long straggly hair and looked very unkempt with 'distinctive bushy eyebrows'.

Amy White explained, 'He said something to us in a different language. We thought it was French but then he started talking to us. We were just joking about, saying that all we knew in French was "*bonjour*" and "*au revoir*". He said something also and then he sniggered quietly to himself and went down the stairs away from us.'

Asked if she would describe the eyebrows of the man in the dock as 'bushy', Miss White turned to Montes and said, 'Yes,' then added, 'He looked as evil in the newspapers as he did on that night.'

The court next heard a statement from Caroline's school friend Ann Jasper, now 21. She had been so haunted by events and an overwhelming feeling of guilt that she had been unable to appear in court personally. 'Why didn't I wake up and save her?' she said in her statement. 'For the past eight years I have been asking myself that question. If I hadn't been asleep, I could have scared the man off and Caroline would not be dead. It's almost unbearable, knowing that I could have saved her.'

Police then told the court that, during interviews with Montes's family, his brother-in-law, Andreas Moro Blanco, told them how Montes had used the shocking description that he was a man whose 'favourite meal was little girls aged 11 or 12'.

Then it was the turn of the medical experts to explain the suffering of Caroline Dickinson. Montes looked down throughout their testimony. Major Thierry Lezeau, from the Rennes police, told the court he was convinced Caroline stopped breathing by the time Montes left the hostel after the attack.

'The asphyxiation was significant and harsh. I believe she stopped living very quickly,' he explained, before adding that it was his 'clear conviction' that Caroline had been smothered with cotton wool taken from the room of Kate Wrigley, the schoolgirl who had been attacked by Montes two hours earlier in St Lunaire.

Medical experts also confirmed that Caroline was not under the influence of any toxic substance and had succumbed, a very short moment after the rape, to a 'brutal syndrome asphyxic', caused by obstruction of the respiratory tracts, without strangulation.

Caroline's death involved 'terrible suffering', according to another expert, Professor Marie-Annick Le Gueut, who stressed the relevance of the lesions noted on the victim's genitals.

Montes then refused to look at photographs of Caroline's corpse, exclaiming, 'Photographs of Caroline? It is not possible! It is horrible!'

The presiding judge was appalled by the defendant's reaction and admonished him, 'You play the startled virgin?'

Montes had been comprehensively humiliated.

35

The trial of Francisco Montes was the most high-profile case in France for many years, avidly followed by the British journalists who attended the court in Rennes in force. Many local people also turned up each day to watch the proceedings on a giant screen set up in a marquee in the building's central courtyard.

On the fifth day, the court heard from Dr John-Michel Masson, a psychiatrist who treated Montes while he was in custody in 2002. Dr Masson described the Spaniard as a 'violent sexual pervert' who was not mentally ill and would probably have killed again. He also confirmed to the court that Montes had abnormal anxieties about cleanliness and sexual impotence. But, he added, Montes had never shown regret or remorse. 'He is in many ways a classic sexual pervert. In cases of sexual perversity of this kind, the crimes inevitably get progressively worse. They can end in murder, as this one did. Montes is a very dangerous man, one of the most dangerous I have met in 34 years' experience.'

Another psychiatrist, Armand Martorell, told the court that when Montes spoke about the attack on Caroline Dickinson he was 'like a naughty child who felt guilty about having broken a pot of jam'.

The court also heard testimony from Montes's former friend Eduardo Suarez, who said the suspect had shown him a photograph of Caroline and boasted about having sex with her. He said that Montes was 'very proud' of the picture of Caroline. Suarez also testified that Montes told him he had seen Caroline playing in a garden with friends before he had sex with her in a youth hostel, and had described the 13-year-old as 'a real china doll'.

But Caroline's mother later raised doubts about Suarez's evidence. Asked by Judge Doroy whether Caroline had packed for the trip alone or they had done it together, Sue Dickinson told the court, 'We packed her bag together. She had no photos at all, except for her passport. To my knowledge, she has never had a photo taken in a white shirt and dark skirt. There is no school picture of that nature.'

Eduardo Suarez also told the court that Montes had shown him other pictures, which he claimed had been given to him by different girls. The judge asked whether Montes had said he had been to bed with all the girls in the pictures.

'Absolutely,' said Suarez. 'That is what he said to me.'

The court then heard about the trip the two men took to Barcelona, during which the car they were travelling in was broken into. Suarez said Montes's violent reaction to the theft was so extreme that he then ended their friendship.

Following this testimony, the case was adjourned until the following Monday, 14 June, when lawyers for all sides would deliver their closing speeches. After that, the jury would be sent to consider its verdict, which was expected sometime on the Monday evening.

On the final day, the prosecutor described Montes as a remorseless and dangerous deviant, adding, 'It sends shivers down the spine. Someone who has crossed Europe for 20 years to satisfy his sexual urges and fantasies. Someone whom we find in France, in Switzerland, in Spain, in Holland, in Germany, in Britain. Someone completely out of the ordinary.'

M. Aubry said also that Montes was a dangerous repeat offender who showed no signs of wishing to reform, and urged the court to hand down a life sentence. 'Taking into account the seriousness of the crime and the nature of his personality, what else could I ask for?' he asked. 'It would be illogical, you would be taken by surprise, if I asked you for anything else.' He asked the court to stipulate that Montes be offered no chance of parole for 22 years.

There were no tears, not even a flicker of remorse from Montes as the prosecutor demanded his imprisonment. There was, said M. Aubry, no redeeming feature in the accused's character, nor in the manner in which he had committed his crime, to warrant a lesser sentence.

'This is a man who has devoted his life entirely to his sexual deviance,' the prosecutor declared. 'What has he done with himself, apart from wander around the youth hostels of Europe looking for 13-year-old girls to rape, searching for a few brief seconds of sexual pleasure? He has never shown remorse, he has never called for help. No. This is someone who is capable of raping and killing a young girl, and then of walking away calmly leaving almost no trace.'

Prosecutor Aubry also said that neither Montes's troubled personality nor his consumption of alcohol and anti-depressants on the night of the crime amounted to an excuse. 'He is entirely responsible for his actions,' he said.

Much of the debate on the last day of the trial still focused on Montes's intent. Did he mean Caroline to die when he assaulted her in the youth hostel at Pleine-Fougeres on in the early hours of 18 July 1996.

Turning towards Montes, the prosecutor looked straight at him as he said, 'Pressing very strongly with a hand and a wad of cotton on your victim for some considerable time, you must know that asphyxiation is the likely consequence. That constitutes a murderous intention. It is a complex action. You have to block the nose and mouth of someone who isn't far off adulthood.' He continued, 'To maintain this gesture you have to apply force. You cannot do that without meaning to. You have to want to do it.'

Herve Rouzaud-Le Boeuf, the Dickinson family's lawyer for nearly eight years, then told the court there was no doubt of Montes's murderous intentions. Montes, he reminded the jury, had returned frustrated to Pleine-Fougeres that night after failing to gratify his sexual urges during an almost identical assault on another British schoolgirl at a hostel in St Lunaire, 40 kilometres away. The girl's roommates had woken up and switched on the light, forcing him to leave.

'I am completely convinced that after his failure at St Lunaire he was determined to obtain satisfaction, come what may,' said M. Rouzaud-Le Boeuf. 'There was an absolute determination and ferocity to succeed. He wanted his pleasure, whatever the cost to his victim. It was imperative that she did not cry out.'

Court-appointed defence lawyer Fabian Lahaie then tried to counterbalance this argument by pointing out to the court that there was no sign of a struggle, which indicated that Montes was unaware of the damage he had caused. Lahaie claimed the charge should have been reclassified as 'rape leading to death', which would mean a reduced sentence.

Lahaie also insisted there was nothing in their client's past to suggest he had intended to kill Caroline. He said the prosecution had exaggerated its case. 'On the strength of this evidence, I cannot see a homicidal intention,' he said. 'The facts to which Mr Montes has admitted are grave enough. Why inflate them into what they're not?'

He asked the jury to reject the charge of murder and judge Montes for the lesser and rarer crime of death as a result of rape. 'Extreme vigilance has to be paid to the outcome of any crime. It is true there was a death, but that does not mean there was intent to kill,' added the defence counsel.

Before the jury retired, Montes was asked if he had anything to say. 'I have nothing to say,' he said. 'I am ashamed.'

Montes then sat crumpled in a heap in the dock. He didn't have to wait long for the verdict. Just four hours later, the jury returned. Montes looked at the ceiling as Sue Dickinson broke down in tears when Judge Doroy read out the jury's verdict of 'guilty of murder preceded by, accompanied by, or following, rape'.

The presiding judge then told Montes that he would be sentenced to the maximum 30 years in prison and would not be eligible to apply for parole for at least 20 years. She also awarded John and Sue Dickinson £23,000 damages each and £16,500 to their daughter, Jenny. The money would be provided out of public funds and would help the family pay for their hefty legal bills. Detective Superintendent Andrew Pierce, of the Devon and Cornwall police, spoke of his 'delight' at the verdict. 'There is a great feeling of satisfaction. But, more than that, a feeling of delight for John and Sue and Jenny Dickinson, who have campaigned for justice for Caroline over so many years,' he said.

Less than 24 hours after the end of the trial, Devon and Cornwall detectives requested a copy of Montes's file from the court so that they could cross-reference exactly when he was in Britain and compare the information with yet more unsolved crimes that fitted his behavioural profile. The force also checked immigration records, bank statements, benefits records, rent payments and employment details to discover where he was at any specific time.

Montes's DNA had already been checked against the national database, which produced no matches. But then many of his attacks had been carried out when DNA samples were not even taken at the scene of a crime. 'At the moment we are not in a position to link him through forensics or method of attack to any outstanding crimes,' said one Devon and Cornwall police source. 'But we cannot dismiss the possibility that other victims have not come forward.'

The Devon and Cornwall police then asked forces bordering London's Metropolitan police area to likewise re-examine their files on outstanding sex attacks and attempted abductions. Police in Worcestershire also trawled through their files to determine whether Montes had committed any crimes on their patch. A spokesman for the West Mercia force said officers had had a preliminary look through their files but there appeared to be no cases linked with Montes. 'There are no unsolved cases that appear to be relevant to this offender at this time, but we will review all intelligence that we are sent,' he said.

In Limerick, Ireland, 24-year-old Valerie Jacques – who had escaped abduction by Montes in the Loire Valley – was happy there would at last be some peace of mind for her family. Montes had stalked Valerie – then 14 – during her visit to Bleres with the Laurel Hill School in 1994. Now the young mother of a one-year-old daughter, Valerie was glad Montes would spend the rest of his days behind bars. She said, 'Hopefully, there will now be some closure for the Dickinson family, they deserve it after eight long years.

'My story is on record and I just want to get on with my life now. I am glad this chapter is finally over. What happened to Caroline is so terribly sad and needless. I am sure if I hadn't woken up when I had I would have suffered the same fate.' Valerie added, 'The fact that Montes was released so soon after what happened to me is terrible. Surely the police should have kept an eye on him. To think they didn't make much of an effort to stop this man makes me angry and very sad.'

Under French law, Montes had ten days from the end of the hearing to say whether he wanted to appeal and a full retrial would be automatically held with a fresh jury who would consider all the evidence and hear all the witnesses. It was in Montes's interest to appeal to seek to reduce the 20-year wait for parole, although there was a slight risk the maximum period before parole might be increased to 22 years if the appeal went against him. But, as one reporter at the trial commented, 'He is such a bizarre person there's no knowing what he will do.'

Montes did indeed exercise his controversial right to an appeal, which meant that two of the girls who woke up to find Caroline Dickinson's body in the youth hostel would have to attend and be cross-examined in person by his lawyers this time. The entire, disturbing case would now be exposed once again to the world.

36

On 21 June 2005, Francisco Montes's appeal against his conviction was held at the court in St Brieuc, Brittany. Back in the dock, Montes first of all apologised to the Dickinson family for forcing them to relive their torment in court for a second time. To the jury of eight men and four women, he said, 'I am appealing because I want to explain what happened on that day. I had no intention of killing Caroline and I'd like to say it's hard for the family to come back here, but you need to know the truth of what happened on that day in Pleine-Fougeres.'

Then he admitted killing Caroline, although he insisted, 'But I had no intention of killing her. It was an accident. It was the result of the rape. I didn't go into her room to kill her. I didn't cover her mouth to kill her.'

Montes admitted being high on Afranil, which made him 'feel like Superman'. Then he told how he went to the hostel and entered the room. 'I lay on the floor and saw there was a young girl… I put my hand over her mouth. I wanted to cover her mouth so that she would not cry out. I killed her but had no intention of killing her. It was an accident, a misfortune.'

At one stage, Montes broke down in court, weeping uncontrollably, before getting off his chair and trying to hide behind the dock's wooden panelling. Still handcuffed to the dock, he appeared wide-eyed with panic and then angered the judge by refusing to answer any more questions.

After being confronted with further evidence by the prosecutor, Montes gave a single nod of his head, which seemed to concede for the first time that he had stalked Caroline and her school friends from Mont St Michel. But, when asked for further details, Montes hung his head in shame and muttered, 'I have nothing more to say.'

Judge Buckel then snapped at Montes, 'I didn't particularly want to hear your case, but may I remind you it was you who asked for this appeal and you must face the consequences. You can't run away all the time as soon as it suits you. The parents and sister of Caroline Dickinson are in court, in case you'd forgotten. You have a responsibility to them.'

Montes was then asked about the cotton wool found near Caroline's body and insisted that he'd bought it in London. 'This cotton comes from the Boots store of London. It was in my car,' he told the court.

The presiding judge, Fabienne Doroy, then snapped back at Montes, 'You invented this [last] explanation during the night?'

Montes replied, 'Today I tell you the truth.'

'You are an unhappy victim of the legal system,' came the dry reply from Judge Buckel, clearly losing his patience with Montes.

In a moving testimony designed to ensure Montes did not wriggle out of his sentence, Caroline's father then told the court he hoped his daughter could finally rest in peace. John Dickinson said, 'You all know that we did not want to be here but Montes's exploitation of the French judicial system and our determination to see through the process for Caroline has required us again to suffer the pain of listening to and thus reliving the events of 18 July 1996. We came here expecting to hear his grounds for that appeal but none appears to have been offered. It has seemed as if the offender's rights have overshadowed those of the victims.'

John Dickinson told the court that he would be haunted to his grave by visions of his daughter's ravaged body lying in the mortuary. 'Life has been stuck on the same page for nine years. I haven't been able to start afresh. I had counselling because of an inability to sleep, due to visions of Caroline's damaged body in the morgue, which will haunt me and always will. Life as we knew it ended when Caroline lost her life. We have tried to rebuild our lives but it's not the same, because an important person is missing.'

He then rounded on Montes in court for reneging on a promise to say why he killed Caroline. In response, Montes turned on the Dickinson family, seated only a few yards from the dock, and shouted, 'I had no intention to kill. I killed her and I take that responsibility but I did not have the intention to kill. I did not think the other girls would wake up in the room and I didn't want Caroline's death. There was a sexual urge I could not control but no urge to kill. There was no murderous urge by somebody who kills for pleasure. I have problems in my head but no urge to kill.' He added, 'When I went out of the youth hostel I did not know Caroline was dead.'

Then Jenny Dickinson explained her feelings about her sister's murder: 'I think I just shut down. It was six years before

I could talk about it to anyone, not even my closest friends at school. I have seen a counsellor but I still find it difficult to speak about it.'

As Jenny spoke to the court, Montes appeared ashen-faced and even wiped a tear from his eye. Just then she added, 'It took a long while for me to believe Caroline was dead and I felt very lonely. I only came to accept it at the funeral.'

Before the jury were sent out to consider their verdict, Montes once again apologised to Caroline's family, saying, 'What I did was awful. It was horrendous. I cannot be pardoned. I am sorry and I regret my actions but I didn't intend to kill your daughter... I want your daughter to be with you at home. I think of my son and if somebody had done that to my son I would think like you.'

Then he made a plea to the jury, claiming he was not a 'clever criminal or the ruthless predator that the prosecution describe'.

Montes's lawyer, Patrick Elghozi, told the appeal court that Montes was mentally ill and in need of treatment. 'He must be punished for what he did, that is rape resulting in death, but not more,' he said.

Under the French appeal system, the jury of eight men and four women would deliberate with the three appeal judges and then cast their votes in secret. The three judges also voted. A majority decision of ten out of fifteen was needed for a verdict.

On 22 June 2005, the jury and the three judges in St Brieuc rejected the appeal brought by Montes against his conviction for killing Caroline Dickinson.

Reading from a specially prepared statement outside the court, John Dickinson told reporters, 'We hope our search for justice for Caroline is at last complete and that she can be allowed to rest in peace. We did not want to be here, but

Montes's exploitation of the French judicial system and our determination to seek justice for Caroline has required us again to suffer the pain of listening and thus reliving the events of 18 July 1996.'

Then, a few days later, the Dickinsons were appalled when Montes announced he was intending to appeal for a second time. The family immediately issued a new statement through Devon and Cornwall police in which they said they were 'very disappointed' by the announcement. It stated, 'We understand Montes has only given his intention to appeal. He still has three weeks to lodge his reasons for that appeal.'

The following day Patrick Elghozi washed his hands of Montes and said he believed it was highly unlikely the appeals court in Paris, the Cour de Cassation, would grant him another trial. The lawyer said, 'It will not consider the facts of the case or Montes's claim that he didn't intend to kill Caroline Dickinson. It will only consider points of law and the procedural aspects of the previous hearing or hearings.'

US immigration officer Tommy Ontko, whose actions led to the arrest of Francisco Montes for the murder of Caroline Dickinson, was honoured with a Children's Champion award on 3 November 2005 at Number 10 Downing Street, in the presence of Prime Minister Tony Blair.

Mr Ontko had been nominated for the award by Sir John Stevens, the former Commissioner of the Metropolitan Police, who cited his outstanding contribution to the efforts of London's police force to resolve this notorious case. The award recognised those who have made a positive difference in the lives of children in Britain.

Back at his home in Detroit, Tommy Ontko, now 55, had a picture of Caroline Dickinson on his office wall. 'I am glad we put our hands on him, but it had nothing to do with civic duty. It is our job to keep the bad guys out of the United States,' he said. 'Her picture reminds me how important what we do can be.' On the wall opposite the familiar picture of the Cornish schoolgirl were family photographs of three more grinning youngsters. They were Ontko's own children – Holly, 23, Karri, 28, and Ryan, 20. 'Caroline would have been the same age as Ryan if she were alive, and just three years younger than Holly,' he explained. He said he was spurred on in his hunt for her killer by the thought that there, but for the grace of God, go all parents. 'You tend to think that those kinds of trips with teachers and chaperones are the safest kind they can take,' he said.

In Pleine-Fougeres, the youth hostel where Montes murdered Caroline Dickinson was still in business. A sign attached to the entrance frequently indicated 'no vacancies'. In the courtyard, children still looked at maps and talked excitedly about the day ahead visiting the sites of Bayeux and Mont St Michel. On the surface, it seemed as if life was normal, despite the awful killing of Caroline Dickinson.

Yet the close-knit Breton village still bore deep scars. Villagers talked effusively about forthcoming fetes and a recent lotto winner in their midst, but at any mention of Caroline a look of suspicion flashed across their faces. 'We don't want to talk about it,' said one resident. 'We need to move on with our lives now.'

The staff at the hostel where Caroline died were sometimes asked about the room where the killing occurred, but they always refused to say which one it was. 'It's not good for them to know or for us. We need some closure,' explained one member of the youth-hostel staff.

The village's reluctance to talk about '*la petite Anglaise*' was understandable. Many of the men were still recovering from the shock of being DNA-tested by police. 'Just to have to give a sample made me feel guilty. I couldn't sleep for two days. I was petrified they might find something,' explained Bernard Cronier, 55.

In the village square, elderly women continued to fill their panniers with local produce from the market. They all agreed that Montes should have been given the death penalty but remained completely bewildered as to why it all happened. As one resident said, 'She didn't hurt anyone. She didn't do anything wrong. What happened to Caroline can't be described as atrocious. It goes beyond that. It was something that can never be justified. Ever.'

Endnote

'Our investigative tradition is less rooted in scientific proof than Britain's and there is a kind of in-built suspicion of science among the French intellectual classes.'

Police investigator Jean–Pierre Michel

In the case of Francisco Montes, the triggering factors that provoked him to rape and kill innocent females were scarily predictable. Caroline Dickinson was killed because she would have posed a threat to his liberty if she had lived. Others were treated with similar disdain. We will probably never know precisely how many victims are out there.

There was no foolproof way of knowing exactly what would send Montes into a murderous, sex-crazed frenzy. Essentially, he was a combination of two types of serial murderer as defined by experts. He qualified as a 'hedonistic killer' because he seemed to have little motive beyond his own pleasure. He raped and molested because it felt good. Inflicting death may have provided Montes with the ultimate high – a source of intense, primary, sexual pleasure. But there was also an element of the 'power seeker' about him because he seemed to need to assert his supremacy over a helpless victim, to compensate for his own deep-seated

300

feelings of worthlessness by completely dominating another human being.

Many believe nothing could have been done to stop Montes doing what he did, unless he had been locked up for ever from the moment he was judged to be a psychopathic personality. It's a sobering thought to realise that there are a lot of people with similar obsessive traits who are not even judged to be psychopathic in the first place.

Montes obviously suffered from an abnormal personality. As a result, he treated people differently from the way a 'normal' person behaves, and in turn people treated him differently. His difficult relationship with his parents is a prime example. It is certainly true that at times people like Montes feel superior to the rest of the world. But people like him are defined by distinctive behavioural patterns.

That's where the paranoia comes in. It is the single biggest constraint in their lives. Today Montes's early obsessiveness would be treated with psychotherapy instead of drugs and then perhaps he would never have discovered the potent combination of the anti-depressant Afranil and alcohol that he put to lethal effect.

It is also possible that deep down Montes may really have wanted to be caught, despite his obvious ability to deny this wish to himself. This man was impulsive. He was also a psychopath, yet he did seem to have a conscience. The evidence seems to suggest that he really did care at certain moments. The trouble is, his impulses overtook his will and his need for sex dominated everything.

Today the psychiatrist who treated him in Gijon, Dr Felix Margolyes, says that people like Montes should be locked away because nothing can be done to cure them. He said, 'This illness set him apart. His obsessions were like a way to manifest his character.'

Now that we have absorbed the appalling catalogue of crimes committed by Francisco Montes, it is clear that he was – and still is – a classic animal of his species. Some serial killers thrive on striking without warning, and in a similar way Montes felt the urge to snatch someone off the street or break into a building and find a victim. But he derived no pleasure from the actual luring of his victim into his clutches. Often he couldn't even be bothered to lull them into a false sense of security by tricking them into lowering their defences. Many who encountered the man personally say he had no idea how to charm people, so his only chance really was the element of surprise.

The most important step for Montes was to enter his victim's lair and ensnare her before she had time to react. Seeing the full horror on her face meant nothing to him. Having entered a victim's room, Montes had only one aim – sexual satisfaction. He actually preferred it if she was not even conscious. An element of guilt is evident in this not wanting to be exposed to the look of horror on his victim's face. That was why, when he was in court, he refused to look at photos of Caroline Dickinson taken after her murder.

In Montes's case, it seems the killings sometimes occurred simultaneously with the sexual assault. It had not always been like that, but there is a strong possibility that in some cases he watched the last breath come out of his victims in order to bring on his sexual climax. This was the acme of pleasure that he had been building towards since the first time he fantasised about murder and sex as a teenager. Eventually this kind of sexual assault became the only way he could guarantee any real, lasting pleasure. The killing and raping became synonymous with the sexual climax. To prolong that experience and help him relive it in later fantasies, he sometimes stole a souvenir, a totemic object associated with the victim. In some cases, it was a photograph; at other times, he would try to take money or other possessions.

In the aftermath of the killings and rapes, Montes undoubtedly experienced a great deal of emotional letdown – similar perhaps to post-coital sadness. Sometimes it left him with such a severe headache that he seriously considered suicide. But once that feeling had passed he renewed his desire to murder and rape again, to try to sate what was in effect an insatiable need for a fix of fresh, young flesh.

Back in the 1980s and 1990s, America was widely believed to be the prime domain of serial killers, but we shouldn't forget that they can come from anywhere. This sexual predator, for example, was from Europe and passed through its borders and beyond without even being noticed.

Serial killing emerged as an epidemic in the United States towards the end of the 19th century, while in Britain in the late 1880s Jack the Ripper became perhaps the most notorious – and mysterious, since his identity remains unknown – serial murderer in history. His 'Whitechapel Murders' garnered many pages of horrendous news coverage in late-Victorian times, but the next big serial-murder story came decades later and returned the spotlight to America. The name of Ed Gein, the serial killer who was dubbed the original 'Psycho', first exploded in the media in the 1950s with his butchering of dozens of victims and his penchant for making clothing from their skin.

For several decades, the 'thrill killers' seemed to be confined to the big cities of the United States: Los Angeles – Charles Manson, Richard 'Night Stalker' Ramirez and 'The Zodiac Killer'; New York – 'Son of Sam'; Chicago – John Wayne Gacy; Texas – Henry Lee Lucas; Seattle and vicinity – Ted Bundy, Edmund Kemper and 'The Green River Killer'; Milwaukee – Jeffrey Dahmer.

But in the 1980s the world was appalled by a serial murderer who came not from the US but the USSR – Andrei Chikatilo – and Britain was represented by the monstrous killers Dennis Nilsen and Fred West. In the following decade, it is estimated, up to a dozen serial killers – including Francisco Montes – passed through mainland Europe and Britain. Many of their crimes went unnoticed and, as already described in this book, Montes might never have been caught if it had not been for a sharp-eyed American immigration officer.

As you will have discovered reading about the life and crimes of Francisco Montes, serial killers are not analytical geniuses, beyond good and evil like Nietzsche's superman. They aren't even homoerotic fruitballs with sex-change obsessions like something out of *Silence of the Lambs*.

Most, like Montes, are sad, white loners. And few are legally insane. They often drink beer and work in normal jobs. And, unlike Montes, many even have wives or girlfriends (or both), and not many of them have psycho-killer tattoos on their foreheads. But Montes proves, if proof were needed, that the serial-killer epidemic has become a worldwide phenomenon.

More than 50 per cent of the world's serial killers are white men aged between 24 and 35, which made Montes a 'classic' in every sense of the word when he first began stalking his prey. Criminologist Michael Newton, who compiled the stories of 544 serial killers in his book *Hunting Humans – An Encyclopedia of Modern Serial Killers*, says that at least one third are nomadic transients wandering between countries and killing randomly. Montes fits that bill perfectly.

Experts who examined Montes were never able to truly nail down his real motives for killing and raping because he chose never to confess to his many other crimes, committed over a period of almost 30 years. Sometimes he selected and stalked his intended victims in the way that other serial killers have done in the past. But, while there were some sado-sexual overtones in his murders and sex attacks, it must never be forgotten that he actually befriended one of his victims after changing her life forever.

Initially, Montes fed off his victims' fear and agony, like most known serial killers. It was the only power he ever had. But, towards the end of his 'reign', he seemed obsessed with their not being conscious, which suggests he could not face the consequences of his actions.

Caroline Dickinson's murder not only lays bare the reluctance of the French police to carry out DNA testing, but also shows up failings in international police co-operation. French investigators received help from their British colleagues, although Interpol-London failed to follow up on a request for information about Montes's stay in Britain. Moreover, Spanish police did not immediately report Montes's links to various sex attacks in Spain.

True, tracing Montes was in some ways like looking for a needle in a haystack, but DNA evidence should have been the magnet to extract the needle from the haystack's depths.

Montes has always refused to admit his involvement in any of the dozens of attacks and killings linked to him down the years – with the exception of Caroline Dickinson's murder. The killer, who as a child blamed everything on his parents, had a complete inability to take responsibility for his crimes. As an adult, he continues to blame society for his problems and refuses to even concede his possible involvement in other crimes.

This author wrote to Montes in Fresnes Prison, in France, to see if he was finally prepared to face up to his evil deeds but police, lawyers and psychiatrists all advised me that it would be a complete waste of time because Montes refuses point-blank to talk about his previous crimes. I never got a reply.

Montes even continues to claim that he was wrongly convicted of Caroline Dickinson's murder. He doesn't deny needing to have sex with her but in his strange, amoral world he still believes that this doesn't make him guilty of causing her death. Many believe that when he boasted to his only friend, Eduardo Suarez, about his 'girlfriend called Caroline' he really had convinced himself that they were genuine lovers because this ensured that he would never feel guilty about her murder.

At one stage, there were real fears that Montes would escape his responsibilities by committing suicide, but experts believe it is unlikely he would ever go through with such a threat because it would be like admitting his guilt for all those other crimes. 'Committing suicide would be a tacit confession that he was guilty,' explained one eminent psychiatrist. 'Unless Montes actually takes responsibility for his crimes this seems highly unlikely.'

So, for the moment, Francisco Montes remains incarcerated within the grim confines of a French jail, watched around the clock in the hospital wing. Some still believe he will one day wake up and decide to get everything off his chest, but until that time comes, the relatives of the loved ones whose lives he has so cruelly destroyed will continue to be emotionally tortured by not knowing the truth about what really happened.

Under French law, Montes could be released in just 16 years, rather than the minimum of 20 years mentioned immediately after his trial. This revelation only slipped out some months after his conviction and many believe that Montes is working towards an early release, convinced that if nothing else can be proved against him he could get out of prison before he reaches his seventieth birthday.

> *Twinkle, twinkle, little star,*
> *How I wonder what you are,*
> *Up above the world so high,*
> *Like a diamond in the sky.*
> *Twinkle, twinkle, little star,*
> *How I wonder what you are.*

These were the last words of Caroline Dickinson.